Design for Multimedia Learning

Design for Multimedia Learning

Tim Boyle
Manchester Metropolitan University

PRENTICE HALL
London New York Toronto Sydney Tokyo Singapore
Madrid Mexico City Munich Paris

First published 1997 by
Prentice Hall Europe
Campus 400, Maylands Avenue
Hemel Hempstead
Hertfordshire, HP2 7EZ
A division of
Simon & Schuster International Group

Typeset in 10/12pt Times from author's disks

Printed and bound in Great Britain by
T.J. International Ltd, Padstow, Cornwall

Library of Congress Cataloging-in-Publication Data

Boyle, Tom.
Design for multimedia learning / Tom Boyle
p. cm.
Includes bibliographical references and index.
ISBN 0-13-242215–8 (cased)
1. Interactive multimedia. 2 . Computer assisted instruction.
3. Media programs (Education) 4. Instructional systems—Design
I. Title.
LB1028.55.B69 1997
371.3'34—dc20 96-41423
CIP

British Library Cataloguing in Publication Data

A catalogue record for this book is available from the British Library

ISBN 0-13-242215-8

1 2 3 4 5 01 00 99 98 97

Contents

Preface

My childhood village is on the shores of Belfast Lough. Our lane ran the short distance from the main road to the sea, and our house was the last in the row. During winter storms the sea would lash the buttress wall. The spray leapt high in the air and swept down the lane. Coming home from school we hid in the shelter of the first house and timed the spray. At the right moment we raced down the lane and scrambled into the doorway. We became very good at this and seldom got wet. Multimedia learning is not something new. It is woven into the fabric of our childhood.

The technology is new, and it is powerful. Multimedia links the interactive power of the computer to the presentation impact of pictures, sound and motion. It can be delivered on consumer PCs, and multimedia networks beckon us into the future. This frightens and alienates some people. They see it as technology versus nature, but they are wrong. It is a technology of enablement. Multimedia computers help us to capture and amplify powerful natural processes of learning. Educational multimedia design, at its best, creates something that is both dazzlingly new and deeply familiar.

There is a social and economic need for what educational multimedia can offer. Our education and training systems were shaped to meet the needs of an industrial society. For many people the natural processes of learning seemed to dry up in the formalities of traditional schooling. The new information society needs people that learn and adapt quickly. Great corporate institutions need to be lithe and nimble to survive and prosper. Multimedia educational technology seeks to satisfy the challenge of this future by recapturing the power of childhood.

The audience for this book, in one sense, is very clear. The book is aimed at educational multimedia designers and students of educational multimedia design. In another sense the potential readership is very varied. This reflects the emergence of a new discipline that has attracted people from many different backgrounds. The book does not have a static audience but one whose dynamic development has been a major factor influencing the development of the book. This makes the area very exciting. There is the clamour of a construction site, and much of its attendant confusion. The contributors to this act of construction come from quite different directions. The perspective from each line of approach is initially different. Some aspects of the work seem obvious; other aspects seem challenging, perhaps even mysterious. Those entering may decide to take the guided tour, and follow the themes as they are laid out sequentially in the book. Other may prefer to strike out to investigate what interests them, skipping around areas of worthy but familiar endeavour.

The panorama of the book for the approaching reader is laid out into four major areas. The first area, mapped in Part 1 of the book, sets out the thematic structure of work in the field. The style of exposition is to identify key issues and describe exemplar systems. This provides the opportunity to appreciate in depth the issues pursued. The discussion begins with a review of developments leading to modern work in educational multimedia. The main areas of work examined then include: information retrieval, construction tools for learning, simulation and virtual experience, and structured learning.

The next three parts of the book organise the process of constructing multimedia learning environments into three major types of activity. These are: conceptual design, presentation design and project management. Conceptual design is the framework of educational principles on which the attractive surface of a multimedia system is built. It provides the 'deep structure' of principles that ensure effective learning. This topic is dealt with in Part 2 of the book. This part reviews the major work in this area, clarifies the central concepts, and systematises our knowledge by employing the innovative concept of 'design action potential' networks.

Presentation design (Part 3) involves the surface appearance of this system. This concerns screen design and media integration. The design of each of the contributing media forms is discussed and exemplified – text, graphics, sound animation and video. The tools used to create multimedia systems are reviewed and assessed. Readers familiar with particular disciplines may wish to skim through particular sections and concentrate on the less familiar media domains.

Part of the excitement of exploring a new area is to break away from old, tired disciplines and follow pure inspiration. After falling down a few holes, however, suitable guidance and control systems begin to seem a good idea. Multimedia developers have rejected many of the 'staid' methodologies of software development as unsuitable and stifling creativity. There are signs now that the discipline is developing project control structures adapted to the needs of multimedia development. This issue is discussed in Part 4 of the book.

Interactive multimedia learning is a fascinating area. The need to integrate ideas from so many fields is both frightening and exhilarating. The challenge is to think in fresh ways, and to build the selective coherences of a new discipline. This book provides a systematic introduction to this dynamic area. I hope it is provocative and fun to read.

Acknowledgements

A book on multimedia by its nature reflects the contributions of many people. Without their help this book would not have been possible. Two people made a particularly sustained contribution. Ian Reid took my sketches and produced most of the drawings in this book, and was unfailing polite when I pestered him. Sue, my wife, spent many hours after her own long day's work typing up my drafts. We have both reason to celebrate the completion of this book!

The wonderful thing about multimedia teams is that your individual inadequacies can become unimportant. You can express what you are good at and your colleagues complement this contribution and amplify it into something that can stun and impress. I would like to thank all my colleagues, and the students from whom I have learned, who worked on the CLEM, Braque, VirCom, DOVE and Ceilidh Notes systems. I particular I would like to thank John Gray, a formalist with imagination, Pete Kelly who developed the VirCom system, and Martyn Davies who programmed the CLEM system, developed Braque and worked on the Ceilidh Notes Shell.

Colleagues from the wider educational multimedia community have supplied screen shots for the book and given permission for the use of illustrations of their systems. Peter Fowler, head of the Learning Methods Unit at LJMU, kindly supplied screen shots for three of the figures in the colour insert – Plates 3, 4 and 6 – from the Cytofocus and Liverpool City of Architecture systems. I would like to gratefully acknowledge the permissions given to use the following illustration, listed in the order that they are presented in the book:

Figure 3.1 'Web screen from the Computers in Teaching Initiative Support Centre'; permission for reproduction granted by Joyce Martin and the CTI Support Service.

Figure 3.4 'The SpeakEasy tool'; permission for reproduction of screen shot from the KIE system granted by Marcia Linn. Screen shot downloaded from the KIE Web pages at 'http://www.kie.berkeley.edu'.

Figure 4.1 'Screen from Murder One'; permission for reproduction granted by Hugh Gibbons, from Gibbons H. (1992) Murder One - developing interactive simulations for teaching law, *CTISS File*, No. 14, Oct. 1992.

Figure 4.2 'The EcoDisk Project: Map of the Reserve'; permission for reproduction from the EcoDisk CD ROM granted by Living and Learning (Cambridge) Ltd.

Figure 4.3 'Opening screen from the HeRMiT system'; permission for reproduction granted by Association for the Advancement of Computing in Education (AACE) from Feifer R. G. and Allender L. T. (1994) It's not how multi the media, it's how the media is used. In T. Ottmann and I. Tomek (eds) *Educational multimedia and hypermedia 1994, Procs of Ed Media '94*. AACE.

Figure 4.4 'Screen from the 'X' system'; permission for reproduction granted by Richard Millwood, from Millwood R. and Mladenova G. (1994) Educational multimedia: how to allow for cultural factors. In P. Brusilovsky, P. Kommers and N. Streitz (eds) *Multimedia, hypermedia and virtual reality*. LNCS 1077. Springer. My thanks to Richard for supplying screen shots for this figure and for Figure 7.2.

Figure 5.6 'The Molehill environment with the Interface Guru visible' from Alpert S. R., Singley M. K. and Carroll J. M. (1995) Multiple multimodal mentors: delivering computer-based instruction via specialized anthropomorphic advisors, *Behaviour and Information Technology*, 14, No. 2, 69-79. Permission for reproduction granted by Taylor and Francis Publishers. My thanks to Sherman Alpert for supplying the screen shot.

Figure 6.1 'A screen shot from the SMALLTALKER system'; permission to reproduce the illustration granted by the Association for the Advancement of Computing in Education (AACE), from Chee Y. S. (1994) SMALLTALKER: a cognitive apprenticeship multimedia environment for learning Smalltalk programming. In T. Ottmann and I. Tomek (eds) *Educational multimedia and hypermedia 1994, Procs of Ed Media '94*. AACE. My thanks to Chee Yam San for the supply of the screen shot.

Figure 7.2 'An arcade game context: the opening screen from the 'X' system', from Millwood R. and Mladenova G. (1994) Educational multimedia: how to allow for cultural factors. In P. Brusilovsky, P. Kommers and N. Streitz (eds) *Multimedia, hypermedia and virtual reality*. LNCS 1077. Springer. Permission for reproduction granted by Richard Millwood.

Figure 7.4 'The policeman and boy set-up' reproduced from *Children's Minds* by Margaret Donaldson; permission for reproduction granted by HarperCollins Publishers Limited.

Figure 7.5 'Scaffolding support for learning activities'; permission for reproduction of screen shot from the KIE system granted by Marcia Linn. Screen shot downloaded from the KIE Web pages at 'http://www.kie.berkeley.edu'.

Figure 10.2 'Example of an Authorware development screen'. Macromedia Inc., Copyright © 1995 Macromedia Inc. All rights reserved . Used with permission.

Figure 10.3 'Multimedia ToolBook'. Asymetrix Corporation, Copyright © 1990-1994 Asymetrix Corporation. All rights reserved. Used with permission.

Figure 10.4 'The opening screen of Macromedia Director'. Copyright © 1995 Macromedia Inc. All rights reserved . Used with permission.

Figure 11.1 'The ToolBook 3 tutorial screen layout'. Asymetrix Corporation. Copyright © 1990-1994 Asymetrix Corporation. All rights reserved. Used with permission.

Figure 12.5 'Video editing in Digital Video Player'. Asymetrix Corporation. Copyright © 1993, 1994 Asymetrix Corporation. All rights reserved . Used with permission.

Colour Plate 8 'Colour manipulation in PalEdit tool'. Screen shot reprinted with the permission of Microsoft Corporation. Copyright © Microsoft Corporation, 1991-1992. All rights reserved.

For permission to use screen shots incorporating Netscape Navigator - Netscape Communication, Copyright © Netscape Communications Corporation. Printed by permission of Netscape Communications Corporation.

I would like to thank the reviewers who gave helpful feedback, and colleagues who have read and commented on various chapters in the book. Finally, my thanks go to Viki Williams and Jackie Harbor from Prentice Hall who shepherded me through the process and brightly accepted my continued excuses for missing deadlines.

Dedicated to my family – the source of stability and inspiration

We shall not cease from exploration
And the end of all our exploring
Will to be arrive where we started
And know the place for the first time

T. S. Eliot

Chapter 1

Introduction

Why write a book on the design of multimedia learning environments? The answer is that there is a need to be met, and that need is best met by a book. The need is to construct a deep understanding of the design principles that should guide this area. Jacobs (1995) comments that paradoxically innovation is quite rare in this highly innovative area. Developments in this area have been driven by the technology. The technologically possibilities of multimedia can be quite dazzling. Computer based learning environments often opportunistically exploit these possibilities. There is nothing wrong with opportunism, but it is not enough. We need a principled understanding to guide the effective use of the new technology. The central aim of this book is to contribute to the development of that principled framework.

Figure 1.1 gives a simplified schematic overview of the main components involved in the development of an interactive multimedia learning environment (IMLE). This provides a starting point for an exploration of what is involved in constructing IMLEs. The outer layers of the diagram (represented by the boxes) point to the basic knowledge and skills that feed into a project. One the one hand there is multimedia design knowledge; on the other there is knowledge of the domain. Design knowledge and skills are in turn broken down into two main areas. Conceptual design involves creating the deep learning architecture of the system. This involves structuring interactive options for the learner. It also involves, in consultation with the domain expert, the structuring of the domain knowledge. Presentation design deals with the realisation of the system as a computer based artefact. This involves issues such as screen layout, colour schemes and the detailed use of the individual media.

The central layer points to the process of developing a multimedia project. The process is usually one of iterative design. Initial design conceptions are instantiated as mock-ups, or as prototypes in an authoring system. The design features of the system are evaluated and this formative feedback is used to guide the next stage of

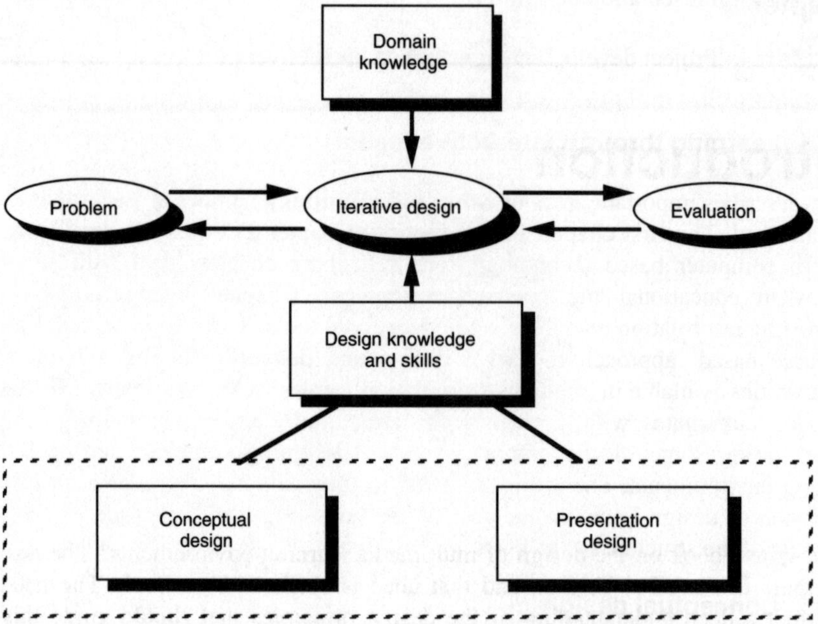

Figure 1.1 A schematic overview of the principal factors in IMLE design and development

development. Project development proceeds in a productive spiral where design, implementation and evaluation are dynamically interwoven.

This diagram identifies three areas of knowledge and skill required for the effective design and delivery of multimedia learning environments. These three areas involve conceptual design, presentation design and project management. There is a fourth area on which these three are predicated – a knowledge of good examples and work in the field. The book is structured into four parts. Each part deals with one of these topics.

Structure of the book

The four parts of the book are:

- Part 1: Learning through interactive media
- Part 2: Conceptual design

- Part 3: Presentation design
- Part 4: Project development, evaluation and delivery.

Part 1 Learning through interactive media

Part 1 describes important areas of work, and identifies a number of issues that need to be addressed. The first chapter in this section (Chapter 2) traces the development of modern computer based technology. The remaining chapters deal with significant themes in educational multimedia development. Chapter 3 reviews two areas: multimedia information resources, and educational tools. These fit in with the popular 'resource based' approach to IMLE design and delivery. Chapter 4 explores the opportunities available in interactive simulation, games and virtual reality. This part of the book culminates with a chapter on 'structured learning environments'. These studies tackle some of the central issues in designing complete computer based learning environments. The work reviewed in these chapters provides a base for the discussion of design issues in the rest of the book. Figure 1.2 provides a schematic overview of the structure of the book.

Part 2 Conceptual design

The two central parts of the book deal with conceptual and presentation design. Conceptual design is concerned with a trinity of issues:

- content structuring
- the structuring of interactivity
- creating a coherent compositional frame.

The discussion of these issues should be treated separately from presentation level concerns. Only in this way can we construct conceptual design principles that are independent of particular presentation constraints. The same conceptual design principles should inform IMLEs implemented in two-dimensional or three-dimensional formats.

The discussion of conceptual design in Part 2 is divided into three chapters. Chapter 6 provides a review and critique of traditional CAI (Computer Aided Instruction) and the dominant modern approach – constructivism. Constructivism emphasises the active role of the learner. Learners are viewed as constructing their own knowledge of the world. The task for designers is to create environments that support these constructive processes. The following two chapters develop a line of argument for a more declarative approach to representing design knowledge. A synthesis is derived in which 'context' is the central explanatory concept. Based on work in film analysis and

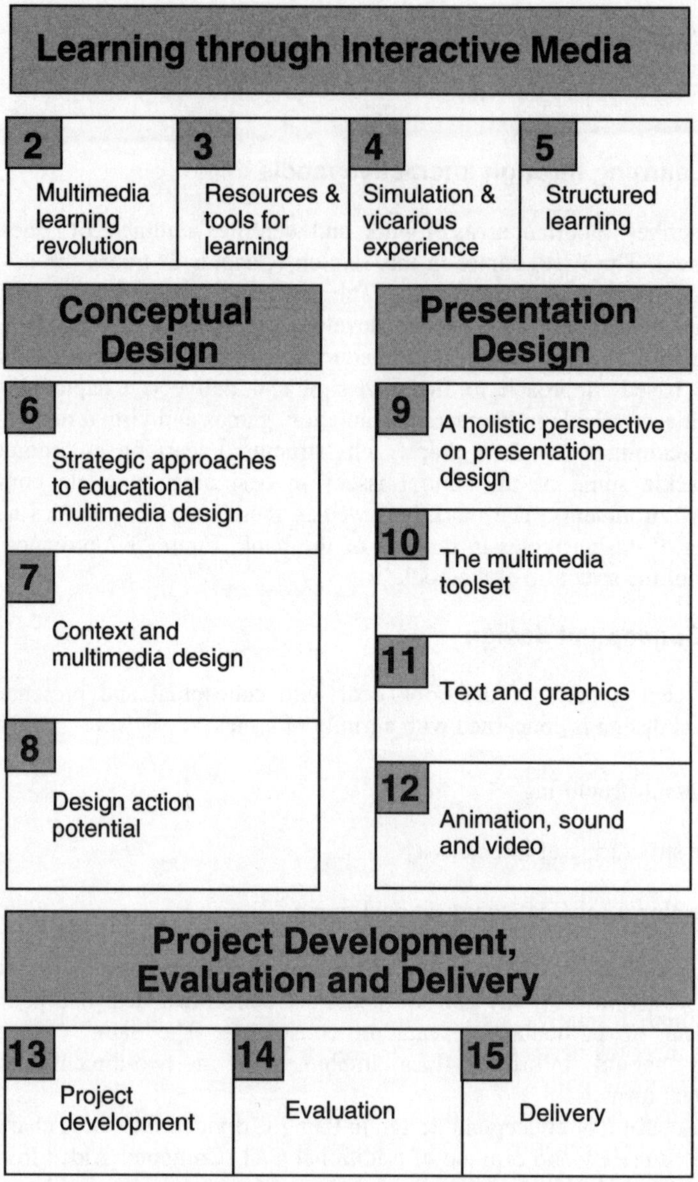

Figure 1.2 Overview of the structure of the book

linguistics it is argued that there are three macro-functions inherent in all communication contexts. The first two macro-functions involve the structuring of communication content and the structuring of interactivity. The third macro-function concerns the creation of a coherent 'Gestalt'. In Chapter 8 the idea of 'design action potential' networks is introduced as a way of representing the options available in these three areas. These networks aim to capture in a systematic manner what *we can do* in design.

Part 3 Presentation design

Part 3 of the book deals with presentation design. The choices made in conceptual design have to be realised using the media available. Presentation design involves choices in the use of the various media. It also involves decisions about holistic presentation features such as screen layout and media integration. The first chapter in this part (Chapter 9) deals with these holistic aspects of presentation design. It reviews characteristics of human perception and discusses principles of multimedia composition. Chapter 10 provides a review of the multimedia toolset. Detailed information about tools can change very rapidly. The aim of this chapter is to establish the framework of choice, and to illustrate authoring paradigms. Chapter 11 deals with the design of text and graphics, including colour composition. Chapter 12 then discusses the dynamic media of animation, sound and video. These time based media produce their own problems for multimedia integration. Video, for example, is a multimedia phenomenon in its own right. This chapter discusses how these media may be restructured to provide flexible interactive access within a wider multimedia context.

Part 4 Project development, evaluation and delivery

The final part of the book deals with project development, evaluation and delivery. Chapter 13 discusses the main issues in project development. This includes the overall structure for managing development, and issues such as the capture and communication of design ideas. Evaluation is a critical factor in the effective development and delivery of IMLEs. The discussion of evaluation in Chapter 14 covers a range of evaluation techniques: observation, interviews and questionnaires. It discusses both formative and summative evaluation, and how evaluation should be framed to meet the needs of different interested parties. The final chapter in the book, Chapter 15, deals with system delivery. Poor delivery can undermine the effect of good design. It is a critical issue for the effectiveness of IMLEs. Chapter 15 outlines different delivery scenarios. It deals with packaging the system, and ensuring effective delivery in an organisation. This involves ensuring an adequate delivery infrastructure, and dealing with the key groups of users.

Reading the book

The book may be read in linear sequence, or the individual chapters may be accessed in a more flexible manner. Each part of the book deals with a significant domain of knowledge. Part 1 presents a review of work in the field. For those who are fairly new to the field this is the obvious place to start. The first chapter (Chapter 2) provides an overview of influences on the development of educational multimedia. Each chapter then deals with a significant area of work, as represented in Figure 1.2. There is a general move towards a tighter pedagogical focus as one moves through the chapters. However, the order of reading the chapters may be varied.

Part 2 provides an analysis of issues in conceptual design. There is a fairly clear narrative flow from the first to the last chapter. This part of the book is thus best read in the order presented. It assumes a knowledge of a variety of multimedia systems, such as those covered in the first part of the book.

Presentation design, covered in Part 3, is treated as a separate layer from conceptual design. Much of this material is relevant to the design of multimedia systems generally. This is where novice designers often want to start. There is a general movement in these chapters from overall aspects of design, through the simpler forms to the dynamic media types. However, there is a large degree of freedom in the order in which these chapters may be accessed.

Part 4 deals with project development, evaluation and delivery. This seems the logical order to follow on first reading. However, it is easy to directly access specific sections concerned with techniques of evaluation or particular aspects of delivery.

Part One

Learning through interactive media

Chapter 2

The multimedia learning revolution: from teaching machines to learning environments

A number of strands have fed into the weave of modern multimedia learning environments. There is first of all traditional computer assisted learning, and the substrands within this tradition. The advent of widely available hypertext provided a challenge based on new technology which supported user centred flexible browsing systems. Overlapping but making its main impact slightly later was multimedia technology. The richness and variety of the tools and materials available to the designer were dramatically transformed. These developments in turn are part of a much wider revolution in the communication and cultural shape of society. This chapter traces some of the significant influences feeding into the revolution in the design of interactive learning environments. It provides the backdrop to the exploration of specific themes later in the book.

2.1 Computer aided instruction (CAI)

Learning technology is a term which is currently in vogue. However, the term aptly captures the spirit of the first attempt to provide machine based teaching systems advocated by the leading behaviourist B. F. Skinner. The central feature of Behaviourism is extreme reductionism. There are two main aspects to this reductionism. The ‘scientific’ study of psychology is reduced to the study of overt, observable behaviour – cognition is regarded as an ‘epiphenomenon’ that is not central to the explanation of behaviour. The explanation of behaviour is then reduced to the study of certain fundamental laws of learning. For Skinner the most important form of learning was operant conditioning. The central premise of operant conditioning is that behaviour is shaped by its consequences. Behaviour is thus 'shaped' by the pattern of reinforcements (or rewards) in the environment.

This framework provides the basis for a very 'technical' approach to problems of applied psychology. There is an emphasis on a very clear, operational definition of the targets to be achieved. This approach had a strong influence in education in the form of 'behavioural objectives'– specifications of desired learning outcomes in terms of measurable behavioural targets. This desired behaviour can then be 'shaped' by arranging the reinforcement of a series of intermediate steps that lead to the target behaviour. This conception provided the direct impetus for the first teaching machines. These were originally mechanical machines that presented material to learners in a carefully defined order. By rigidly optimising the presentation of learning material, it was argued, you could optimise the process of learning.

The wider availability of computers in the late sixties and seventies provided a more powerful medium for delivery. The rigid paths of the early machines were replaced with branching systems, i.e. systems where different paths could be followed depending on the responses of the learner. The tradition of formal design of computer based teaching systems remained very strong. In the mid sixties Gagné's book *The Conditions of Learning* was published. This provided a formal systematisation of learning theory which was very influential in shaping approaches to CAL design. This formal approach laid the basis for 'instructional design'. This emphasised a highly disciplined approach to design. You first analyse the target behaviour to systematically decompose it into its constituent skills. This decomposition is used to derive a sequence of content. Simpler skills are practised and mastered before more complex ones. This systematic structuring of the curriculum is matched by a pedagogical emphasis on systematic drill and practice. It is an extremely precise procedural model of the instructional domain. As Laurillard (1993) points out, this approach was very successful. It provided a formal, systematic guidance for the designer of CAL and CBT (Computer Based Training) systems. This approach has been carried over by some into the design of multimedia learning environments (O'Toole 1993).

2.2 Logo and constructivist learning environments

A very different approach to computer support for learning was advocated by Papert (1980). The tradition from which Papert derived his ideas was very different to that of instructional design. Papert had worked for two years with Jean Piaget, the father of developmental cognitive psychology. Piaget developed a sweeping intellectual framework for what he called 'genetic epistemology' (Piaget 1970). He was concerned with how the child came to develop knowledge of the world. There are two great traditions in epistemology. The empiricist tradition argues that our senses give us accurate information of at least key aspects of the world. The rationalist tradition, by contrast, emphasises pre-built rational structures which enable us to make sense of the world. Both these traditions have had marked impacts on the modern human sciences. Behaviourist psychology was very much in the empiricist tradition; modern language analysis was much influenced by Chomsky's idea of an inbuilt rational language acquisition device. Piaget took a radical third position. He argued that the child, through interacting with the world, *constructs* knowledge of the world. This constructivist view of learning and cognitive development provides an important theme in understanding the design of multimedia learning environments. Learners are viewed as active constructors of their knowledge of the world.

Papert took these theoretical ideas as a basis for the design of learning environments which would facilitate the process of cognitive development. To use his own words he developed a number of 'powerful ideas' for the design of computer based learning environments. These ideas were embodied in the design of the language Logo and the learning interactions it was used to support. The aim of introducing children to Logo was not just to get them to learn a computer language, but to assist their cognitive development. The best known feature of Logo is Turtle Graphics. The turtle is a small floor robot which responds to command written in Logo. Alternatively, and more abstractly, the turtle may be represented by a cursor on the computer screen. A program is a set of instructions the child gives to the turtle to do something, such as draw a rectangle or a triangle. In a subsequent program the child may combine these 'procedures' to create more complex shapes, such as a drawing of a house.

The turtle represents one of these powerful ideas. It is a transitional object. Papert was particularly concerned with introducing children to mathematics. Many mathematical concepts seem too abstract, removed and alien for children to grasp. The transitional object allows the children to make sense of tasks in terms of everyday familiar experience, but supports them in moving into the world of the abstract. When children are asked to draw a circle this may at first seem too difficult. So they are encouraged to use their intuitive 'body geometry'. One child can tell another how to walk in a circle. The commands are basically – forward a little, turn a little, and so on. This can them become a program for the turtle. As a consequence of this approach one eight-year-old boy argued with Papert that a circle is really a pentagon with lots of little sides. This is a quite profound mathematical insight. But it also the child's own knowledge – he discovered this insight through working with Logo. It is the child's knowledge, not someone else's. The idea of transitional objects, or transitional contexts, is a crucial one for the design of interactive learning environments for complex, abstract skills.

Within Logo mistakes are treated not as errors but as opportunities to learn. Making errors a productive part of the learning process is another important theme. Several years ago I watched a group of educational psychologists make such a mistake when trying to draw a triangle in Logo. The mistake they made is illustrated in Figure 2.1. They had drawn the first two sides of the triangle and they needed to turn the turtle (represented by an arrow on the screen) to the correct angle for the third side. They gave the command to turn the turtle 45° instead of 135° (i.e. 90° + 45°). The dashed line

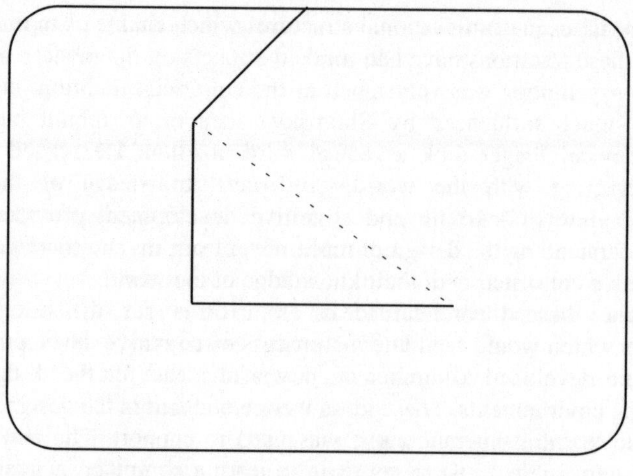

Figure 2.1 The psychologists' mistake

in Figure 2.1 indicates the effect aimed at; the solid lines show the shape created. When they issued the command to draw the final side the turtle shot off the screen. What was interesting was the reaction to the basic mistake they made. They did not look embarrassed and freeze up; they burst out laughing and then animatedly started debugging the problem, i.e. discussing what had gone wrong and correcting it. This treatment of mistakes is important in facilitating active, constructive learning.

Papert developed another idea which is highly relevant to modern IMLE design. 'Microworlds' could be developed with Logo to let the child actively explore certain abstract concepts. For example, in a 'Newtonian' world the children could manipulate objects and see how they behaved. Papert argued that this provided a better basis for coming to terms with Newtonian physics than abstract descriptions in textbooks. Multimedia technology provides the basis for much more sophisticated microworlds than can be created in Logo. The concept of microworlds provides a potentially very powerful technique for constructing sophisticated interactive learning environments.

Logo provided not a teaching regime but a child centred learning environment based on a constructivist psychology. There is a series of penetrating insights which are still salient for modern IMLE design. Over and above these conceptual insights there is a strategic view that the overall challenge is the one of transforming a culture. If this latter point fails to be appreciated then all the multimedia CAL systems in the world will have only a minor impact. The chances of cultural transformation are now much greater than in 1980. Multimedia technology is making an increasing impact. I only have to watch my seven-year-old son on his games machine to remind me of that. This decade will see a revolution in multimedia and telematics which will affect home and work as well as education. Within the educational sphere a central challenge will be to produce high quality educational artefacts; the concepts associated with Logo have important insights to offer in this endeavour.

2.3 Minimalism

Minimalism represents a challenge to systematic instructional design from a different direction. The main tenets of this approach are set out in Carroll (1990). Carroll and his co-workers were concerned with how adults learn to use IT systems, such as word processors. They carried out a number of empirical studies which led them to reject the formal systems approach to instructional design. Instead they proposed a much more dynamic user centred approach. The name they gave to this approach is 'Minimalism'. The central idea is to minimise the amount of explicit instructional material and instead to support 'natural' patterns of learning. This approach was originally concerned with paper based learning material. The principles developed, however, are important for the design of computer based interactive learning environments. Unlike many others they started with the process of learning and worked back to the technology. This approach was later extended to develop CAL systems (Rosson et al. 1990).

The Minimalist principles were derived from the task analysis of people learning to use IT tools using instructional materials based on traditional systematic instructional design. They found that the traditional approach worked poorly. They observed that people were dynamically trying to make sense of the situation rather than following a rigid series of steps. As Carroll (1990) puts it, 'they were too busy learning to make much sense of the instructions' (p. 74). The users seemed to want meaningful interaction with 'real' tasks rather than formal drill and instruction.

A series of design principles for an alternative 'minimalist' approach to instruction was developed. The aim was to exploit people's natural sense making propensities, and to produce highly user centred learning environments. The first principle emphasised was to get learners started quickly on real tasks. The creation of a personally meaningful agenda took precedence over any systematic curriculum. Support should be provided for exploration, reasoning and improvisation. Incomplete materials, for example, with mechanisms to support completion by the learner, encouraged this active style of learning. Error recognition and recovery should be strongly supported. As with Logo, learning from mistakes was viewed as an essential part of active learning. By contrast intrusive instructional materials were to be reduced to a minimum. Minimalism thus emphasises supporting dynamic, user centred learning, and provides a set of design heuristics to construct learning environments which support this approach.

Given the user centred emphasis Minimalism also emphasised a high degree of freedom of access to learning materials. Learning material should be highly modular – a structure of small self-contained units. Learners could then choose the units useful to support their activity, rather than being constrained to a predefined learning sequence.

This idea links very nicely with the concept of hypertext and hypermedia. Hypertext provides a natural technology for implementing this design feature.

2.4 Hypertext and hypermedia

The hypertext wave, which hit in the mid to late eighties, offered a new software technology and a related conception of how information space should be structured. This approach supports highly flexible access and navigation through an information space. The original hypertext concept was advocated by Vannevar Bush in 1945. He envisaged a system, called 'memex', which would help individuals deal with the information explosion. The memex would provide associative access to items in a vast database. Any item could be caused at will to automatically select a link to an associated item. The user could thus peruse the database following a dynamic association of ideas.

Our traditional modes of organising information have a strong linear element – stories, books and video. The idea of a hyperstructured information space was to replace linear structures with a network of nodes of information. The user would have considerable freedom of access to individual nodes and to traversal between them. The user could thus structure the information access which suited their needs at a particular time.

In the sixties Engelbart implemented a number of hypertext features as part of the Augment system. The aim of the project was to develop tools which would augment the intellect of people. Ted Nelson invented the term hypertext around this time. He envisaged a system called Xanadu where a vast database of world information would be available to individuals. Developments, however, were limited by the technology available at the time.

The idea of a hypermedia system is illustrated in Figure 2.2. The black circles are used to indicate hot spots on the screen from which jumps to other information can be made. One of the buttons at the bottom of the screen will be a 'backtrack' button. This enables the user to retrace the series of jumps made to reach this node. Other standard buttons may support linear navigation ('page forward', 'page back') and standard hierarchical jumps, e.g. going back to a contents screen.

In the 1980s a number of commercial hypertext systems became available. Reviews of these systems are given in a number of sources, e.g. Hardman (1990), Barker (1993) and Nielson (1990). In 1986 the GUIDE hypertext authoring system was released for the Apple Macintosh, followed by a version for IBM PC compatibles. The greatest impact, however, was made by the release of HyperCard for Apple Macintosh computers in 1987. HyperCard was bundled free with every Macintosh sold. It combined hypertext features with the graphical user interface of the Apple computer. It provided an easily available, powerful authoring tool which became very popular. Ambron and Hooper (1990) provide a catalogue of systems developed using HyperCard.

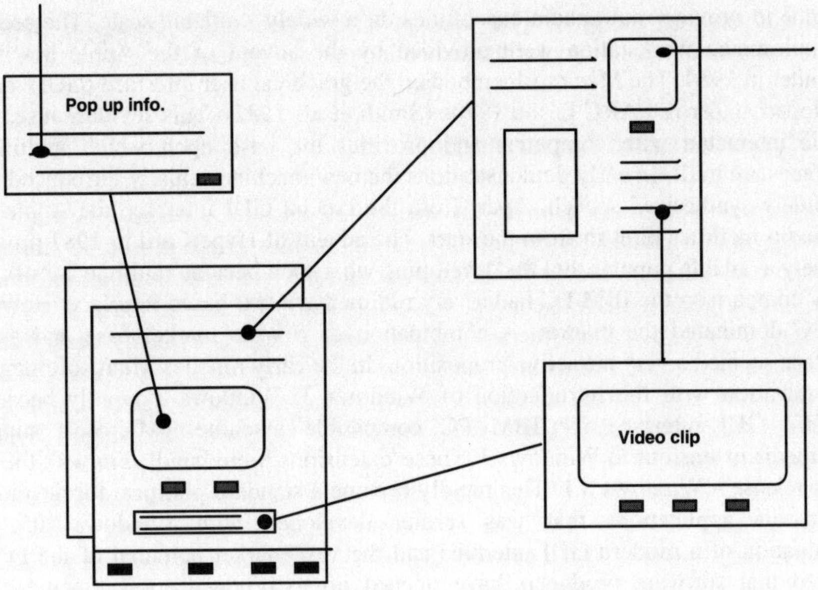

Figure 2.2 Example of a page based hypermedia system

An interesting development is the Microcosm system developed at the University of Southampton (Hall 1993). This provides a sort of meta-hypermedia tool. Information developed in a variety of different application may be linked using Microcosm. This is based on the separation of the links from the information stored at the nodes. This allows the links to be processed separately as data and provides a powerful and flexible mechanism for open hypertext linking. It thus harks back to the original idea of open access to large information bases.

The hypertext wave was soon overtaken and reinforced by developments in multimedia technology. Multimedia personal computers began to become increasingly available. Hypertext rapidly moved into hypermedia, where the nodes of information may be of any media type.

2.5 Affordable multimedia workstations

In the nineties personal computers have been transformed into multimedia workstations. This provides the base for the implementation of multimedia learning environments. In this education is riding on the wave of the general multimedia revolution in personal computing. The two main platforms for this mass market are the Apple Macintosh and the Multimedia PC (MPC). The Apple Macintosh was the first machine to provide multimedia capabilities on a widely available scale. The seeds of the multimedia workstation were provided by the advent of the Apple Macintosh computer in 1984. The Macintosh embodied the graphical user interface (GUI) design developed at Zerox PARC in the 1970s (Smith et al. 1982). This revolutionised how people interacted with computers and provides the base upon which multimedia interfaces are built. In early demonstrations the new machine actually introduced itself in crudely synthesised speech. Apart from the crucial GUI interface the Apple Mac had audio facilities built in from the start. The advent of HyperCard in 1987 provided a widely available popular tool for developing what soon became multimedia 'stacks'.

By comparison the IBM PC had a very rudimentary text based interface. However, the PC dominated the market. A combination of a wide market base and a GUI interface seemed a very attractive proposition. In the early nineties Microsoft managed this transition with the introduction of Windows 3. Windows 3 rapidly became a standard GUI interface for IBM PC compatible machines. Microsoft supplied multimedia extensions to Windows 3. These 'extensions' were bundled in with the next major release – Windows 3.1. This rapidly became a standard platform for developing multimedia applications that was further developed with Windows '95. The combination of a modern GUI interface and the vast market potential of the PC has ensured that software producers have queued up to produce applications for this platform.

In 1990 Microsoft and a number of major companies got together to define the MPC standard. This specified the capabilities that a computer should have to qualify as a 'Multimedia PC' (MPC). The entry standard was originally set quite low to provide multimedia upgrade capabilities for a wide range of standard PCs. The details of the standard, and its various entry levels, are discussed in Chapter 10. The essential elements were the addition of a good quality sound card and a CD ROM drive. Windows with multimedia extensions provided the basic software tools to exploit the capabilities of the enhanced hardware.

Powerful software tools and hardware add-ons rapidly became available for both platforms. Apple provided software video control through the QuickTime system. Microsoft later released Video for Windows as a relatively cheap software video playback systems for Windows. The basic framework of the multimedia desktop workstation is now well established. Crucially for education these workstations provide not only a development platform but also a mass delivery platform for multimedia systems.

2.6 Back to the future: the Internet and the World Wide Web

The Internet and the World Wide Web have sent shock waves through the entire computing industry. They provide the entry into the electronic market place of the future. This market place will be based on multimedia networks. The Internet and the Web provide the foundation on which this new market place is being built. This transformation is being driven by technological and commercial factors. Billion dollar industries see the 'information superhighway' as crucial to their commercial prosperity. This revolution heralds new standards in content production, distribution and sales. For education it opens up the prospect of developing 'national learning infrastructures' based on the new multimedia networks (Twigg 1994).

The Internet is a global network of networks made possible by common protocols for information exchange. The origins of the Internet are in the defence research networks in the USA. These networks were designed to be fault tolerant so that in the event of war the destruction of individual nodes would not bring down the network. This produces a very flexible and adaptable network structure. These protocols (standards for communicating between computers) later become very widely used. This enabled the development of an 'Internet' of networks either using or providing interfaces to these standard protocols. From the mid nineties this network began to attract enormous commercial interest. This was sparked off by a second major development – the advent of the World Wide Web.

The World Wide Web acts like a global, distributed hypermedia system. It provides a standard for structuring applications as hypertext documents that can be 'published' on the Internet. The Web originated in 1989 at CERN, the European high energy physics research centre, as a means of distributing information between geographically separated research groups. Mosaic, the first graphical browser for the Web, was released in 1993. The Web has developed at a phenomenal rate ever since. For most users the Web is the application interface to the Internet.

The Web comes close to realising the hypertext dream of the early visionaries. For users the Web application is presented as a standard hypertext document on the screen. Clicking on a marked link spot in that document can cause a jump to material held on a local hard disk or on a computer half way round the world. The advantage for the author is the speed and ease of producing these documents. The basic authoring technique is to use a mark-up language (HTML) to provide formatting instructions and place links to other documents. This makes it comparatively easy to create content that can be distributed world wide.

From a multimedia perspective this approach can be rather limiting. However, the Java language, released in 1995, supports the creation of full interactive multimedia applications. Java has been adapted with amazing speed as a standard tool by major software producers. This supports the development of highly interactive multimedia applications that can be integrated into Web documents. Distributed 'virtual reality' systems can be created using VRML (Virtual Reality Modelling Language). This tool permits the creation of three-dimensional worlds that can be accessed over the Internet. Hypermedia jumps can be between these worlds and standard Web documents. With the further creation of high level productivity tools the Internet offers great opportunities for multimedia authoring and distribution.

Gates (1995) declared that the Internet is not the information superhighway. He was undoubtedly correct. Through a series of transformations, however, the Internet may well transform itself into the information superhighway. Negroponte (1995a) provides an illuminating series of sketches of what this future might look like. The impact on education and training will be enormous. It will permit planning for national learning infrastructures and 'virtual' learning communities (Bates 1994). The quality of the content provided will be crucial. The early wave of slotting material into the technological possibilities afforded by HTML must be superseded. The electronic superhighway will provide a great opportunity space for well-designed learning applications. Good design, however, does not emerge opportunistically from using the technology. It requires creative insights and good, deep design that can be mapped on to the opportunity space available. The major theme of this book is to explore and clarify the nature of good design for educational multimedia.

2.7 Summary

This chapter has reviewed a number of strands that have contributed to the development of modern learning technology. Papert pointed out in 1980, which now seems a long time ago, that the challenge of changing learning environments is tied up with the question of cultural change. Frameworks for fundamental change have been proposed in both America (Twigg 1994), Britain (MacFarlane 1992) and Europe (Van den Brande 1993). The wider cultural and organisational changes will rely on the production of well-designed high quality learning materials. The creative clash of different media and the traditions associated with them opens up exciting possibilities. But where can we derive the frameworks that will guide the design of multimedia learning experiences? In the next three chapters we will look at a variety of ways that multimedia learning techniques can be used. This provides a survey of some of the main issues that have been tackled. At the heart of good design are good exemplars. The review of exemplars of different types of multimedia systems is thus an ideal place to start.

Chapter 3

Resources and tools for learning

3.1 Introduction

Multimedia technology can be used to support a variety of learning settings. Any division across these settings has to be primarily for descriptive purposes. Education is complex and multimedia is a hybrid form. It is often the 'hybrid' adaptations that underpin the most effective learning environments. A list of basic topics, however, may be drawn up that provides a descriptive framework. These main topics are:

- information dissemination and retrieval
- tools and composition support
- simulations and vicarious experience
- structured skill and knowledge acquisition.

These first two areas of educational multimedia are discussed in the present chapter. Information dissemination systems provide multimedia resources for information retrieval and browsing. Multimedia encyclopaedias and reference works provide prototypical examples of this type of application. These multimedia resources extend the richness of the learning environment. A range of software tools may empower learners in analysing and manipulating retrieved material and in constructing their own artefacts.

The succeeding chapters deal with the two other major categories of multimedia learning. 'Virtual experience' systems aim to immerse the user in environments that provide realistic simulations of real-life or imagined learning contexts. Some of the most striking examples of multimedia learning technology are represented in this category. The technological sophistication of these systems varies from basic simulations through to full virtual reality. A similar educational intuition underlies these systems – that experience and involvement in the target situation provide a powerful basis for authentic learning. The next category, structured learning environments, is discussed in Chapter 5. In many ways this represents the greatest educational challenge. How can we combine tutorial guidance and student centred learning in structured, complex domains?

A central issue in exploring each of these domains is the nature and quality of the interactivity supported. Piaget (1970) argues that we construct our knowledge of the world through interacting with the world. Knowledge is neither pre-given, nor stamped in by the impact of external stimuli. It is constructed and validated through interaction. A central issue in interactive multimedia design is the nature and quality of the interaction. The technological possibilities of interactive multimedia offer great scope for productive innovation in this field.

3.2 Information dissemination and retrieval

3.2.1 Information retrieval

This has been one of the most prevalent uses of multimedia in educational settings (Heppel 1993, Romiszowski 1993). This type of use is supported by CD ROM based encyclopaedias and reference 'books', e.g. 'Microsoft Encarta', 'The Multimedia Encyclopaedia of Mammalian Biology', 'Multimedia Musical Instruments'. This in many ways is a natural hypermedia application. There is a clear traditional format – the encyclopaedia or resource book – which lends itself to multimedia enhancement and hypermedia cross referencing. The new multimedia resources can be integrated into well established teaching approaches, such as project work in schools, with minimal disruption. It therefore provides an attractive multimedia resource for many teachers.

Nielson (1990) reviews a number of applications where this information retrieval function is the dominant one. These include on-line help and manuals as well as dictionaries and reference books. Some of these uses have now become standard. For example, the Microsoft Windows operating system uses a hypertext format as the standard for on-line help. Software applications developed to run under Windows follow this standard help format. One of the first multimedia information resources in Europe developed specifically for schools was the BBC Doomsday book. More than one million volunteers, mainly schoolchildren, collected information about their local communities. The system was released on two interactive video disks in 1986. The technology at that time, however, was too expensive for most schools, and this severely limited the use of the system. Commercial CD ROM based systems, however, are increasingly finding their way into schools and this information dissemination function has become widely accepted.

There are interesting issues about how to compare, process and structure the information that has been retrieved. Often these issues are left to the tutor to supply as part of the overall learning environment. But there is clear scope for extending systems to support these processing functions. The 'Chronoscope', a prototype system for viewing impressionist art, explores issues of how to structure the retrieved information. The information consists of reproductions of impressionist art stored in the Musée d'Orsay in Paris, and supporting material. The pictures are organised on a 'time line'. The viewer can have different size views on this time line, and can select particular pictures and bring up information about the artist. The authors argue that the time line gives a 'virtual space' for the representation of time that facilitates a conceptual grasp of how design evolved over this time period (Hodges and Sasnett 1993).

3.2.2 Informational retrieval from the World Wide Web

Viewed over the long term, disk based storage may represent a transitional technology in the sphere of information retrieval. There are already available vast network based information resources that are open and comparatively easy to use. The Internet provides a global 'network of networks' which gives a revolution in access for the computer user. The World Wide Web (or Web for short) organises information on the Internet as a set of hypertext documents. Each document consists of content and links. As these links can point to any other document on the Web this produces a vast distributed 'hyperbase' of information. For example, in Figure 3.1 each piece of underlined text acts as a link that provides a jump to a specific resource. The resources listed are the various CTI (Computers in Teaching Initiative) Web sites. These sites hold information about computer based learning technology applied to specific subject areas.

A number of features have contributed to the phenomenal growth of Internet and the Web:

- Platform independence. The underlying protocols mean that these systems can be accessed from all the popular hardware and operating systems platforms.

- Flexibility brought about by the server–client approach. The server machines send information to the client machines. The information to be sent can be minimized by letting the client software (browsers like Mosaic and Netscape) carry out the work of presenting attractive graphic interfaces.

- Ease of authoring. The hypertext features of Web documents are produced by mark-up symbols embedded in the documents. The client software interprets the mark-up symbols and manages the local display. The mark-up language is HTML (**H**yper**T**ext **M**ark-up **L**anguage). This is very easy to use thus almost anyone can author a document for 'publication' on the Web.

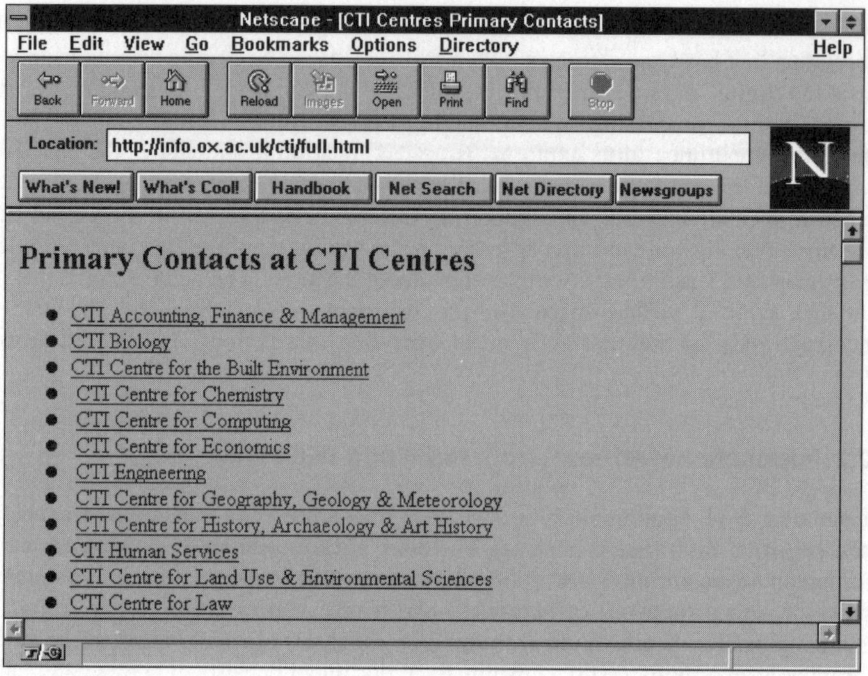

Figure 3.1 Web screen from the Computers in Teaching Initiative Support Centre

There is a plethora of books on the Internet and the World Wide Web. Krol (1994), for example, provides a comprehensive introduction to the Internet. Several books introduce the Web and HTML authoring (e.g. Ford 1995). The focus of the present discussion is how these facilities contribute to the development of effective learning environments. To answer this question the Internet and the Web need to be considered as a new opportunity space. These developments represent a revolution in access. How can this access be best used to achieve effective learning?

Darby (1995) describes his experiences of using the Web with students. They were asked to search the Web for up-to-date information on modern computer technologies. Darby comments, 'My students were initially intrigued and fascinated by Gopher and the World Wide Web'. Then an assignment was set for which they needed to find answers to specific questions. The initial euphoria rapidly evaporated. The available search engines proved far from satisfactory. Access times were frustratingly slow, and when information was downloaded it was often found to be unsuitable. The students, however, continued to acknowledge the potential of the Internet and World Wide Web.

The finding reported by Darby is not very surprising. Information scientists have struggled for years with the problem of conducting effective searches on conventional bibliographic databases. The normal technique has been for a skilled librarian to help the end user conduct the search. Attempts to provide computer based support for this process have revealed the complexity involved (Belkin et al. 1987, Ingwersen 1986). The initial euphoria of tutors in providing access to these networked resources needs to be succeeded by a realistic assessment of the problems involved, and the development of techniques and tools to support the effective use of these resources.

Many researchers are asking pertinent questions about how information retrieval is to be supported and integrated into the wider learning experience. The following section describes a model of 'resource based learning' as a means of organising this function. Several important questions still remain. These issues are addressed in the subsequent discussion.

3.2.3 Resource based learning

Information dissemination and retrieval have to be integrated into wider educational activities. The most common proposal for integrating the wealth of information available into education is resource based learning. This is a very general approach. A central theme is the creation, retrieval and use of computer based resources. Hall et al. (1995) provide a sharper picture of how a resource based approach may be conceptually organised. Their approach is based on the idea of 'open hypermedia systems'.

In traditional hypertext systems the links to other resources are embedded in the material. Most material on the World Wide Web, for example, is based on HTML. In an HTML document the anchors are embedded in the document as it is created. In an open hypermedia system the links are separated from the data and stored in a separate link database. These links can be easily changed, and different link databases set up to satisfy different requirements. By freeing the content from the links it becomes easier to use the content as a flexible, reusable resource. This potentially provides a much more powerful architecture for resource based learning. This architecture is illustrated in Figure 3.2.

This conceptual model consists of a series of layers. The base layer consists of the collection of resources. These may be held on local hard disks, local network servers, CD ROMs or the World Wide Web. The primary educational decisions about the selection and use of resources are made at the top layer. This layer relates to the educational context in which the resources are to be used. The selection and configuration at this layer may be made by a course team of local trainers or tutors. This facility to create an educational artefact from pre-existing resources may be extended naturally to students and trainees. This 'authoring' of educational resources is achieved through the facilities provided by the middle layer, the link management layer. Educational 'authoring' becomes focused on the reuse of electronic resources. In this approach the information retrieval function plays a key role in the conceptual framework for learning technology.

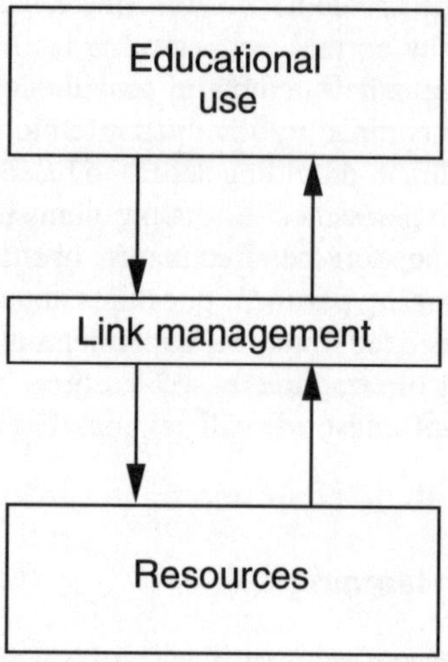

Figure 3.2 A layered approach to resource based learning

This conceptual framework is supported by a sophisticated tool – the Microcosm system developed at the University of Southampton (Hall 1993). This tool supports the integration of information created in a variety of original applications, e.g. word processors, graphics packages and multimedia authoring tools. The data files remain in the native format of the application that created them. The links for accessing information are held in a separate link database. This holds information on the source of the links, the destinations, and the type of each link. Different link databases may be created by different tutors to suit their own purposes. Front ends may be created in other applications, such as ToolBook, to create structured learning environments which use the information provided through the link database.

The concept of layering is a very important concept in computer science. The ISO (International Standards Organisation) model, for example, divides computer communications into a set of separate layers. Each layer provides a self-contained service to the layer above it. This architecture is also manifest in natural systems such as human language. The phonological layer in language is separately organised from the lexico-grammatical layer. The result is considerable flexibility and power. The proposal for resource based learning based on a layered approach is thus very interesting. The 'education layer' could use the material held at the resources layer in a highly flexible fashion.

There are a number of problems with implementing this approach on a wider scale. The de facto standard for the creation and dissemination of hypermedia resources is the World Wide Web. The documents for the Web are based on HTML. In this approach the links are embedded as mark-up symbols in the documents. These documents vary widely in purpose, quality and size. There are clearly problems in 're-purposing' these documents to create a coherent learning environment. It is much easier to do what comes naturally: browse, and then afford this more educational significance than it warrants. A second key issue, which is central to the concerns of this book, is the structuring of the 'educational use' layer. Talk of resource based learning often finesses this issue. By permitting almost any practice, resource based learning succeeds in giving very little guidance about the design principles to be applied. The layered approach, however, does provide a clear framework for relating resources to educational use. If it can be implemented, this framework offers many advantages in economy and productivity.

3.2.4 Critical reflections on resource based information retrieval models

Hammond (1995) argues that many of the mistakes made when computers were first introduced into schools are being repeated with CD ROMs. His comments are equally applicable to network based information retrieval. The initial introduction of computers was dominated by the idea that the introduction of computers would itself provide general educational benefits. It is now often uncritically assumed that access to vast stores of information by itself will bring broad educational benefits.

A key criticism Hammond makes is that information may be confused with knowledge. He asks – how far do critical faculties emerge as opposed to surface understanding? It has been claimed that hypertext is a natural augmentor of intellect because it parallels the free association of ideas in the mind. It is amazing that this notion has gone comparatively unchallenged for so long. If the mind was organised on the basis of free association it would be chaotic, a biological failure. Psychological research has repeatedly shown that the key feature of the mind is that it imposes selective coherence on the world. This is the nature of how we understand and adapt. There is a creative interplay between the 'chaos' of association and the structured complexity of understanding, but achieving this high level coherence is crucial. A primary function of education is to 'educate' people to be more penetrating in the *selective* coherences they construct. A naive view of the Web and hypertext undermines what education is about: the construction of coherent knowledge. A question that needs to be asked is – does hypertext encourage deep or shallow learning? The answer, no doubt, is … it depends. We need to clarify these dependencies. What is good practice and what is bad practice in exploiting the vast information resources now available?

Henderson (1995) has argued that the information available on the Web is often inadequate for learning. He states that the dominant 'information base' model is too limited. 'There is little ability or effort to organise, contextualise, and develop coherent educational experiences' (Henderson 1995, p. 2). He argues for the development and dissemination of specific structured educational programs. This approach does not contradict the resource based approach. However, the focus is quite different. The emphasis is upon high quality, coherent learning environments rather than ease of access and reuse. The key question is – what is the quality of the educational experience? A pure resource based approach relies on the local tutor to supply that experience. Henderson argues for the need to design and provide high quality educational programs at source.

3.3 The computer as a tool

There are a number of approaches to using the computer as a tool. General tools, like word processors and spreadsheets, have been used to aid learning. A range of studies reporting the educational use of these 'worldtools' is given in Underwood (1994). There is a more direct set of tools (sometimes referred to as 'mindtools') developed specifically to enhance problem solving and learning. Several types of mindtools are reviewed in this section. The discussion begins with concept mapping tools. These provide support for problem solving by mapping ideas to a graphical form. The discussion then moves on to a range of software tools developed specifically to support learning.

3.3.1 Concept mapping

One of the commonest forms of mindtool is concept mapping. Concept mapping is a graphical display of conceptual knowledge. Concepts are represented by nodes in a network. The relationship between the concepts is indicated by the labelled links between nodes. Concept maps may be divided into different types such as linear chains, hierarchy maps and spider maps (West et al. 1991). Spider maps may be used to organise initial ideas. Figure 3.3 shows a spider map which I drew to outline initial ideas for this section. A hierarchy may be used later to impose a clearer structure on a set of ideas. Concept maps can be drawn out on paper. Computer based tools, however, may support the more sophisticated use of these techniques.

Trapp et al. (1992) performed a claims analysis on three representative knowledge mapping tools. The claims analysis aimed to explicate the claims such tools make about the nature of learning. These claims were then related to the psychological principles that might support or refute such claims. The three systems reviewed were Learning Tool (Kozma 1992), Semnet (Fisher 1992) and KNOT. These tools differ in their ease of use and power of representation. Learning Tool supports the use of direct manipulation to create networks. It also supports recursive networks; a node may open out into another network. Semnet uses a different interface style, menus and dialogue boxes, to create a network. KNOT provides a facility to create a network from proximity ratings of concepts produced by the user.

These tools can support a wide range of learning activities. A learner may use them to assimilate new knowledge or revise for exams. A tutor may use the network to diagnose a student's level of understanding. Different tools have different strengths that might best suit certain activities. Trapp concludes with support for the general

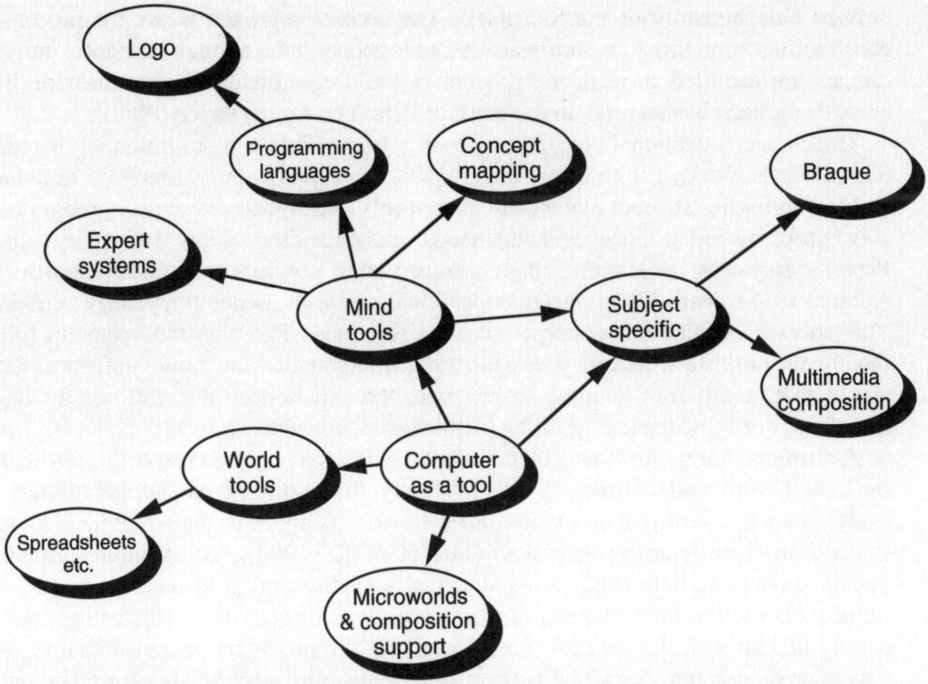

Figure 3.3 Spider map for the initial structure of this section

principles of knowledge mapping and supports the availability of a variety of tools. There are some qualifying issues in assessing concept maps. Learners often find difficulty in using concept maps (Reader and Hammond 1994, West et al. 1991). The counter argument is that the purpose of mapping is not to make learning easier but make it more effective (Jonassen and Marra 1994). This issue points to the central thrust behind these tools. Learning, it is argued, takes place *through* the process of using the tool. Bruner (1964) has argued that systems such as mathematics act as cognitive amplifiers. They enable us to solve problems that would be impossible to solve otherwise. The extent to which computer based knowledge mapping tools satisfy this function remains to be empirically verified. Jonassen and Marra (1994) suggest some caution in the power we attribute to concept maps. They argue that they are simply one of a range of tools one may use to augment cognition.

3.3.2 Construction tools for learning

There are two broad approaches to designing software construction tools for learning. The first approach uses construction tools to support an educational process that is defined independently of the tool itself. The second approach views the process of constructing something as intrinsically and deeply educational. Insights into the domain are acquired through the process of building structures using the tool. This second approach has its roots in the work of Papert on Logo (Papert 1980).

The classic educational construction tool is Logo. This is a programming language designed specifically for children. Papert (1980) was particularly interested in helping children to master abstract mathematical concepts. He argued that writing programs to solve problems led to a deeper mathematical understanding. Kafai (1996) picks up on Papert's emphasis on learning though constructing programs. He used Logo to get children (8–11 year old) to design educational software games for younger children. This software dealt with concepts such as fractions. The children spent up to six months on projects where they designed and implemented their own software. Kafai argues that, apart from learning to program, the experience gave children a deeper, more integrated understanding of the mathematical concepts.

A different, but by no means incompatible, emphasis is placed on tool use in studies by Linn (1996) and Guzdial et al. (1996). In these studies the learning tasks are analysed into a series of activities. Specific tool support is then provided to help students in these learning activities. Guzdial et al. (1996), for example, provide a graphical editor to help engineering students visualise design ideas. This is one of a set of tools used to help students in the whole range of activities. This use of tools is closely tied up with the idea of 'scaffolding', i.e. the provision of transitional support structures in learning. A general support strategy is to identify key learner tasks and to support these activities by using specially designed tools. The important concept of scaffolding is examined in more depth in Chapter 7.

3.3.3 Tools for collaborative learning

A number of tools has been developed to support communication and learning in groups. Linn (1996) describes a tool used to structure and support electronic discussion in learning groups. This tool, called SpeakEasy, guides students to indicate the function of their contribution, e.g. challenge to a previous contribution (Figure 3.4). The aim is to get the students to reflect on and plan their offering to the group discussion. These group discussions are part of a wider project based learning environment in which the students learn about scientific enquiry.

Guzdial et al. (1996) report the use of two tools to support collaborative learning in groups. The first tool supports brainstorming ideas and planning. The students gather round a single computer, and the system helps to structure and record the problem solving process. The tool presents the students with a whiteboard consisting of a series of named columns where the students can enter ideas about different aspects of the problem. The second tool works in a similar way to Linn's SpeakEasy. It structures asynchronous communication by asking the students to identify the function of their contribution. Students can use this tool to link their text notes to other media, such as diagrams. Notes can also be linked to WEB based material to support the presentation

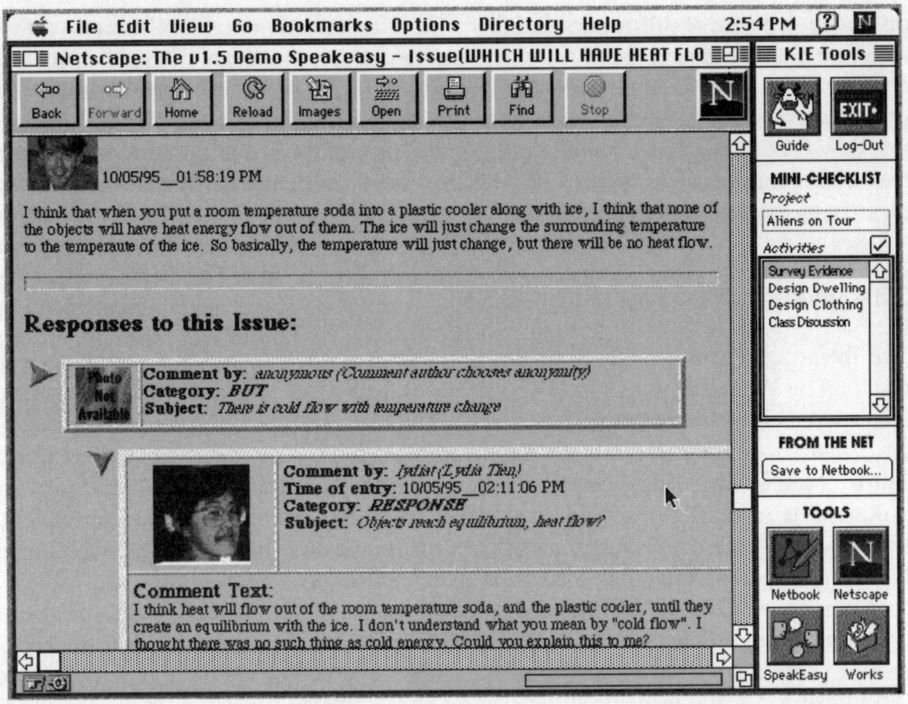

Figure 3.4 The SpeakEasy tool

and discussion of ideas.

In both these studies the communication tools are provided as components of a wider learning environment. The CSILE system has been developed as 'a computer-supported environment in which collaborative discourse is the primary medium for knowledge advancement' (Scardamalia and Bereiter 1996, p. 36). The CSILE environment consists of a communal database and a set of tools for the creation, linking and retrieval of notes. Shared authorship is implemented through turn taking and editing privileges. Structures are provided to support group criticism through electronic communication. An Internet version of the system has been constructed to link groups in several countries. Scardamalia and Bereiter (1996) report that the system has been extensively evaluated (mainly with the 10–14 age group) with very positive results. Many multimedia projects are reported as prototypes with limited evaluation. This study comes out well in this respect.

The 'Collaboratory Notebook' is a similar system to CSILE (Edelson et al. 1996). It also is implemented as a networked, hypermedia database. The students are provided with a fixed set of page types for recording information. These page types are based on a task model of scientific enquiry. The student, for example, can enter hypotheses on one page type, or evidence on another. This framework provides learners with a structure for organising their activities and group communication. Each page type contains hints on suitable follow-up activities. Edelson et al. (1996) argue that collaborative learning enables learners to accomplish tasks and develop understandings that they could not achieve alone. Furthermore, they propose that the need to articulate and communicate ideas provokes students into organising what they know and identifying gaps in their understanding.

3.3.4 Multimedia composition tools

The theme of learning *with* technology as opposed to learning *from* technology is taken up by Weingrad et al. (1993). They developed a tool to enable children to create their own multimedia compositions. They argue that students would be empowered by tools that support the creation of multimedia artefacts. The group developed a tool called 'MediaText'. They describe this as being 'to various media what a word processor is to text' (Weingrad et al. 1993, p. 542). The tool supports multimedia composition through a powerful set of easy-to-use media controls. All the main media types are supported, including the use of sound and video.

Weingrad et al. (1993) report the results of an exploratory study carried out at a Community High School in Ann Arbor, Michigan. The tool was used in a variety of classes – English composition, Physics, Science and Society – and a course on 'Multimedia: art and technology'. Teachers and students were very interested in the use of MediaText to create alternative forms of assessment. A multimedia composition seemed preferable to many of them to in-class exams. The results of this study point to a number of themes for further investigation. The first was the observance of two styles of composition labelled 'Annotated Text' and 'Integrated Composition'. They believe that the Integrated Composition style, where the message content is distributed across the media, may encourage greater understanding. They also propose that the incorporation of more materials that are meaningful outside the classroom would encourage cognitive engagement. This theme is echoed in the use of another multimedia tool 'Constellations' developed by Goldman-Segall to support participant ethnographic research (Goldman-Segall 1991, Goldman-Segall et al. 1994).

3.3.5 Domain specific tools

Tools may also be developed to support working in specific domains. An example is Braque, a tool used to support the learning of program design (Boyle and Davies 1996). The traditional approach to teaching program design is to use some form of 'stepwise refinement'. A problem is broken down in sub-problems. These problems, in turn, are broken down in a stepwise fashion. The result is a tree structure representing a hierarchy of levels of decomposition of the problem. The bottom nodes are small enough to map clearly on to program code. These structures are normally represented by one of two notations. Structure charts present a graphical representation of the

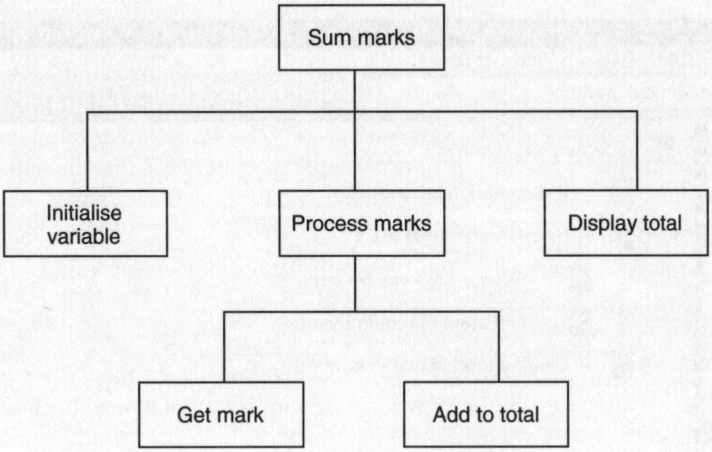


```
Sum student marks
          Set running total to zero
          Repeat processing  individual student marks
               Get the mark for the student
               Add mark to running total
          Display the total of the marks entered
```

Figure 3.5 Paper based structure chart and pseudo-code

structure. Pseudo-code or Structured English use text to provide a more detailed reflection of the problem breakdown (Figure 3.5).

There are a number of problems with this traditional approach. These problems may be distilled into three main areas: problems with the notation, problems with using paper based representations and problems with the design method. The first two problems provide a clear setting for developing a computer based tool. The third area is more problematic. It suggests that the tool may have to act as a catalyst in changing the content of the course. This reflects a tension in the development of computer based tools. Are they to be used to improve or transform the old way of doing things?

Paper based representations are cumbersome to maintain. Braque aimed to produce a computer based tool with a notation developed specifically to aid learners. This notation was created through a create–test–refine cycle. Candidate notations were mocked up using drawing packages and a series of formative tests was conducted. The notations were further refined based on the feedback received. The notations that resulted from this approach are presented in Figures 3.6 and 3.7. Figure 3.6 presents an example of the top 'goal decomposition' layer. The tree structure is turned on its side. Layers of indentation are colour coded as they move from left to right across the

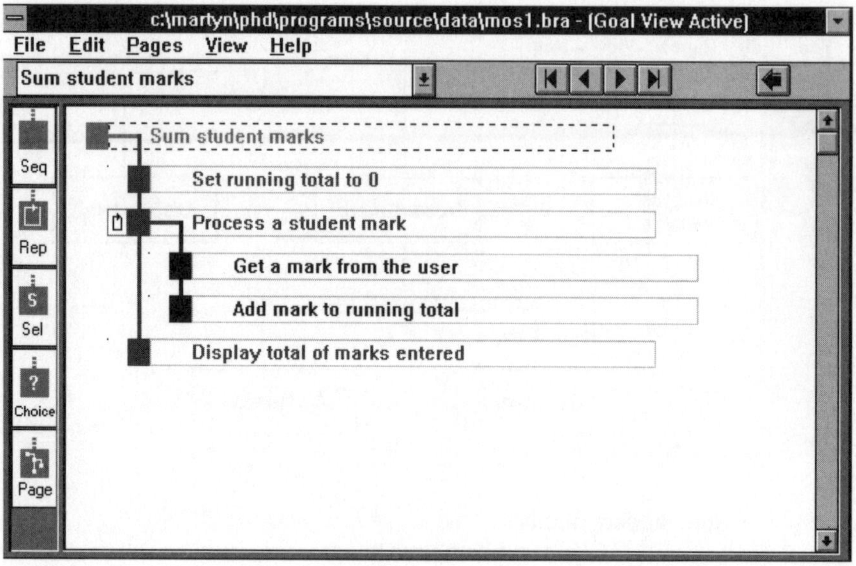

Figure 3.6 Goal level interface in Braque

screen (see Plate 7 in the colour insert). The aim was to produce strong perceptual representations of design structures.

Braque presents three views of the evolving design. The 'goal oriented' layer is a variant of structure charts. By turning the tree on its side structured English comments can easily be added to the design. Learners often have problems mapping from this high level goal decomposition to the procedural structure of the programs. Therefore, a second 'flow level' notation is presented to help students make this transition (Figure 3.7). This view is automatically generated by the program from the goal tree created by the student. The third view is simply the structured English on its own. This can be transferred directly into the editor of a commercial compiler environment. This produces the skeleton around which the student can build his program.

A full set of controls is provided for the student to create and edit a design. The goal tree is built using a drag and drop method. The student picks an icon from the palette at the left of the screen and drags it into position (Figure 3.6). The program automatically draws the connecting lines and sets the indentation colour. The student can double click on the node and add comments to the node via a dialogue box. The overall design can be edited. Nodes can be deleted or moved. Whole sections can be moved using the drag and drop method. Comments can be changed at any time. The page icon allows the creation of new pages. The design can thus be built up in a structured way over several pages. Each page maps to a procedure at the code level.

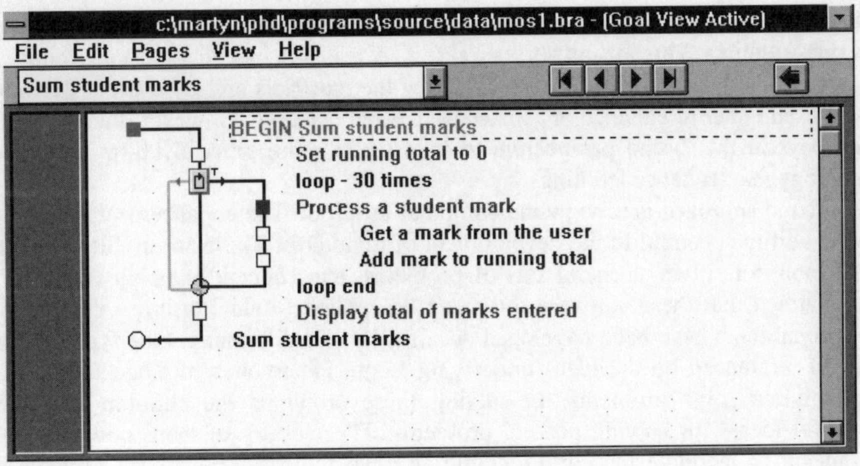

Figure 3.7 Flow level representation in Braque

I have used Braque for over two years in a class on programming and program design. Braque is used in the lectures to illustrate the design of programs using a computer linked to a projector. The system is also mounted in the programming laboratory and the students are free to take copies home. There has been a marked improvement in the quality of the designs produced both in the assignments and in the exam. A questionnaire given to the first group of sixty students reflected a high degree of student confidence on a series of design questions. It seems clear that a computer based tool that is specifically designed to aid learning can lead to clear improvements in student learning.

3.4 Summary

This chapter has reviewed the use of multimedia technology to provide resources and tools for learning. One of the first activities was to convert traditional encyclopaedias and reference works into a multimedia form. The original material was enriched by the addition of good quality graphics, sound and video. Hypertext cross-referencing provides a natural enhancement of the normal mode of access of these materials. The advent of the Internet and the World Wide Web provides vast networked resources. Performance limitations mean that the Internet cannot normally deliver the performance achieved from a CD ROM. However, the Internet is viewed by many as the market place of the future. Education should benefit substantially from the wider social and commercial forces pushing the development of the global networked society. Commentators like Henderson (1995), however, have called for the development of more educational materials for use over the Internet.

Resource based learning has been proposed as a framework for exploiting these new opportunities. This idea is very attractive. A resource can be almost anything, and resource based learning does not specify how the materials are to be used. Resources can be used either to enhance or replace traditional teaching. However, there is a need to go beyond this broad perspective to investigate more precisely how multimedia technology may enhance learning.

A second approach is to view the computer as a tool. The enhancement of problem solving ability is central to the development of mindtools. These are usually computer based tools for solving general sets of problems, e.g. concept mapping tools. It has been claimed that these software tools can be applied to aid learning. A number of educational tools have been developed specifically to aid learning. One type has been strongly influenced by the ideas underlying Logo. Papert viewed Logo as a tool to help children solve problems. In solving these problems the children discovered 'powerful ideas' for solving general problems. The mastery of these powerful ideas was meant to facilitate the child's cognitive development. Another set of tools has been developed to support goal based learning activities. In this approach a task analysis of the topic, e.g. scientific enquiry, leads to the identification of a number of key learning activities. Software tools are then developed to support these activities. Support is provided for both individual and collaborative aspects of the learning process. A specific theme within this approach is to use composition tools to learn the new skills of multimedia literacy.

This tradition of developing software tools has had an important impact on the educational use of computers. Themes from this tradition feature prominently in the discussion of strategic approaches to multimedia design in Part 2 of this book.

Chapter 4

Simulation and vicarious experience

4.1 Introduction

One of the most powerful uses of multimedia is to immerse the user in a learning environment. The key to this approach is achieving the imaginative engagement of the learner. Three variants of this approach are discussed in the chapter. There are clearly overlaps between these approaches. This descriptive framework, however, helps to delineate some of the important themes in this area. The three approaches are:

- simulation
- games
- virtual reality.

A learner may acquire skills and knowledge through the vicarious experience provided by acting in a simulated environment. The form of the user's activity varies with the domain and the learning approach adopted. The discussion in this chapter covers systems used for both exploration and more structured learning.

A second powerful way to promote engagement is the use of gaming structures. These structures may be based on arcade games or adventure games. Examples of both approaches are reviewed. There is a clear continuum from simulations to games. The HeRMiT system reviewed in the chapter illustrates the use of business simulation in a game-like context.

The ultimate expression of simulation is full virtual reality (VR). This is potentially one of the most powerful media for educational systems. In this chapter VR is approached not from the technological point of view but from the perspective of imaginative engagement. The discussion reviews the different levels at which this engagement may be promoted. Often VR systems are developed to fit the technology, e.g. virtual walk throughs. As the technological possibilities open up we need to ask how can these resources be more effectively used to promote learning.

4.2 Simulation

Simulations can be used to support vicarious experience in real or imagined worlds. They may support observation, exploration or task based activity. In a passive simulation the learner simply observes the operation of the simulated system. There are various systems for algorithm animation, for example, that provide visual simulation of the operations within a computer. The user can observe the changes in data structures as an operation is performed. The lack of interaction, however, can be frustrating, especially when combined with a lack of control over animation speed. Purely passive simulations have a limit to their cognitive utility and motivational engagement.

A significant step forward is to allow the user to actively explore the simulated environment. 'Dans le Quartier St. Gervais' uses simulation to create an exploratory learning environment (Schlusselberg 1993). It tries to provide a degree of cultural and linguistic immersion for French language students. Like the 'navigation' project this was developed at MIT under the umbrella of the Athena project. The language students can simulate a visit to the Quartier St. Gervais in Paris. By clicking at icons on a map of the neighbourhood the students can go to a particular location. They can walk down the street or enter certain building and listen to talks given by the residents. The talks are given through video sequences. There are multiple paths thorough the quarter and the users can choose which path they wish to follow. The students can 'explore' the neighbourhood and get a feel for the culture as well as the language.

In task based simulations the user interacts with the simulation to achieve some effect or goal. The classic example is the aircraft simulator. In this case great expense is taken to create as accurate a copy of the real world situation as possible. The simulation also allows the practice of operations that would be very hazardous in real life, or which would only occur in emergency situations. The idea of computer based simulation is a powerful one. It can be activated by limited use of graphics and text, or it can lead through to virtual reality and the irony of simulating situations that do not exist.

The Murder One project provides a nice example of the educational use of simulation. This is a multimedia simulation of the investigation and trial of a murder case. The aim was to put the students in role of practising lawyers. Gibbons (1992) says that the term 'artificial reality' captured this aspiration. The students handle the whole case. They have to interview witnesses, prepare the case and present it at trial. At the end of the exercise a trial verdict is given. The characters in the case are represented by line drawings on the screen. The students asks questions from a list, and the character 'interviewed' replies in digitised speech (Figure 4.1). The face of the

Figure 4.1 Screen from Murder One

character moves in synchronisation with the speech to present a reasonable analogue of a person speaking. The simulation is not a canned exercise. It is an interactive environment where the plot unfolds depending on the choices made by the students. The students have to prepare a case against time, present it and try to win the verdict.

Gibbons (1992) argues that this approach does not substitute for other types of learning. It adds a new element that was otherwise absent – learning by discovery. The dominant response of the students seemed to be that it was instructive and fun. The application was developed by four people – two law professors, a programmer and a graphic artist, and it was implemented in HyperCard.

The EcoDisk represent another interesting use of simulation. This project has gone through several phases of development. The original system was implemented using an 8 bit BBC computer and a laser disk. A later version was implemented using HyperCard with a CD ROM as the storage device (Riddle 1990). The EcoDisk is a simulation of a nature reserve in the south of England (Figure 4.2). A range of options is available to the user. They can take a walk through the reserve; the views along the walk are represented by fifty-five pictures, each offering seven different directional views.

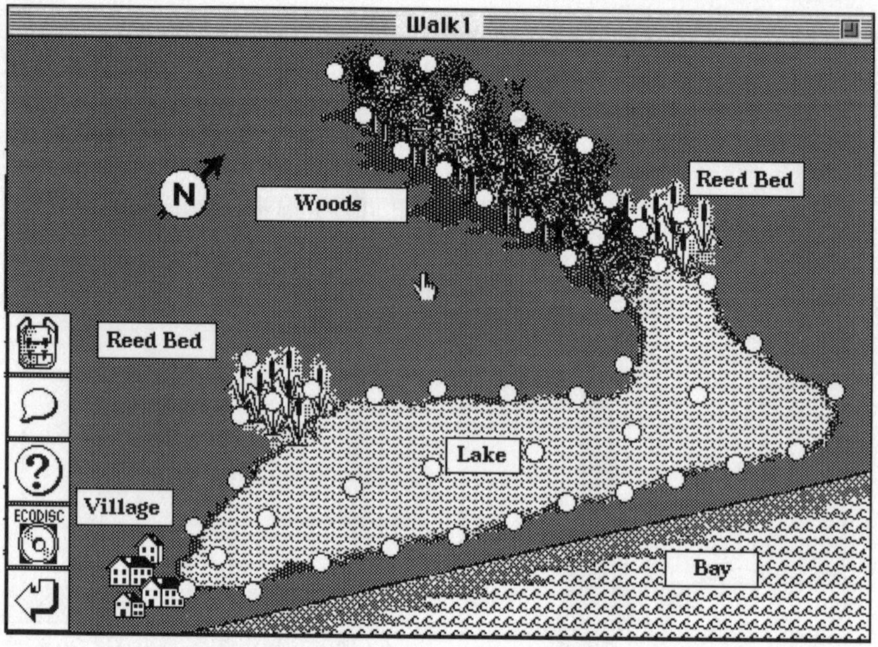

Figure 4.2 The EcoDisk project: map of the reserve

The user can collect samples from different areas of the reserve. For example, netting sites can be set up on the lake. Clicking on a net reveals the catch, and a count of the fish can be entered in a table. The user can play the role of a Trainee Reserve Manager. The task is to use the variety of information sources available and formulate a plan for the future of the reserve. The CD ROM of the system version is available in a range of European languages, and there is extensive learning support for teachers in the form of worksheets, templates, role playing activities, etc.

The 'Navigation' system, developed by the Visual Computing Group at MIT, makes extensive use of video to create a realistic training environment for learning navigation skills. This aims to:

...integrate the two aspects of knowledge, theory and experience, by presenting the theoretical components of navigation in the context of a simulated experience.

(Hodges and Sasnett 1993, p. 89).

The screen represents a boat navigating the waters around the coast of an area called Hurricane Sound. A videodisk holds a database of 1000 panoramic views of the area. The boat moves through the environment from point to point on a 4 yard grid. This gives a sense of motion through the environment. Part of the screen display is used to

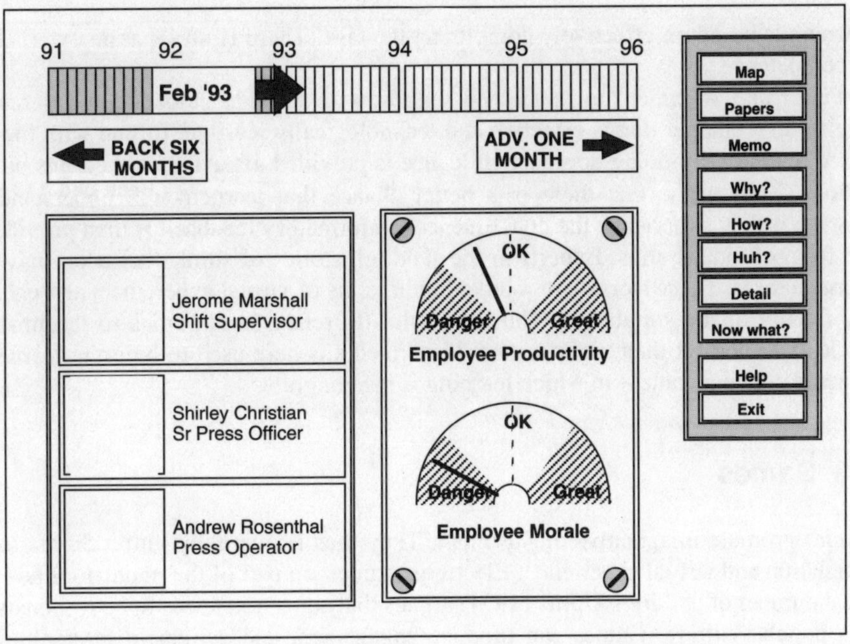

Figure 4.3 Opening screen from the HeRMiT system

represent the scene. On the other part of the screen the user can access the tools and materials needed to navigate, e.g. compass and maritime reference books. Hodges and Sasnett (1993) comment mainly on design and technical issues in creating realistic surrogate travel. They do not report how this system was integrated within a wider learning environment, or how successful it was in use.

The idea of task based simulation is developed further by Feifer and Allender (1994). They identify a number of problems that may limit the effectiveness of case based reasoning. Good simulations are hard to build, especially for social domains, and proposed solutions must be technologically feasible. There is a need to provide guidance to prevent users floundering, in a manner that preserves the active, driving role of the learner. Finally, there is the problem of perceived fidelity. The learner may not believe that the simulation is an accurate reflection of the real world situation.

Feifer and Allender (1994) put forward a well developed argument for a CaBLE approach (Case Based Learn-by-doing Environments). This approach uses a game-like simulation to create motivating tasks. In the HeRMiT system, for example, the user plays the role of a manager making human resource decisions in a company (Figure 4.3). The CaBLE approach emphasises learning by doing. The learner retrieves information, makes decisions and gets feedback on the consequences of those actions. The situation evolves dynamically depending on the user's decisions. Assessment of learning is based on effectively completing the task. There is no separate external test of competence.

Feifer and Allender are concerned with how to provide guidance and perceived fidelity in a manner that is effective and technologically feasible. In line with the task based, learning-by-doing approach guidance is provided **after** the user carries out the actions. They argue that there is a better chance that learners will understand the mistake if they experience the consequences. Informatory feedback is then provided in the form of videos clips. Experts in the field tell stories of similar mistakes and their consequences. These stories are motivating in terms of virtual experience, and enhance the fidelity of the simulation. The learner has to relate these stories to the mistakes made and interpret their significance. Hypermedia is here used to help the learner on demand and in a context in which learning is meaningful.

4.3 Games

Games promote imaginative engagement. They thus fit naturally into a discussion of simulation and virtual experience. Electronic games are part of the popular culture of a great number of children. Upitis (1994) argues that education needs to be responsive to this popular culture. Games can produce engagement and delight in learning. They thus offer a powerful format for educational environments that are attractive and motivating.

The E-GEMS project seeks to build on these advantages to promote the use of learning games for maths and science (Klawe et al. 1994). One objective of this project is to exploit the possibilities offered by commercial games such as Sim City. These games often involve problem solving and sustained effort to achieve the goal. A second objective is to create educational games specifically designed to support learning in maths and science. This second objective is echoed in the 'X' system developed by the Ultralab group (Millwood and Mladenova 1994). The domain for this game is a rather dry one – multiplication tables. The aim is to make this rather dry area interesting and engaging. An arcade game format is adopted. The views of parents, teachers and children were gathered to aid in the design of the system. The children wanted a number of arcade game features included. There is a score panel, for example, giving the points for the current question and the cumulative points gained. These are very high numbers, typical of those given in game formats. The children also wanted pressure. This is an interesting demand. It is difficult to envisage teachers or parents demanding this feature. The 'pressure' is implemented as a cartoon character. This character starts off looking happy and relaxed. As time goes by without an answer the character becomes increasingly nervous and begins to sweat (Figure 4.4). A successful answer switches the character back to a happy mood. An added feature is that the children can customise the environment. They can add mnemonics to help them recall answers. For example, a child may add a drawing of a chess piece and attach it to the question – 'What is 8 × 8?' Cross-cultural testing in the UK and Spain confirmed that many of these design themes were successful.

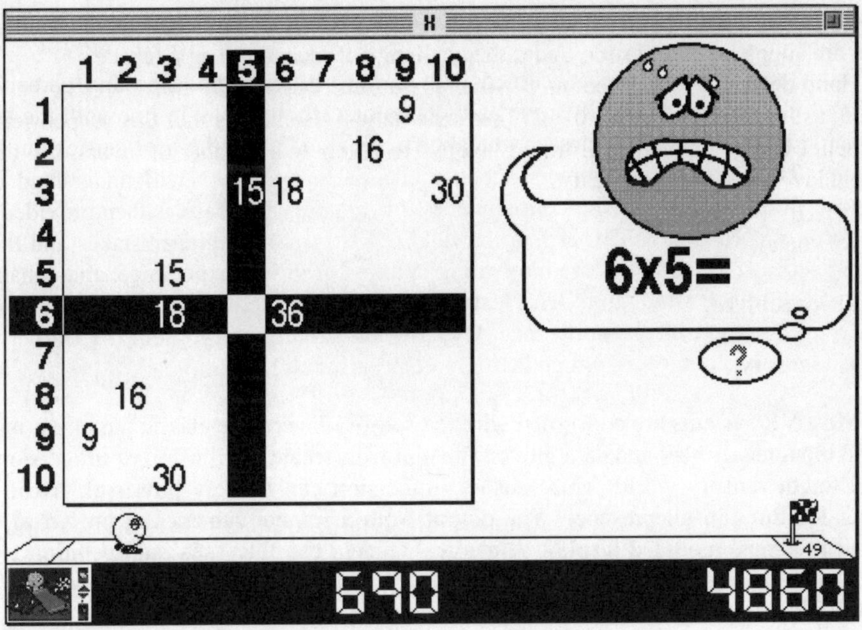

Figure 4.4 Screen from the 'X' system

Arcade game features provide one approach that may be very successful with children, though perhaps less so with adults. Adventure games provide a broader format. Karyakin et al. (1994) describe an adventure game interface to a learning environment for the natural sciences. They argue that this frees the student from tension, increases motivation and supports collaborative learning. A number of specific tasks can easily be incorporated into the game plot. The students have to make measurements and solve a variety of puzzles in order to succeed in the game.

4.4 Virtual reality and virtual experience

Virtual reality seems to be the most powerful extension of simulation based systems. In virtual reality (VR) we are inside the simulation. This creates a unique vantage point for learning. In technological terms, however, we have a marked discontinuity at this point. There is a move to three-dimensional, multi-sensory interfaces. How do we maintain continuity with other forms of interactive learning environment? Hand (1996) argues that there is a strong continuity if we approach the issue from a psychological rather than a technical viewpoint. Though Hand's concern is not particular to educational environments it provides the basis for a more unified approach to learning environment design. It supports the development of principles that are supple and not brittle under the challenge of technological advance.

Hand defines VR as something *'which is not real, but may be considered to be real while using it'* (Hand 1996, p. 107, author's italics). He argues that this suspension of disbelief can be created at different layers. He points to a number of layers, but three broad layers may be demarcated:

- social
- cognitive
- sensory.

Most VR systems are concerned with the sensory layer. The classic paradigm is the head mounted display and data glove. The aim is to create the illusion of immersion in a different sensory world. This sensory immersion can be very powerful. It can be extended through telepresence. The output from a remote camera can be fed as the input to a head mounted display. A medical student can then 'see' an operation from the operating surgeon's point of view. This provides powerful new raw material for developing learning environments. Hand, however, argues that VR can be delivered on layers higher than the sensory one. Sensory immersion may not be necessary for these higher levels of immersive involvement. He points to the sense of immersion produced by the traditional media of books, theatre and films.

These higher layers are important for learning environment design. The film 'The Tree of Wooden Clogs' works largely by emersing the viewer in the village life it depicts. In one scene an old man is telling a ghost story. The carriage draws up at a graveyard. Suddenly the ghost appears! A young boy falls backwards off his seat with shock. Since they are in a stable he falls in some cow dung, and all the villagers burst out laughing. The boy's experience for Hand is virtual reality. A ghost theme park, with full technological paraphernalia, might well fail to achieve the same effect in a modern child. There are different ways of achieving effective immersion in an experience.

If we apply this argument to the simulation studies reviewed we see that some of these achieve virtual experience. Murder One seeks to immerse the student in dealing with a law case. Gibbons actually uses the term 'artificial reality'. Feifer and Allender, through their business game and war stories, try to seduce the learner into the illusion of the real thing. I find an interesting correspondence between this study and the film 'The Tree of Wooden Clogs'. At Ed Media '94 Feifer and Allender showed a video illustrating the use of the system. In the video one of the war stories was told. It was about a hard-working secretary who did not get her annual bonus. She was sometimes late for work because of child care problems. A mediocre secretary got the bonus because her time keeping was OK. When I remember this story I 'see' the secretary bursting into her boss's office. She slams down the extra work she has been doing on his desk, and tells him never to expect her to do unpaid overtime again. She will work nine to five just like the other secretary. I can 'see' this scene in the same way that I can see the carriage stop outside the graveyard in the ghost story. I have to remind myself that these scenes were not actually presented. All I heard were the stories. The impact is as great if not more so than actually seeing the scenes. It is like the old adage that plays are superior on radio than television because the pictures are better.

Following these arguments we need to look at design principles for creating effective virtual experience. Many of the systems that do not use classic VR technology create highly effective virtual environments. However, as VR technology becomes more widely available these principles must carry over to exploit these possibilities. Sensory illusion is not an adequate basis for creating effective learning environments. It will require guiding principles geared to meeting educational and training objectives.

The greatest educational focus in VR at the moment is in training complex physical skills. There is, for example, considerable interest in training for surgery. We would expect that as VR technology becomes more mature there would be extensions to a much wider range of applications. In selecting the technological options for creating virtual experience we will have a range of techniques available. In some projects, like Murder One, video may be more effective than VR techniques. In other applications sensory and perceptual immersion may be more appropriate. In meeting the new technological opportunities and challenges we need a set of principles for education and training. This should guide us in how best to exploit the technological opportunities available. The studies reviewed in this chapter provide significant contributions to this goal. Part 2 of the book approaches the topic of design principles in a more systematic manner. As more esoteric technology becomes widely available we should be able to apply these principles in shaping the technology to create effective learning environments.

4.5 Summary

The development of multimedia technology has opened up rich possibilities for learning based on 'virtual' experience. Simulations can support both exploration and case based learning. Simulations are excellent for relating the abstract to the concrete. Formal linguistic skills can be practised in the context of use. Abstract theories about navigation or conducting investigations can be grounded in vicarious practice. There is a danger, however, of becoming beguiled by the technology. We must ask how effective is a particular simulation in promoting learning. What is learned well through simulation, and what needs are best met by other means? Unfortunately, assessment of the effectiveness of these systems is often fragmented, subjective and anecdotal. There is rich range of techniques available, but we still need to fully evaluate their strengths and limitations.

Game formats are a powerful way of promoting engagement. There are two fairly distinct variants in arcade games and adventure games. Arcade type games are most often used with children. They can be used, as in the 'X' system, to package rather dry topics in a rather more exciting format. Adventure games open up a wide range of possibilities, and naturally overlap with case based simulations.

The use of full VR for learning has been more rare. The effort required to build such systems has been a disincentive. Wider access to systems such as VR with QuickTime and VRML (Virtual Reality Modelling Language) should promote much wider use of these techniques. The central question from an educational perspective must remain – how is learning better promoted using this technology? One of the most exciting possibilities is the creation of new imaginative worlds. Playing with atoms, however, may not necessarily lead to better learning. How to structure and promote learning is the key question. The technology, no matter how wonderful, simply provides the materials that require shaping by a deep understanding of the nature of learning.

Chapter 5

Structured learning

...beneath the rhetoric of 'giving students control over their learning' is a dereliction of duty. We never supposed students could do that with a 'real' library; why should they be able to do it with an electronic one?

(Laurillard 1993, p. 206)

5.1 Introduction

Laurillard criticises the popular emphasis on 'resource based learning'. She argues that it has a lot more to do with the limitations of computers and the complexity of learning than 'pedagogical high mindedness'. A 'structured learning' approach places responsibility back onto the designer for the structuring of learning interactions. In these systems there is often a clear target competence to be acquired, e.g. mathematical or programming skills. These tasks cannot be tackled adequately by giving the students the 'resources' and letting them get on with it. A key element is guidance from an expert tutor in the domain. A central challenge for these approaches is to incorporate this expert guidance without undermining the creative initiative of the learner.

This section discusses three areas of work on tutorial learning. The first area is traditional intelligent tutoring systems (ITS). These predate the multimedia era. They attempt to emulate a human tutor who can diagnose and respond to the needs of individual students. The aim is to provide learning tutorials that are *adaptive* to the needs of learners. The main challenge in this approach is the production of intelligent software. The second approach – guided discovery learning – by contrast, places the emphasis on supporting and exploiting the intelligence of the learner. The learning interactions and content are structured to facilitate the active discovery by the learner of the target skills and knowledge. The emphasis in this second approach switches from intelligent software to intelligent learners. The third area discussed seeks to provide a synthesis of the strengths of the first two approaches. In this approach intelligent software components are embedded within learner centred environments. One of the most interesting innovations is the use of 'intelligent agents' who act as assistants to the learner. Adaptive assistance is thus provided under learner control.

5.2 Intelligent tutoring systems

At the plenary session at CAL '93 there was a discussion on intelligent tutoring systems. The chairman turned to the audience and asked whether anyone had seen an ITS used successfully in an educational setting. There was a pause. Then one person spoke up. She had seen an ITS used in a real educational setting. But, she added, the students found it boring.

Intelligent tutoring systems (ITSs) seek to replicate in computer software the expertise of a human teacher. In this paradigm the computer acts as a personal tutor. This field considerably predates the emergence of multimedia computing. Nwana (1990) traces the emergence of this field back to the early seventies. The computing framework within which this field emerged was thus radically different from modern multimedia computing. The aim of intelligent tutoring systems is to generate content and teaching actions that are adaptive to the needs of individual learners. The primary focus is thus on teaching strategies rather than on learning. The central conceptual problems involve the construction of software that embodies the intelligence required for adaptive teaching. These 'intelligent tutors' need to handle three primary tasks:

- generate what to teach the student
- select the most appropriate teaching method
- diagnose and respond appropriately to problems in learning.

The question of mapping the teaching onto the most appropriate media for learning did not arise during the development of this approach. The interface was primarily text based and this provided the main medium for communication.

Although there are a variety of ITS architectures there is general consensus on the need for three main components (Nwana 1990):

- the domain model
- the student model
- the tutoring model.

(See Figure 5.1.)

The domain model should provide an explicit representation of the domain knowledge which an expert possesses. This aspect of constructing an ITS strongly parallels the activities in building a standard expert system. The knowledge has to be elicited from an expert and encoded in an appropriate knowledge representation formalism. A common formalism is a database of rules and facts. This knowledge base, insofar as it is complete, provides an explicit representation of the expert's

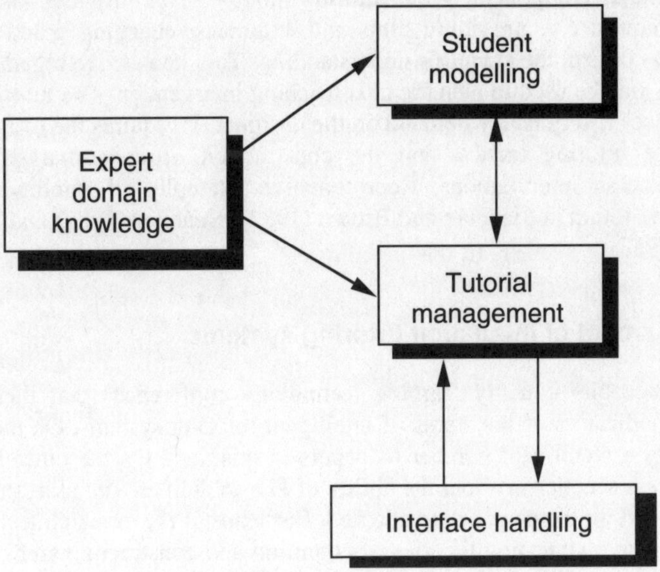

Figure 5.1 Overall architecture of an intelligent tutoring system (based on Nwana 1990)

knowledge of the domain. In an ITS this domain knowledge has two main functions. It is used to diagnose the student's level of expertise in the domain. It is then used to help generate the content that is appropriate to the learner's level of competence.

The second major component of an ITS is the student model. If an ITS is to provide tutoring adapted to individual needs then it needs to have an explicit model of the learner. The student model matches information on student performance against information stored in the domain expert component. It uses this to construct and dynamically update a model of the learner. This model supports two main functions. The first function is the diagnosis and evaluation of the student's level of performance. This information then helps in planning tutoring interventions and predicting the student's likely response.

Two of the most common approaches to student modelling are 'overlay' modelling and the 'buggy' approach (Brown and Burton 1978). In the overlay model the student's knowledge is viewed as a sub-set 'overlayed' on that of the expert. This provides an explicit basis for planning the next teaching intervention. The learner's knowledge, however, may not just be incomplete but erroneous. In many disciplines there are standard error patterns to which learners seem prone. An ITS should be able to recognise the errors and help the learner 'debug' their behaviour. This achievement relies on an explicit representation of these errors, and tactics for dealing with them.

The third major component is the tutoring module. This provides knowledge of tutoring techniques, e.g. providing hints and examples, changing practice tasks or setting tests to confirm the student's understanding. This knowledge together with the student model may be used to plan the next teaching intervention. The tutoring module once again places a very heavy demand on the designer. It requires the explication and codification of tutoring tactics, and the construction of code that can use this knowledge to plan interventions. Representative examples of intelligent tutoring systems may be found in Sleeman and Brown (1982), Kearsley (1987) and Polson and Richardson (1988).

5.2.1 Assessment of intelligent tutoring systems

It is very noticeable at many learning technology conferences that there are two contradictory indicators of the status of intelligent tutoring systems. On the one hand there is usually a significant number of papers in this area. On the other hand many delegates express scepticism about the ability of ITS to deliver. The assessment of ITS work will depend on the perspective adopted. For many it is a research test bed; these research issues involve testing theories of cognition and constructing architectures for intelligent software. The issue of producing deliverable systems is of secondary importance. The perspective adopted in this discussion is how it may contribute to the development of interactive multimedia learning environments. From this perspective there are a number of problems with the traditional ITS approach. These issues may be discussed on three levels.

At the philosophical level there is the problem of cognitive 'reification' – reducing an adaptive process to a cognitive object which generates it. As Bruner (a founder of the cognitive revolution in the fifties) argues, adaptive intelligent action may be distributed across cognitive and contextual factors (Bruner 1990). We may need a transactional rather than a purely cognitive approach to understand intelligent action. Since technology changes and amplifies contextual support mechanisms it may be more productive to concentrate on this area. Thus for both theoretical and practical reasons the traditional ITS approach leading to the 'omniscient tutor' may not be appropriate.

The primary emphasis on teaching rather than learning may be criticised. It may be argued than we need to start with learning and delineate the role of instruction rather than start with instruction and delineate the role of learning. The learning models used in ITS work, e.g. the overlay model, are often too simple. Research on learning reveals transformations in thinking and productive 'errors' which are very difficult to formalise. The domain expert's model is a reification of the expert's view of the domain. The learner's view may be very different. Segal and Ahmad (1991) report that tutors and learners even differ in their choice of preferred textbooks. The richness of the qualitative difference between tutor and learner views cannot easily be captured in formal models.

Finally, at a technical level the ITS approach represents an immensely complex approach to building learning environments. IMLE development has been greatly enriched by contributions from a wide range of disciplines. To provide systems that only expert cognitive scientists could build would seem to be step backwards.

5.3 Guided discovery learning environments

The ITS approach focuses on the computer as a tutor. This led to an emphasis on the development of intelligent software to instantiate this role. The 'guided discovery' approach, by contrast, places the primary emphasis on the learner. The role of computer software is to create an effective environment for learning. The structure of the environment is designed to optimally support powerful, natural learning strategies. Tutorial support is often embedded as feedback contingent on the learner's actions. Individual differences are accommodated by letting the users adapt the environment to their needs. The search in this approach is to discover design principles for constructing these learning environments. Multimedia technology then provides a rich set of resources for implementing these design principles.

Three areas of work within this tradition are reviewed. The authors of the 'Animate' system aimed to produce an 'unintelligent tutoring system'. The use of graphic feedback plays a key role in this system. The MITTS project provides a more systematic and extensive framework. This explicitly tackles both issues of pedagogy (structuring learning interactions) and curriculum (structuring the content to be learned). The third approach, the CORE method, provides a set of design principles which have been implemented in an extensive, fully implemented system.

5.3.1 Animate

The Animate system provides tutorial support for students learning a small sub-set of Algebra (Nathan 1990, Nathan and Young 1990). It deals with equations of the form 'distance = rate multiplied by time'. This includes calculating collision times for objects starting at different times and having different velocities. The key feature of Animate is that it uses students' 'real life' situation based knowledge to help construct and solve formal mathematical equations. The diagnosis and repair of erroneous actions is carried out by the student, not by intelligent software. The role of Animate is to supply the support necessary to carry out that task. Nathan and Young (1990) argue that you do not need an ITS if students have the means to monitor and debug their own actions.

Students are presented with problems and asked to construct the appropriate equations. A keypad type interface presented on the screen helps the student to build the formal equations. In parallel the student can select objects for a simple animation. The equation drives the animation process. The result is an animation showing the consequences of executing the equations the student has built. Since the equations involve movement and collision, mistakes are normally clearly illustrated. The students can use this situational feedback to debug their formal equations. The students may repeat the process. They can also enter partial equations and get feedback.

Nathan and Young (1990) comment that the task of building tutoring systems is so much easier 'when the student is on the designer's side' (p. 242). Improvements in learning come about when students use familiar experiences to make sense of and assimilate formal knowledge structures. The key element is to provide situational support for students to monitor and debug their own problem solving attempts. By enriching the situation we may thus allocate learning functions to 'intelligent learners' rather than intelligent machines.

5.3.2 MITTS : Minimalist Tutorial and Tools for Smalltalk

A full 'guided discovery' tutorial system needs to go beyond the contribution of the Animate system. MITTS highlights a number of issues for guided discovery tutoring (Rosson et al. 1990). This system was developed within the Minimalist tradition (see Chapter 2). Like Animate there is an emphasis on exploiting user's general knowledge and supporting error recognition and recovery. The Smalltalk language is introduced by playing a Blackjack game. The authors believed that the learners would be able 'to leverage off their knowledge of the card game to investigate and learn how the program itself works' (Rosson et al. 1990, p. 426). Error situations were anticipated and recovery support provided.

The MITTS system contains a structured set of design features. These features include support for the structuring of content, and support for learning interactions. The Minimalist approach emphasises getting started quickly on 'real' tasks. Earlier work on general IT skills had emphasised a great deal of freedom in accessing learning modules. Learning Smalltalk, however, represents a significantly more complex problem. This required setting up a structured curriculum for the domain. The approach adopted was a 'spiral curriculum' (Bruner 1975). This approach supports getting rapidly involved in a potentially complex domain. The four instruction blocks cover the same area – playing a Blackjack game – but on each successive pass more demanding features are introduced. The curriculum thus spirals upwards over the same content.

Support was also provided for learning activities in the form of 'scaffolding'. Scaffolding refers to transitional support structures in learning. (This topic is discussed in more detail in Chapter 7.) The system replaced some of the more complex interface features of Smalltalk with simpler features designed to aid learning. The Class Hierarchy Browser in Smalltalk, for example, was replaced by a tool that achieved the same basic functions while filtering out some of the more complex features. This was made as similar in appearance as possible to the real tool to facilitate the transition to using the full system.

In the MITTS system we begin to move towards a more comprehensive framework for tutorial learning. The curriculum is structured; learning activities are scaffolded;

error recovery is supported, and everyday knowledge is used to provide a meaningful framework. The authors report anecdotally that learning progressed at one or two orders of magnitude faster than standard approaches to learning Smalltalk. This system, however, seems to have been primarily a research prototype dealing with a sub-set of Smalltalk. The final approach to be considered provides a structured set of design principles that have been incorporated in a large system that has been in practical use for several years.

5.3.3 The CORE approach

A long time ago, when people had very few words, when someone invented a new word how did they explain it to other people?

(Sarah, aged 8)

The CORE approach provides a set of design principles for the acquisition of competence in relatively complex domains. The method was initially developed for programming. It has since been extended to cover multimedia learning in a number of domains. The traditional university method of teaching programming is to transmit knowledge to students through lectures and textbooks. The students are then required to apply that knowledge in laboratory classes. The main transmission of knowledge is separated from the practical application of that knowledge. This leads to a number of problems:

- A focus on the transmission of rules in such a way as to invite rote learning.
- Premature complexity – it is hard to define a partially true rule. The temptation is to define the rule as fully as possible. This can easily overload the learner.
- Premature abstraction – to define a rule you need a 'meta-language' with its own specialist terms. This language of description can become a major barrier in the learning process. The learners often do not have the 'words' to understand the formal descriptions.
- Passivity: the imposition on the learner of a comparatively passive role and hence the failure to tap more constructive learning styles.

The CORE approach attempts to avoid these problems by fostering a more natural style of learning based on research in language acquisition. There are two overriding themes in natural language acquisition – creative construction by the child, and contingent guidance from mature speakers. The CORE approach adopts these twin themes to construct guided discovery learning environments.

The term CORE is an acronym which captures the four central design principles of this approach.

Context

Objects

Refinement

Expression

The explanation of these principles will be illustrated primarily by reference to the CLEM system. CLEM (CORE Learning Environment for Modula-2) is a large scale learning environment for programming (Boyle et al. 1994). It provides a complete course in the Modula-2 programming language for first year university students. It has been used since 1991 by nearly 2000 students in three British universities. This system is discussed in some detail in order to provide a picture of a full guided discovery learning environment. The CORE approach has subsequently been applied to build systems using a variety of multimedia implementation techniques (Boyle et al. 1996, Boyle and Thomas 1994). These systems are described in subsequent chapters.

Context

The role of the first element 'context' is to set the scene for the learning experience. Like a hinge it has two faces. It helps learners relate new material to what they already know. It also provides a holistic view of the learning experience. It does this by providing an example of the type of skill the learner should have acquired by the end of the learning block. The primary function of setting the context is to provide the learners with an overall orientation without burdening them with technical details.

Research in both developmental and adult psychology has demonstrated the central role of context in facilitating effective learning (Donaldson 1978, Wason and Johnson-Laird 1972). The penetrating insights of Donaldson are discussed in some detail in Chapter 7. In the CLEM system each learning block has a 'Context Program' presented at the start. This program introduces the new material highlighted within a full working program. The program frame around the new constructs is familiar to the learner from previous learning blocks. Figure 5.2 shows one of the simplest context screens. In CLEM colour is used to highlight the new constructs (red text as against black text for the rest of the program). Unfortunately this is not reproduced clearly in the black and white copy; the highlighting feature is more clearly illustrated in colour Plates 1 and 2. The student can view the output of the program at the click of an icon. Alternatively the students can compile and run the program. The new constructs and skills are thus set in a complete, meaningful program. When students are tackling technical details in the body of the learning block they can relate the details to the whole. The context program thus acts as an example based 'advance

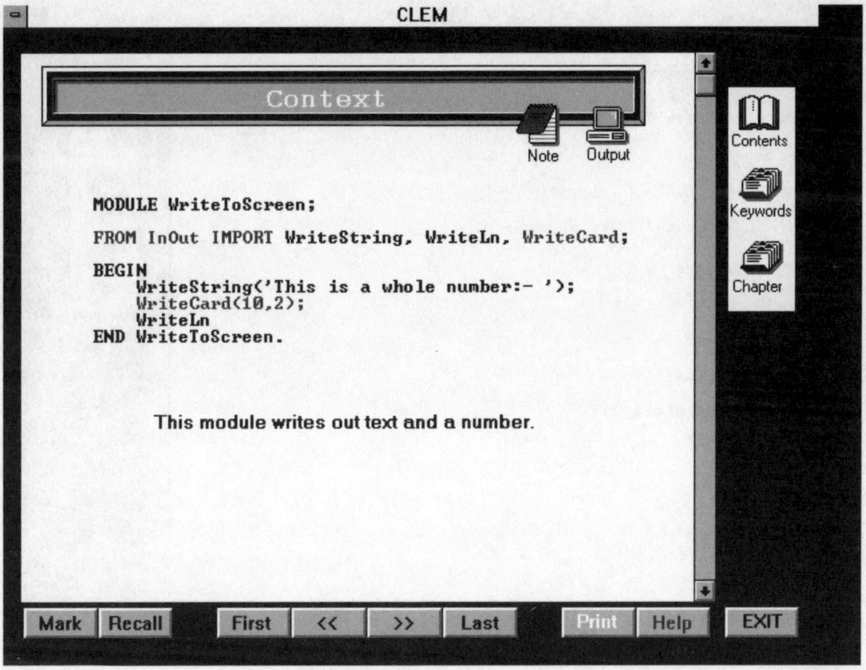

Figure 5.2 A Context screen from CLEM

organiser'(Ausubel 1968, West et al. 1991). Such advance organisers seem to have their strongest effect when users are dealing with unfamiliar technical materials.

Objects

A central concern of the CORE approach is to replace a didactic exposition of rules with a more natural form of learning. The learners should be able to infer their own rules, or other forms of cognitive representation, based on their experience of the relevant material. The approach adopted was influenced by studies of language development. Children learn from examples in context. They construct interpretations based on these examples and then gradually refine their understanding though feedback received from mature speakers (De Villiers and De Villiers 1978, Kuczaj 1986). Rosch and her colleagues have convincingly demonstrated the importance of central exemplars in concept representation in adults (Rosch 1988). In CLEM new constructs are introduced not through formal descriptions but through central examples (Figure 5.3). These examples, or 'objects' from the domain of discourse, provide the basis for the learner to form an initial hypothesis about the construct. The student is

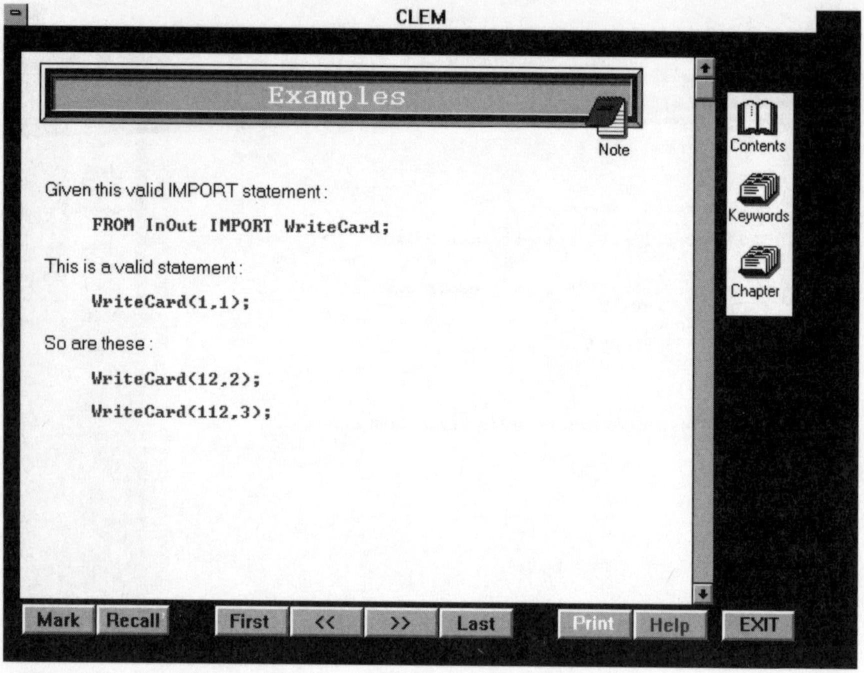

Figure 5.3 An Example screen from CLEM

actively involved in making sense of the new construct from the beginning. This initial conception provides the entry to the next phase – the Refinement phase.

Refinement

The natural propensity to form patterns from examples and then refine this knowledge in the light of further feedback is very strong. For example, my son Sean (then six years old) was watching a tennis match intensely with the score at 40 to 30. The player with the lower score won the point. Sean exclaimed loudly 40 - 40! The play continued. When the next point was scored he exclaimed 50 - 40! Sean then asked me had this player won? I ruefully explained that tennis scoring does not work this way. This capability of inferring patterns together with the ability to use feedback to adapt our knowledge is a powerful form of learning. The central components of CORE dealing with 'Objects' and 'Refinement' seek to provide an environment optimised to support this 'guided discovery' process.

In the CLEM system each presentation of examples is followed by a Refinement section. The student is presented with a carefully chosen sequence of questions. The

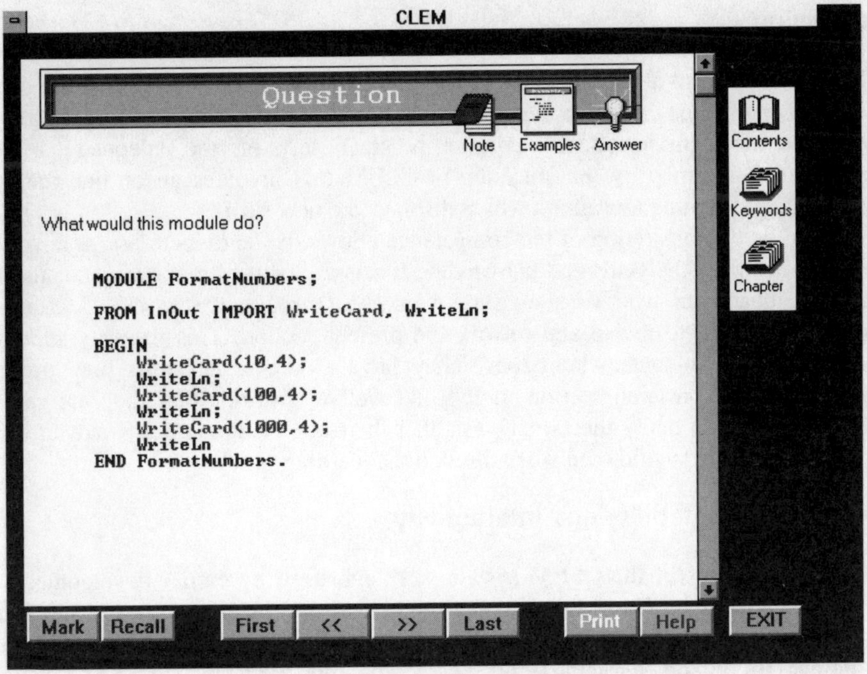

Figure 5.4 A Refinement screen from CLEM

student tries to answer each problem and receives feedback. The Refinement section begins with simple yes/no questions. The questions gradually become more demanding. Figure 5.4 shows one of the last questions in an early learning block.

Note the icons attached to the banner at the top. They indicate functionality available on a Refinement page. The students may study the examples for this section by clicking on the 'Examples' icon. A student notepad is available by clicking the 'Notepad' icon. When ready to answer the student clicks the 'Answer' icon. A pop-up dialogue box appears. When they have completed their input a 'Feedback' card appears. This provides information for the students to check and refine their understanding.

In the CORE approach mistakes are regarded as opportunities to learn. If the students are actively involved in making sense of the evidence and testing out their ideas they will naturally make mistakes. If appropriate feedback is supplied they will also learn more effectively than if they were the recipient of someone else's rules. Complexity is progressively introduced in the problems tackled. Through the Refinement phase the student engages in a guided discovery of the rules and operations of the language.

Expression

The CORE approach allows students to form representations which make sense of the domain to them. This brings up the question of how adequate are these representations. The Expression phase should provide a clear test of the adequacy of the representations formed by the students. In CLEM this involves an on-line multiple choice test, and writing a program which displays the new skills.

The public demonstration of the competence allows the learners to assess how well they have acquired the skills and knowledge. It acts as a sort of gateway. The students receive feedback on whether they should proceed through to the next section, or whether they need to revise and rework the present section. This gateway approach also means that students who believe they have the requisite skills may proceed straight to the Expression section. If they do well it confirms that they are safe to proceed. If they do badly then it suggests that their knowledge is not as advanced as they thought. They should then work through the learning block.

Enhancing adaptability and interactivity

The design features of the CLEM system were enhanced by earlier developments of the CORE approach. These developments included user testing of paper mock-ups (Boyle and Drazkowski 1989), the development of a DOS based learning environment for Pascal (Boyle and Margetts 1992), and an in-depth pre-trial for CLEM involving 22 students over a three month period. The central principles that emerged were the provision of enhanced interactivity and flexibility while retaining ease of use. CLEM was designed as an *adaptable* resource-rich learning environment. The basic concept was that instead of an ITS adapting to the students' needs, the students would be provided with the resources to adapt the environment to their needs. The basic contrast here is between an *adaptive* and an *adaptable* system

Resources had to be provided in a way that made their availability both easy and non-intrusive. One such resource was to allow every fragment of code in the system to be executed. Compiled languages, such as Modula-2, do not permit the execution of isolated fragments of code. CLEM allows users to click on any fragment of code. This is then embedded in a working program presented in a window on the screen. The student can then click on an icon to transfer the code to a commercial compiler environment where it can be compiled and run. The first two steps in this sequence are illustrated in Plates 1 and 2 in the central colour insert. The students can edit the programs before running them. This provided them with a facility to ask their own questions and use the compiler as a feedback resource. In the pre-test it was noticed that this facility was especially popular with the more able students.

A variety of additional resources was provided which the student could choose to use. A pop-up Index Card was provided that displayed the structure of each learning block (Figure 5.5). Each heading on this card is a hotspot. The student could jump directly to any section by clicking on the appropriate heading. Some students, for

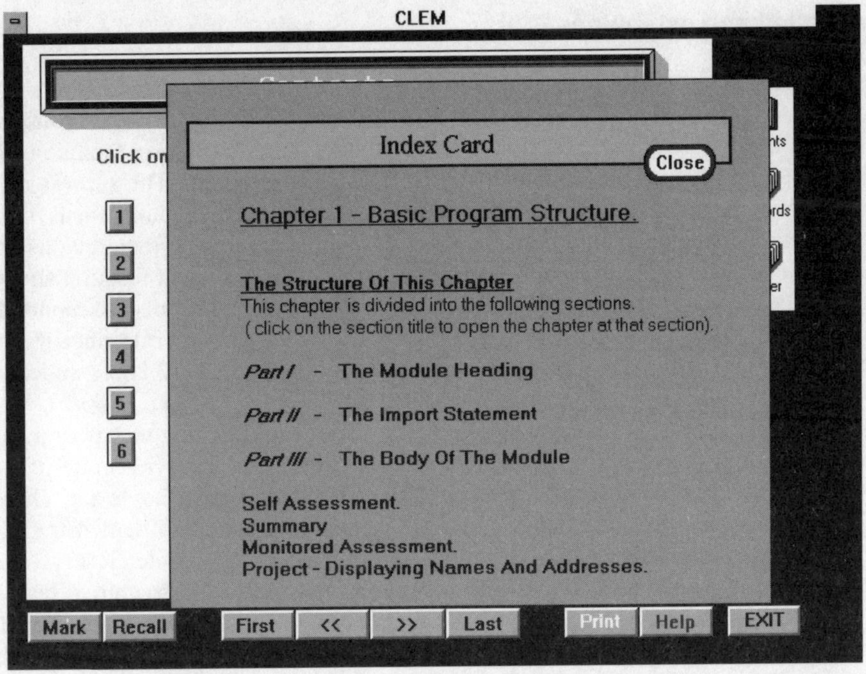

Figure 5.5 Index Card in CLEM

example, preferred to read the summary before tackling the rest of the chapter. Students with prior experience could go directly to the Expression section and test themselves to see whether it was safe to skip the chapter and proceed. A 'Book Index' was also provided that operated in a similar way to an index in a normal book. The student could click on a target term and jump directly to the pages dealing with that construct.

A key design issue is how to provide enhanced resources without producing a complex user interface. The interface to a CAL system should be as transparent as possible. In CLEM the metaphor of an electronic book was used to structure the system. This has the quality of being 'superbly mundane'. A student has a rich intuitive understanding of how books work. Hypertext features, such as jumping from an item to a given page were contextualised as a book index. Extensions such as the ability to pick up and compile code seemed to be intuitively easy to grasp. The idea of 'context' was thus applied at two levels in this system. The context programs set the context for each learning block. The electronic book metaphor set the context for the whole system. Empirical evaluation indicates that this approach worked well. The students rated the system as easy to use, and observation confirmed this.

Evaluation and extensions

A comprehensive evaluation was carried out of the CLEM system (Boyle et al. 1994). CLEM is a large system. It can provide over 50 hours of CAL. It was used initially with 240 students following a first year university module in programming. The students used CLEM as the principal way of learning to program. The success of the system was assessed though observation, a formal questionnaire, focus group discussions and a comparison of course pass rates with a baseline of the previous three years' results. The results were very positive in terms of both student reaction and unit results. Marked improvements in pass rates were achieved. The results are reported in Boyle et al. (1994). The CLEM system has been used on a similar scale since the first intake in 1991. It has now been used extensively by approximately 2000 students in three British universities.

The CORE approach has been applied to a variety of domains using a range of media. VirCom is a system in which students can learn about the architecture of a PC by building a virtual computer. A report on this system is given in Boyle and Thomas (1994). This system makes extensive use of interactive graphics to demonstrate and support users in interactive virtual assembly of a PC. DOVE (Dynamic Observation in Virtual Environment) uses the CORE principles to create a structured learning framework for the systematic observation and recording of animal behaviour. This is a full multimedia system using video, graphics, speech and text. The CORE approach provides the guiding principles on how to structure the learning framework. Illustrations of the DOVE system are given in Plate 5 and Figure 9.6.

The realisation of the design principles depends on the domain and media used. In VirCom, for example, 'context' is set through overview animations displaying the skill to be acquired (see Figure 11.2). The 'examples' of contributory sub-skills are provided through more detailed demonstrations (Figure 12.1). Many of the 'refinement' tasks involve interactive graphics where the user picks up objects, and assembles components on the screen. The 'expression' at the end of a block may then involve the integrated skill covered in the block, e.g. going through all the steps in a virtual assembly of a hard disk drive (Figure 12.2). The separation of conceptual design principles from specific realisation options is necessary if the conceptual principles are to have any generative power. Aspects of the VirCom and DOVE systems are discussed in more detail in Part 3 of this book, which deals with presentation design.

5.4 Adaptive hypermedia and intelligent assistants

This third approach seeks to provide a synthesis of the strengths of user centred environments and intelligent guidance. There are two related sub-strands within this area. The first strand seeks to provide adaptive guidance in hypermedia structured information spaces. The second approach provides intelligent software agents to assist the user in structured learning environments.

5.4.1 Adaptive hypermedia

Brusilovsky (1994) provides a review of research in adaptive hypermedia. These systems can be applied to a number of domains, e.g. information retrieval, advanced help and explanation facilities and educational software. In the sphere of educational software this approach seeks to provide a productive synthesis between hypermedia systems and intelligent tutoring systems (Brusilovsky 1994). An intelligent component is added to a hypermedia system to provide adaptive guidance for the learner. At the same time facilities for user driven adaptation are retained. Achieving the appropriate balance of adaptive guidance and user driven adaptation is a key goal of this research.

Brusilovsky (1994) provides two main reasons for augmenting hypermedia systems with intelligent guidance. The first reason is to provide software which will adapt better to different classes of user. Users differ in goals, background and knowledge of the subject. It would seem sensible to provide different 'views' onto the knowledge for different users. This emphasis on different user views onto the same body of information has long been recognised in database theory. This approach extends to providing different views to learners at different stages of the learning process. The second reason is to provide navigational guidance to prevent users becoming lost in hyperspace.

Hypermedia systems consist of nodes linked into a networked information or learning space. Adaptive support can be provided at two main levels – selection and presentation of content at the node level, or navigational guidance at the link level. The underlying domain model is usually some form of semantic network. The domain is broken down into topics, and the relationships between these topics. This provides a form of knowledge representation which can be mapped well onto a hypermedia system. At the simplest level one topic would map to one page presented to the user. The intelligent components use the information from a user model (most often based on an 'overlay' model) to select and present nodes of information and recommend links to other nodes.

These links may be colour coded or ordered in some visible way to suggest recommendations to the user. A recommended link, for example, may be coloured green. The user is free to survey the choices available and select what is believed to be the best option. One technique for adaptive presentation is the 'more explanation – more details' approach. Each topic can have associated with it more explanation and more details. The user-model is used to guide the choice of more explanations for novices or early learners, or more details (and less explanation) for more advanced users.

This is essentially a research field, and the final balance to be achieved between machine guidance and user choice is not fully clear. There are many conceptual and technical problems to be answered. Are overlay user models really adequate, for example? But the philosophical thrust of this field is a productive one. It offers the promise of sophisticated support for learning within a learner centred framework. To be widely effective, however, these systems would have to solve more than the conceptual and technical problems. They would also have to solve the 'usability' problem. The authoring resources offered would have to be packaged in such a way as to be widely available and reasonably economical to use.

5.4.2 Intelligent assistants for learning

A hypermedia system is optimised for browsing and information access. Whether this is the best structure on which to base intelligent assistance for learning is a more open question. An alternative approach is to provide intelligent agents within a more structured learning framework. A good example of this approach is the Molehill system for learning Smalltalk (Alpert et al. 1995). The name 'Molehill' is meant to indicate the goal of cutting the Smalltalk learning 'mountain' down to size. Smalltalk is a complex object-oriented programming language. The most distinctive feature of the Molehill system is the use of 'Gurus' to coach the user in learning the language. This 'Guru instructional model' has a number of distinct features:

1. The use of multiple intelligent agents: for the Smalltalk system there are two agents. One gives advice in learning the language; the second agent gives advice about the Smalltalk interface.

2. The presentation of these agents as figures on the screen to which the user can relate.

3. The provision of multimodal advice, i.e. using an appropriate mixture of demonstration and voice commentary.

4. The role of the agents as intelligent *assistants* to the learner.

The combination of features leads to intelligent assistance being presented within a learner centred framework. Alpert et al. (1995) argue that this reflects a naturally occurring instructional model, where local experts help learners in a semi-informal mentor–apprentice setting.

The two Gurus used in the Molehill system reflect a conceptual division between learning language concepts and learning how to manipulate the Smalltalk programming environment. The two Gurus are clearly different in appearance – one is presented as male; the other as female. This signals in a salient fashion their different roles. It should help the learner relate to the underlying distinction in knowledge organisation signalled.

The Gurus use multimedia communication: '…the Gurus interact with students not only to *tell* them *what* to do but to *show* them *how* to do it' (Alpert et al. 1995, p. 70). When a Guru is first summoned it appears as a figure on the screen (e.g. Figure 5.6). It introduces in speech the demonstration to be shown. The demonstration may involve animating screen elements while providing an explanatory commentary. A demonstration of an interface operation for example may involve moving the cursor

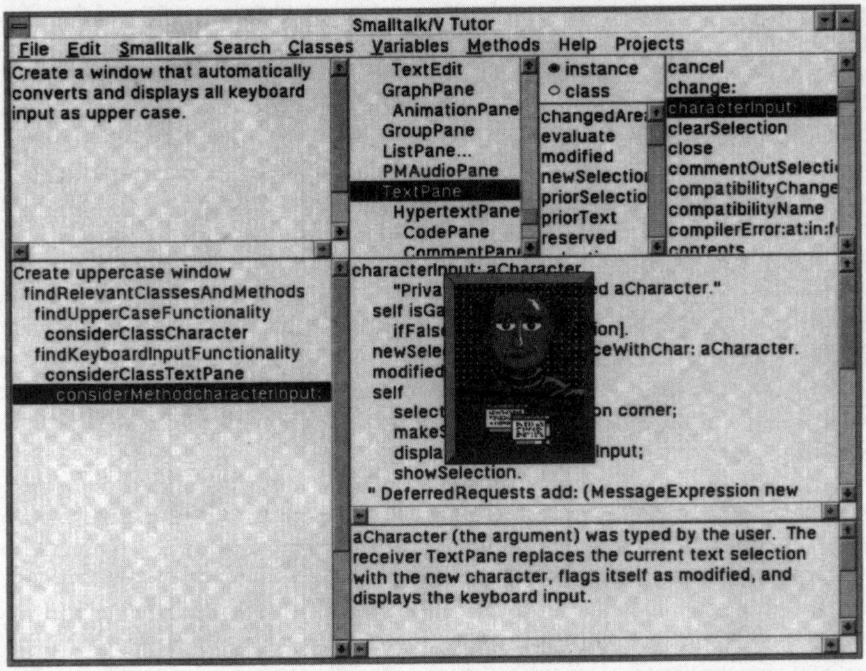

Figure 5.6 The Molehill environment with the Interface Guru visible

across the screen, selecting menu options, etc. The demonstration shows the system in action while the commentary describes the meaning – i.e. what is being achieved.

These Gurus are incorporated in the Molehill environments as intelligent *assistants* to the learner. The central roles of these assistants are to respond to user requests for help, and to suggest help to students when the need is detected. A session begins by the student selecting a programming task from a list supplied by the tutor. The Molehill system then compares the student's problem solving attempts with those of an expert. The system can detect mismatches and suggest remedial strategies. So far this reflects the technology of a traditional ITS system. However, the Guru model also provides an explicit representation of the inferred student plan in solving the problem. This is represented on the screen by the Goal Poster (i.e. it 'posts' goals and sub-goals as they are detected in the student's problem solving strategy). This is represented in the bottom left hand panel in Figure 5.6. The goal-plan representation provides the basis for explicit communication about solving the problem by learner and Guru. The student can request help on any sub-goals by clicking on it. Help is provided using a 'repetition heuristic'. Minimal help (hints and orienting information) is provided initially. More elaborate help, including appropriate demonstration, is provided if the call for help is repeated. The language Guru can also signal an *offer* of help when it detects a problem in the user's plan. In this case a small iconised image of the Guru is placed opposite the sub-goal where the problem was detected. The learner may choose whether and when to use this help

The Guru approach, as with adaptive hypermedia, offers a productive synthesis of traditional intelligent tutoring and learner centred environments. Research into Distributed Intelligent Agents is a burgeoning area of study. Educational technology may well benefit by assimilating useful techniques from this area. The key aspect of this synthesis is that the creative scope of the learner is enhanced, not reduced, by the provision of these resources.

To become practically useful to the wider community of multimedia designers certain issues need to be resolved. The first issue is that systems must be made as robust as possible. The idea of separate intelligent agents for separate sub-domains allows one to scale the size of the problem tackled. One may use much smaller agents than those used in the Smalltalk system. This makes the problem of robust, intelligent components more amenable.

Even when the techniques for producing robust, well-integrated components are mastered there are barriers to the widespread adoption of this approach. Producing intelligent software is a very demanding task. The technology and techniques would have to be developed to make this facility available to other than small groups of specialists. The alternative, the development of a corps of educational knowledge engineers, does not seem an imminent prospect. The issues which are pertinent are thus not just the issue of success but also the question of economy. To have a widespread impact in producing practical multimedia learning environments these twin issues need to be successfully resolved. The strategic framework for tackling these issues has been greatly strengthened by recent work.

5.5 Summary

In this chapter we reviewed three approaches to the development of structured learning environments. The traditional ITS approach tried to develop intelligent software to emulate a human tutor. The emphasis in this approach is the construction of intelligent software to emulate a human teacher. The Zeitgeist of this approach, the computer as tutor, was challenged by the emerging hypermedia and learner centred approaches. The guided discovery approach emphasises using the emerging technology to support the intelligence of the learner. The emphasis switches to learning as the central phenomenon. The most important resources are the abilities the learner brings to the situation. The primary aim of technology is to support and enhance these powerful learning abilities. The guided discovery approach places tutorial support firmly within a learner driven format.

The third approach aims for a synthesis of intelligent tutoring within a learner centred environment. Intelligent agents provide assistance rather than direction to the learner. The clash between learner centred *adaptable* systems and computer based *adaptive* systems is resolved by incorporating intelligent components as resources for the learner. This provides not only a conceptual synthesis but also a basis for technical advance. Smaller, intelligent agents should be easier to build than monolithic intelligent tutors.

'Structured learning' systems deal with the central themes of educational design. The key issues of the structuring of content (curriculum) and the structuring of interactions (pedagogy) are tackled explicitly. The topics are revisited and discussed in some detail in the central chapters on design in this book (Chapters 6 to 8). The work reviewed in this chapter provides an important contribution to that discussion.

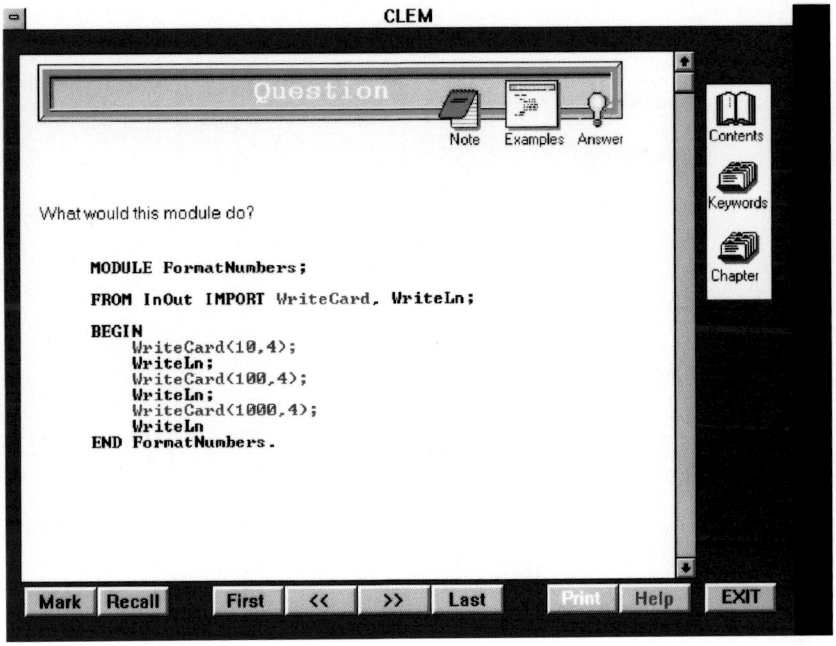

Plate 1 A 'refinement' page in CLEM.

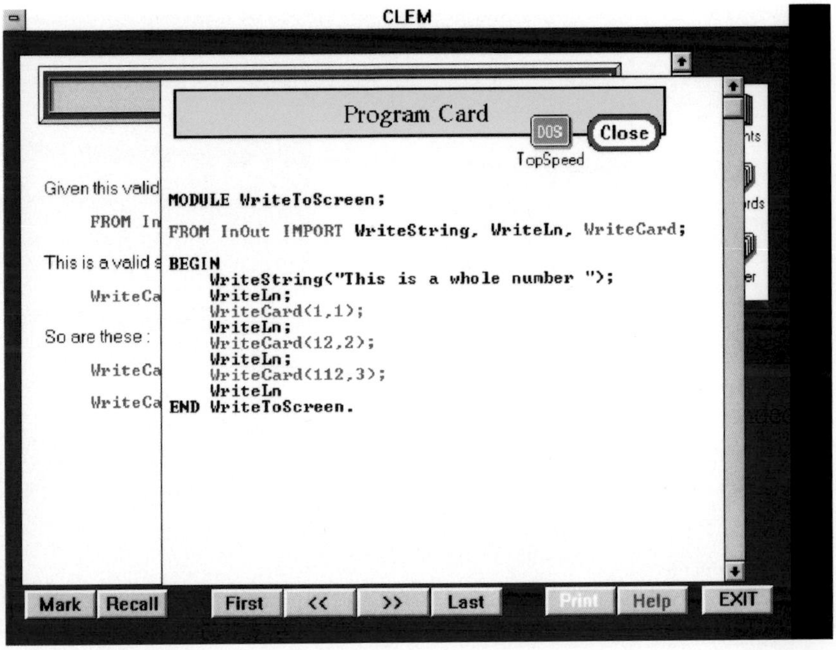

Plate 2 A refinement page with the program card loaded.

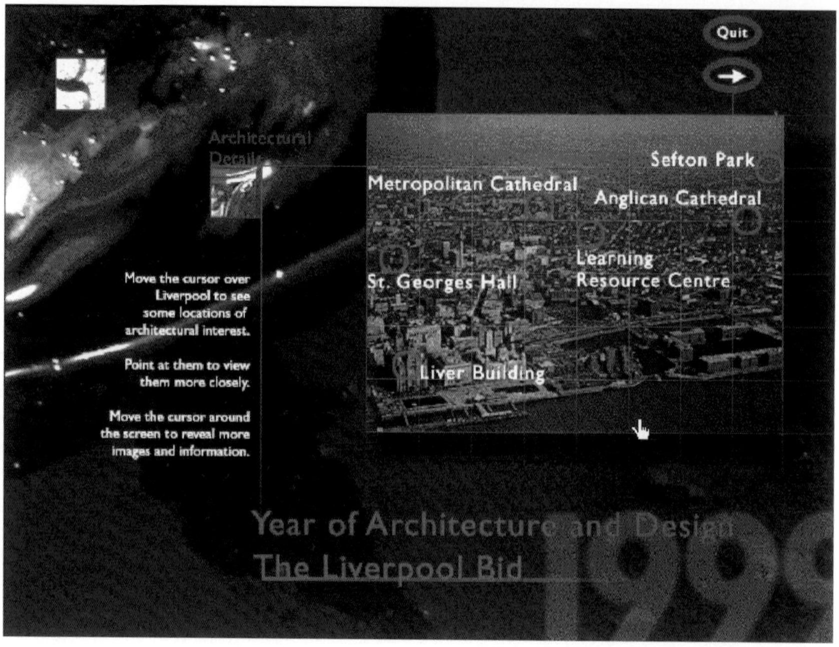

Plate 3 Liverpool City of Architecture CD ROM : by clicking on a red circle the user can zoom in on that building.

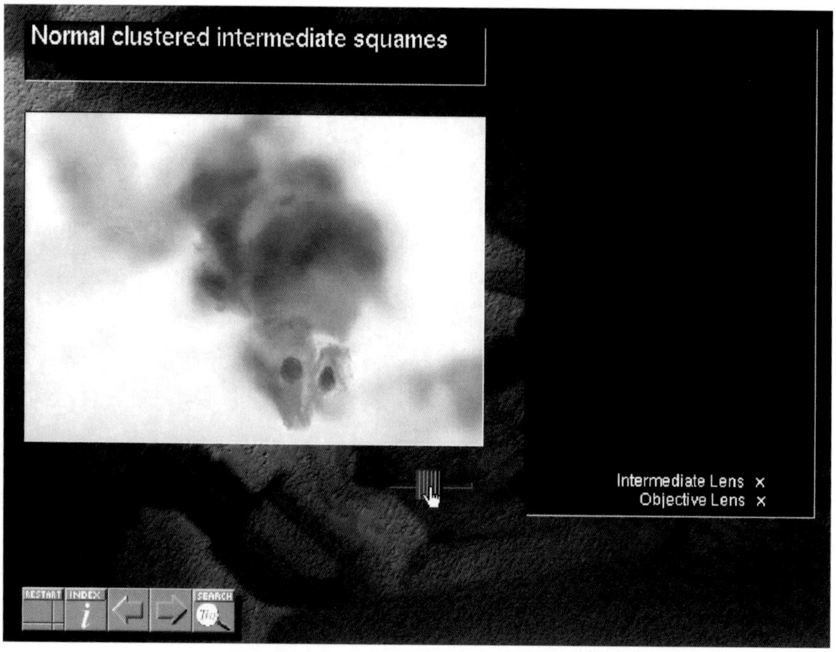

Plate 4 Slide from the Cytofocus system: the user can change the focus on the slide by moving the lever on the screen.

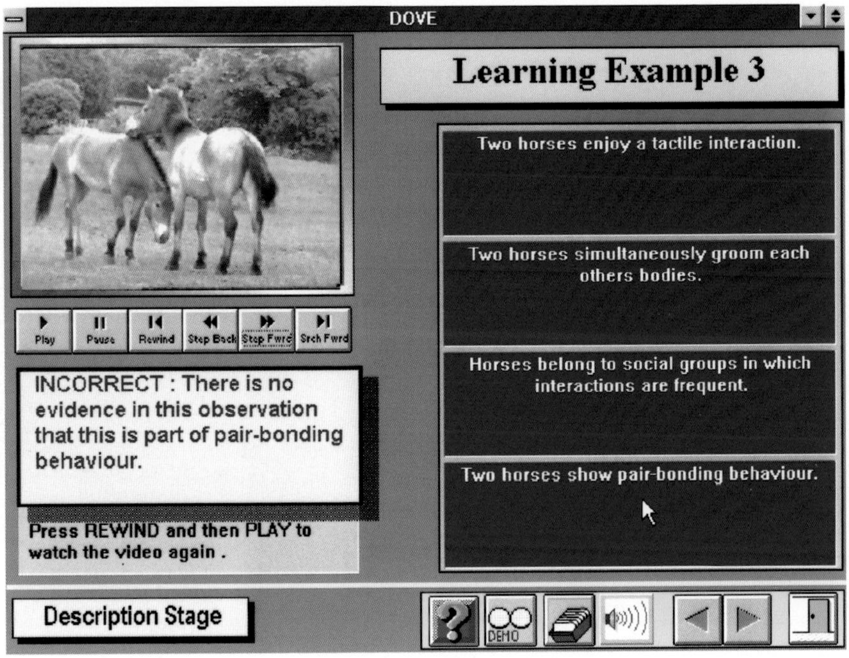

Plate 5 A screen from the DOVE system: feedback has been given to the user.

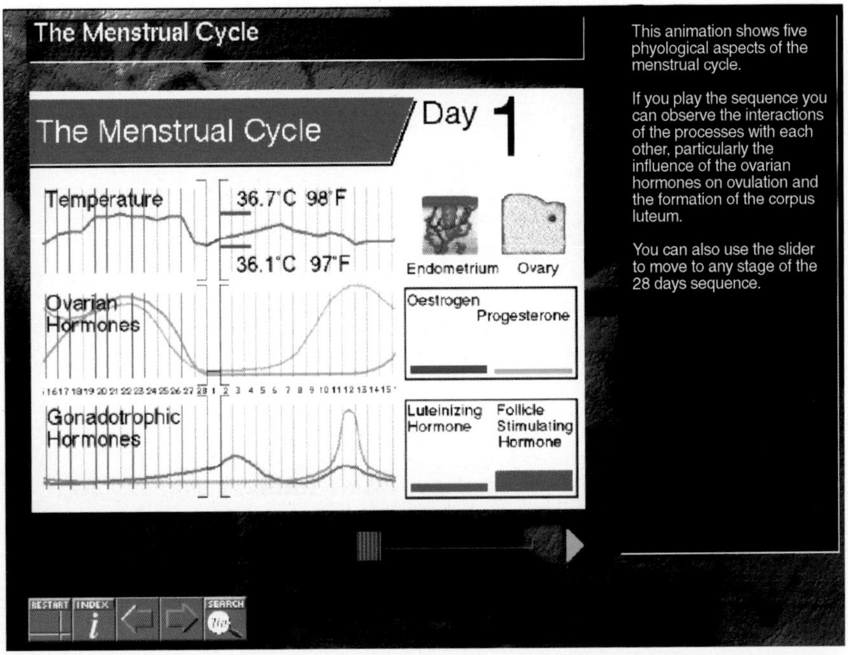

Plate 6 The menstrual cycle: by moving the lever the graphic view can be run through the monthly cycle.

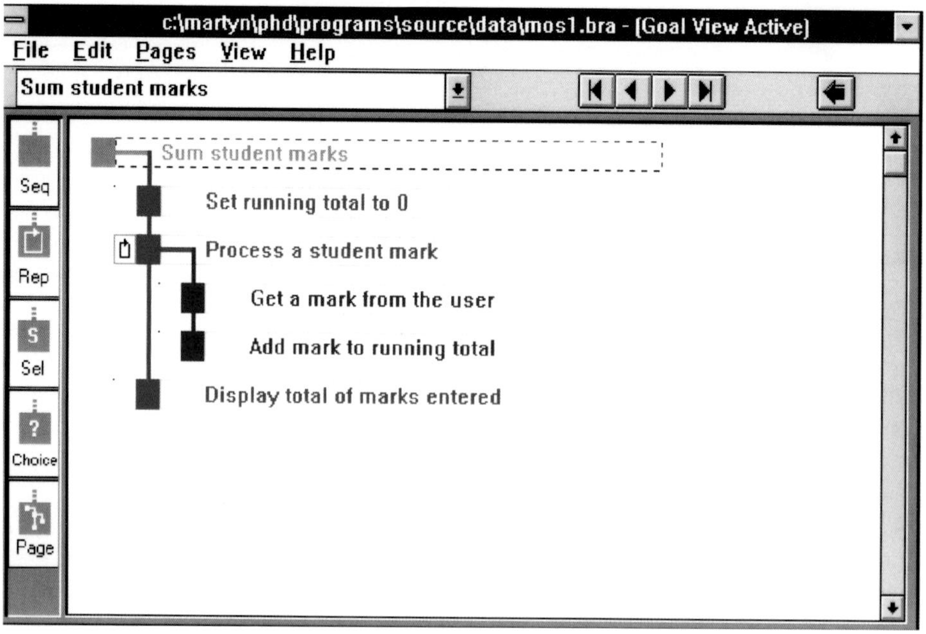

Plate 7 A screen from the Braque system showing the colour coding of the program plan.

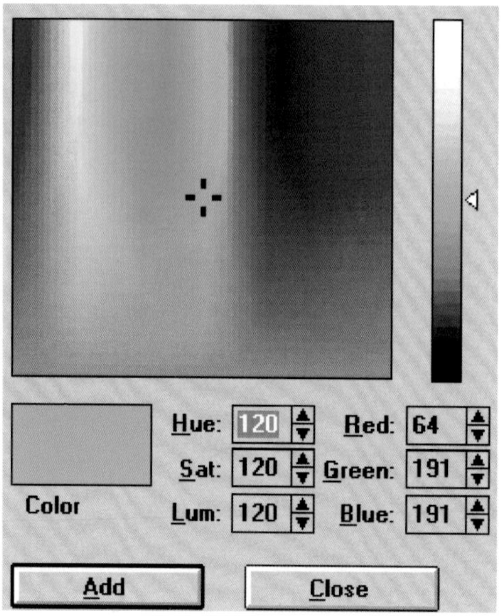

Plate 8 Colour manipulation in the PalEdit tool: the user can change the colour parameters using either the RGB framework or hue, saturation and luminance.

Part Two

Conceptual design

...this is their classical beauty – not what you see, but what they mean – what they are capable of in terms of control of underlying form.

Robert Pirsig (1976) Zen and the Art of Motorcycle Maintenance

Chapter 6

Strategic approaches to educational multimedia design

6.1 Introduction

The design of multimedia learning environments may be considered on two broad layers. The conceptual layer deals with the structural organisation of the learning environment. The present part of the book deals with this topic. This organisation has to be mapped onto a physical form on a computer. The subsequent part of the book deals with this topic of presentation design.

The discussion of conceptual design is divided into three chapters. The present chapter introduces two strategic approaches to the design of interactive learning environments. Traditional CAI (Computer Aided Instruction) emphasises a very systematic approach based on a set of instructional design principles. This was the dominant paradigm for many years. However, this 'instructionist' approach has been overtaken by developments in both computer technology (e.g. hypertext) and educational design. 'Constructivism' has become the most influential approach to IMLE design. Constructivism has a strong base in psychological theory, and offers greater scope for exploiting the opportunities offered by modern technology. A detailed review and critique of constructivism is presented in this chapter.

Cognitive principles may inspire design. However, these principles still have to be converted into decisions about the design of learning situations. The following chapters develop an argument for using 'context' as the focal concept for this design task. 'Context' refers to a holistic interpretation of a situation that guides adaptive actions in that situation. This theme begins with a synthesis of ideas from film theory and linguistics. It culminates in the idea of 'design action potential' networks as a way of formalising knowledge of conceptual design in a non-prescriptive way.

6.2 Instructional Design

Instructional Systems Design (ISD) represents a systematic structured approach to the design of computer based instructional systems. This approach has fallen into disfavour in many quarters. It has been bypassed by many of the developments in hypertext and multimedia. Its premises and framework have also been rejected by antagonistic intellectual traditions such as constructivism. Laurillard (1993) dismisses it as '...not a progressive force' (p. 75). This approach, however, represents a coherent strategy for the design of learning environments. It is informative for a designer to understand this view and the reasons why it has been criticised.

6.2.1 Principles of instructional design

Instructional design has its roots in the work of Skinner and Gagné. Skinner represents the epitome of the behaviourist tradition in psychology. He argued for a formal systematic design of instructional environments based firmly on the principles of behavioural learning theory. Gagné however, realised that learning theory was not sufficiently developed to meet the wide ranging demands of instructional design. In his seminal book *The Conditions of Learning*, first published in 1965, he produced a formal systematic framework of types of learning. There was clearly a gap between what learning theory at the time could offer and what instructional designers needed. Gagné extrapolated beyond the evidence and produced a formal framework to guide teaching practice. This 'creative leap' made by Gagné provided the basis for the subsequent development of instructional design. In the view of its critics it also provides its central weakness. Laurillard's central criticism of ISD is that it '...has only a tenuous link to any empirical base' (p.72).

Instructional design has developed a clear method with a strong element of prescriptive guidance. In this method there are three main stages in instructional development – needs analysis, selection of instructional methods and materials, and evaluation.

The aim of the needs analysis stage is to precisely analyse the nature of the task. This analysis is meant to identify every sub-task the student must do and every piece of knowledge the student must acquire. The underlying assumption is that the systematic analysis of task requirements will map onto the steps the learner will have to go through to acquire the knowledge. This analysis will normally yield a hierarchical classification where goals are broken down into sub-goals, and the content required to achieve the lowest sub-goals is specified. Based on this task analysis the objectives of the teaching program can be specified. These objectives are stated in terms of measurable outcomes. At the end of the analysis stage it ought to be possible to specify a series of tests which will indicate whether or not each learning objective has been met.

When the objectives of the instruction have been fully specified the designer then chooses the instructional methods and resources required to achieve these objectives.

Table 6.1 The nine instructional events

External instructional event	*Internal learning process*
1. Gaining attention	1. Alertness
2. Informing learner of lesson objective	2. Expectancy
3. Stimulating recall of prior learning	3. Retrieval to working memory
4. Presenting stimuli with distinctive features	4. Selective perception
5. Guiding learning	5. Semantic encoding
6. Eliciting performance	6. Retrieval and responding
7. Providing informative feedback	7. Reinforcement
8. Assessing performance	8. Cueing retrieval
9. Enhancing retention and learning transfer	9. Generalising

(Source: Price 1991)

The prescriptions of instructional theory are used to guide this process. Price (1991) states 'In order to ensure that each learning process happens, the CAI author should include a sequence of nine instructional events that "teach" for each objective' (p. 84). These nine instructional events are based on the theories developed by Gagné and his colleagues (e.g. Gagné and Briggs 1979). The nine teaching events are set out in Table 6.1. These events represent a sequence of steps that should normally be followed from 1 to 9. Price, however, comments that the selection of event order should be tempered with common sense.

The development of the instructional framework is expected to be iterative. Prototypes are developed and assessed through formative assessment. The feedback from the formative evaluation is used to tune the prototypes until the required level of performance is achieved. At the end of the development period the instructional program should be tested on a larger sample of the target audience (Price 1991). Satisfactory performance on this summative evaluation means that the program can be released for general use. This instructional design strategy is largely media independent. It could be used to guide the development of a computer based system or a text based open learning programme.

6.2.2 Criticisms of Instructional Design

Instructional design takes a very formal and precise approach to the design of learning environments. The approach is oriented to providing prescriptions of procedural sequences that should be applied to achieve instructional goals. This outlook has tended to be rejected by major developments both in psychology and computer technology. These major developments provide complementary support to each other. In modern psychology learning is viewed as a dynamic process where people **construct** their knowledge of the world. It is not imposed by instructional sequence. Learning, not teaching, is primary. The role of teaching is not to impose knowledge structures but to facilitate this constructive learning process. This leads to a much more learner centred approach to the provision of learning experiences. The following section on constructivism expands on the influence of these ideas. In parallel, but starting at a much later date, has been the development of hypertext and hypermedia. These facilitate users in choosing their own paths through computer based worlds. The *a priori* sequencing of steps for the user is explicitly rejected. The users are empowered to choose their own paths through the computer based system. The views in psychology and multimedia technology tend, to a certain extent, to be mutually supportive and reinforcing. Traditional instructional design is seen as over-prescriptive and mechanical. It does not provide a good base to exploit the possibilities of multimedia technology to create user centred learning environments.

On the positive side Laurillard points to the strong emphasis on needs assessment. She argues that this has been neglected in many areas of educational planning. It also provides a provocative contrast, by its precision in specifying instructional methods, with the much looser approaches now in fashion. ISD may be over-prescriptive. Are some modern approaches, by contrast too vague and woolly? If we are going to reject the formal precision of the ISD approach then we need to justify this in a rational and cogent fashion. Finally ISD placed a strong emphasis on objective assessment. This stakes out a clear position in the debate about the nature of assessment, and it is a position that cannot be dismissed lightly.

6.3 Constructivism

Constructivism challenges the approach of traditional instructional design and proposes a radical alternative. Duffy and Jonassen (1991) argue for a theory based approach to instructional design. This theory concerns the assumptions made about the learner and the learning process that underlie the design of instructional materials. They argue for '…a firmer link between learning theories and instructional practice' (p.9). The 'objectivist' tradition of instructional design is criticised, and a radically different epistemological perspective proposed.

In the objectivist tradition knowledge is presumed to exist in the world independently of instruction. This approach leads to a decisive approach to the three main issues of setting goals for instruction, designing instructional strategies and materials, and assessing the effectiveness of the educational program. Learning becomes viewed as the process of the transmission and acquisition of knowledge structures which exists independently of the learner. Duffy and Jonassen (1991) argue that approaches to instructional design influenced by both behaviourism and information processing fall into this class. The instructional design strategies which emerge from this perspective emphasise the precise identification, efficient transmission and rigorous assessment of knowledge. This approach is characterised in a cartoon at the start of John Carroll's book *The Nurnberg Funnel*. In the cartoon the funnel is used to pour knowledge directly into the head of the recipient (Carroll 1990).

Constructivism proposes a radically different epistemology. The central tenet is that knowledge of the world is **constructed** by the individual. The person through interacting with the world constructs, tests and refines cognitive representations to make sense of the world. Learning rather than instruction becomes the focal issue. There is a range of epistemological variations within the constructivist approach. These vary from a near solipsistic approach, where individuals are viewed as creating their own idiosyncratic meanings, to a balanced approach where the individuals' constructions are shaped and validated by the environment of interaction. Some of the principal variations are described in the following description of the constructivist approach. These variations and their implications for design are discussed in the subsequent review and assessment of this approach.

6.3.1 The principal tenets of constructivism

Cunningham et al. (1993) distil seven main principles which inform the design of learning environments. These principles are set out in Table 6.2. These principles provide a useful framework for summarising the proposals for learning environment design. The following résumé employs this framework, but the order of the headings is changed to provide an easier transition into the constructivist views.

'Authentic' learning tasks

A central constructivist criticism of traditional school learning is that it is disembedded from the child's experience outside the school. The tasks lack meaning for the child. They argue that learning tasks should be embedded in problem solving contexts that are relevant in the real world. Learners must see the relevance of the knowledge and skill to their lives, and the leverage it provides in problems they see as important (Cunningham 1991).The tasks should be problem based or case based. These immerse the learner in a situation which requires the learner to acquire the knowledge and skills relevant to solving the problem (Jonassen et al. 1993).

The Jasper Woodbury videos produced by the Cognition and Technology Group at Vanderbilt University provide an example of materials constructed with these aims in mind (CTGV 1991, 1993). Video is used to create a 'real life' case-based problem situation. The case based approach ensures that the problem solving activities are

Table 6.2 Seven principles for constructivist design

1. Provide experience of the knowledge construction process
2. Provide experience in and appreciation of multiple perspectives
3. Embed learning in realistic and relevant contexts
4. Encourage ownership and voice in the learning process
5. Embed learning in social experience
6. Encourage the use of multiple modes of representation
7. Encourage self-awareness of the knowledge construction process

(Source: Cunningham et al. 1993)

embedded in an unfolding story, i.e. an authentic, context, which nevertheless can be made available in the classroom.

Each video in the Jasper series tells a story which takes about 17 to 20 minutes. The first video is about Jasper buying a boat and making a journey to a place called Cedar Creek. At the end of the stories a problem is introduced by one of the characters and handed over to the children to solve. In the 'Journey to Cedar Creek' video the problem is – can Jasper return home before dark? To solve this problem the children must generate the relevant sub-problems and solve them (CTGV 1991). Relevant sub-problems include finding out how far is the journey, how much fuel is left, how much fuel is required, etc. The information required to solve these problems is embedded in the video. The children have to form their plan, search for the data and carry out the appropriate mathematical calculations to solve the problem. The Jasper videos provide a resource for anchoring learning in an authentic context. This resource may be used in a variety of ways by the teacher. The Vanderbilt group prefer a 'guided generation' approach. In this approach the students work in groups, and the teacher acts to provide support. The teacher has a crucial role in providing the requisite type and degree of support to enable groups to be successful. Research on the nature of appropriate teacher support is continuing (CTGV 1993).

Social context

Social interaction is viewed as the primary source material for the cognitive constructions that people build to make sense of the world. Dialogue and the negotiation of meaning provide the basis for the individual to develop, test and refine their ideas. The traditional didactic mode of transmitting information in de-contextualised settings is rejected. Knowledge is instead regarded as 'situated' in the context in which it emerges. There are two main strands for developing interactive, social contexts for learning (Cunningham et al. 1993). These strands focus on tutor – student relationships and peer group relationships respectively.

The first approach derives from the work of Vygotsky (1962). Vygotsky was concerned with the process of cultural transmission, and its role in cognitive development. One of his profound insights was that processes which are at first social, i.e. based on interaction between two or more people, later become internalised to become psychological. For example, the principles used by the mother to regulate the child's behaviour later become internalised as the psychological principles which structure self-regulation. Language development is seen as crucial to this process. The principles articulated in the social dialogue between adult and child later becomes embodied in the inner language of thought.

The first type of 'collaborative configuration' is thus between a mature partner and a learner. The mature partner provides the principles which the learner assimilates over time through repeated social interactions. This model may be applied to clarifying the micro-structure of teaching and learning. The clearest articulation of this approach is probably Cognitive Apprenticeship theory (Collins et al. 1989). Cognitive apprenticeship emphasises the active role of the teacher in supporting the learner. The learner acts as an apprentice to the master craftsperson in the domain, i.e. the teacher.

In this approach the teacher first provides a model of expert performance in the task. The teacher may do this by talking through a problem solution in mathematics, or the processes involved in composing an essay. The learner observes the model to build up a conceptual picture of mature performance in the domain. The teacher then actively coaches the learner in acquiring the target skills and knowledge. The two primary processes in coaching are scaffolding and fading. The teacher scaffolds the efforts of the learner by providing hints, comments and carrying the parts of the task the learners cannot yet handle. There is a division of labour in learning. The teacher performs the operations the learners cannot yet handle on their own. The teacher then gradually removes this support – the process of 'fading'. This forces the learner to become increasingly independent in their application of skills and knowledge. The final stage is for the learner to engage in independent problem solving in the domain.

The SMALLTALKER learning environment for the Smalltalk computer language is a particularly clear implementation of cognitive apprenticeship theory (Chee 1994).

Figure 6.1 provides an illustrative screen shot. The teaching methods of cognitive apprenticeship are implemented in a one to one fashion in this system. Modelling is implemented by using video clips of teachers accompanied by animation of program processes. This allows the explicit modelling of the new operations. Chee comments that animation is particularly useful for providing concrete representations of processes that otherwise would be invisible. Coaching is provided as students attempt to write programs. The most pervasive form of coaching is information provided in pop-up boxes when the system detects an error. The learning here is situated in the activity of writing a program. Information is provided through visual animation of program processes where possible. Fading is implemented by presenting less detailed help messages as the student becomes more familiar with Smalltalk. The degree of fading, however, is left under student control. If the reduced feedback is not sufficient the student can click a button to select further information.

The central apprenticeship methods of modelling, coaching and fading are extended by a further grouping – articulation and reflection, and exploration. Articulation and reflection help students to gain greater conscious control of their problem solving processes through making these processes more explicit (Collins et al. 1989). The teacher, for example, may question the students to get them to articulate the decision processes they are employing. In the SMALLTALKER system students are encouraged to articulate their knowledge through conceptual questions that require the students to express their understanding. Chee comments on the limits of computers in promoting articulation and reflection as it cannot process the students' answers. Exploration encourages students to become independent problem solvers, where they can generate significant problems as well as solve them. In the SMALLTALKER system an 'Explore' button is provided to facilitate student access to the full programming environment. Here the students can construct their own programs and explore the system.

The SMALLTALKER system provides a particularly clear illustration of mapping from teaching principles to multimedia implementation. The first grouping of teaching methods seems to be handled well in the computer based environment. The power of the computer in making visible abstract processes seems particularly helpful. There are clearly more problems in implementing the principles of articulation and reflection. It might be argued that these would be best pushed out from the computer system into the design of the social environment in which the system is used. This is the approach adopted in other constructivist systems such as the Virtual Clayoquot project (Goldman-Segall et al. 1994).

Cognitive apprenticeship is a 'balanced' constructivist approach. The students are viewed as constructing their understanding within a supportive framework supplied by the teacher. The general constructivist themes of situated learning, authentic tasks and group collaboration are all supported. The particular contribution of cognitive apprenticeship is the emphasis on clear, structured functions for the teaching role. The nature of the teaching/learning interactions is described with sufficient clarity to inform the design of computer based learning environments.

The second type of social collaboration is between peers in a group. The proposal is

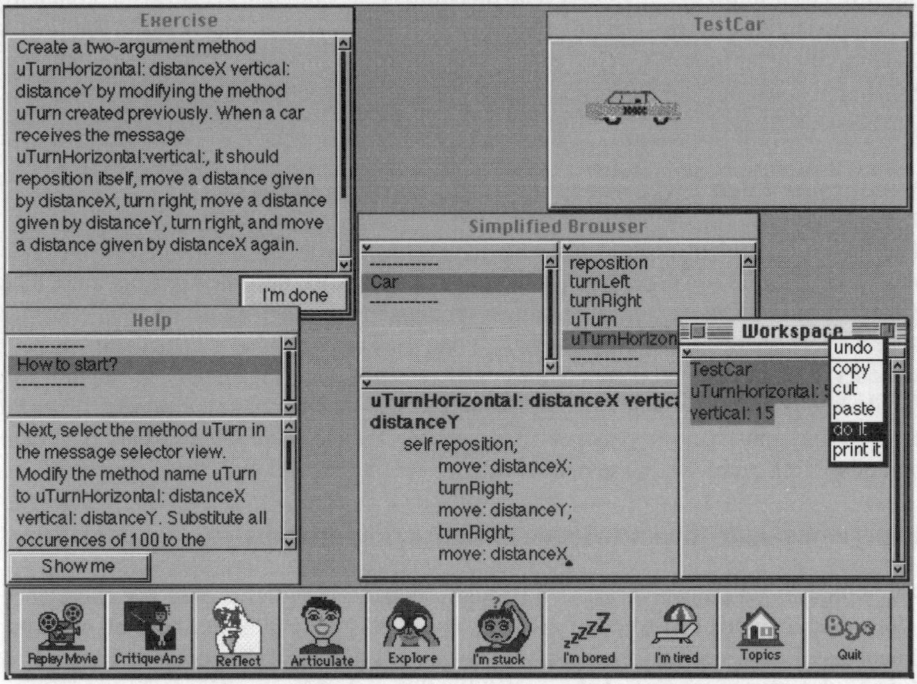

Figure 6.1 A screen shot from the SMALLTALKER system

that individuals can often learn best the processes of knowledge construction, negotiation and refinement in a community of peers. The Virtual Clayoquot project provides an example of this technique as an important strand within a large, authentic case based study (Goldman-Segall et al. 1994).

The children of Bayside Middle school on Vancouver Island have been engaged in a study of the future development of the Clayoquot sound rain forest on the west coast of their island. There are controversial proposals to develop the forest, and this situation provides the backdrop to the study. A central purpose of the project is '…to enable young people to conduct their own research in order to become informed decision makers' (Goldman-Segall et al. 1994). Groups of the teenagers collect data from multiple sources, e.g. field trip experiments, interviews with local people and class discussions. This data naturally takes multiple forms – video, text and sound. The teenagers then analyse this data in the school. Group discussion is encouraged to elicit multiple perspectives and promote the negotiated construction of meaning. A further stage of the project involves the selection and structuring of data to provide learning resources on a series of CD ROMs. The final aim is to build up a distributed community of enquiry by linking the Bayside teenagers through real-time video based links with children in other schools. The central constructivist themes of authentic activity, collaborative learning, and appreciation of multiple perspectives are well represented in this research study.

Encourage voice and ownership in the learning process

The theme of student centred learning is continued with an argument that students should be allowed to choose the problems they will work on. The students must take greater responsibility for their learning experience (Cunningham et al. 1993). Rather than the teacher acting as the task master, the teacher serves as a consultant to help students to generate problems which are relevant and interesting to them. The Vanderbilt group argue that it is not enough to get students to solve problems set by others. They must gain experience in generating their own problems. This is a vital part of solving problems in the real world.

Experience *with* the knowledge construction process

The emphasis on authentic tasks and social dialogue provides a base for experience ***with*** the knowledge construction process. There is a basic question here of what the outcomes of the learning process should be. Conventionally these outcomes would be defined in terms of the knowledge and skills the student has acquired. Constructivists argue that experiencing and becoming proficient in the process of constructing knowledge is more important. In other words it is learning how to learn, how to construct and refine new meaning, which is most important. This approach is illustrated in the Jasper and Clayoquot studies. In each case there is a strong emphasis on learning how to construct knowledge appropriate to the situated task.

Self-awareness of the knowledge construction process

This is the ultimate goal of a constructivist approach. This concept is similar to the idea of metacognition. Problem solving involves the processes of reflecting on problems and searching for solutions. Metacognition is the higher order process of reflecting on our own thinking and problem solving processes. Cunningham refers to this ability as reflexivity. Metacognition has powerful problem solving potential. If we are stuck with a problem we can reflect not just on the structure of the problem, but on the structuring of our approaches to the problem. We can then try to generate alternative, more productive strategies. However, this is viewed not just as a useful problem solving ability, but the ultimate expression of education – the ability to reflect back on what has been created by the process of education. This opens up opportunities to transform our understanding and to 'liberate' ourselves from prior ways of thinking.

6.3.2 The application of contructivism to learning environment design

There are a number of variations within the broad framework of constructivism. The guidelines for learning environment design vary in both nature and precision across these groupings. There are, however, certain fundamental principles in constructivist approaches to design. The central point is summed up by Perkins (1991, p.20):

If learning has this constructive character inherently, it follows that teaching practices need to be supportive of the construction that must occur. The constructivist critique of much conventional educational practice is that it is not especially supportive of the work of construction that needs to be done in the minds of the learners.

The impact of the constructivist approach may be related to the three main activities of front end analysis, selection of instructional strategies and resources, and assessment.

Front end analysis

The primary emphasis is not an analysis of domain facts and knowledge. The emphasis is on the skills and processes required to become expert in the domain – how to operate constructively in the domain. The ability to generate problems, engage in collaboration, appreciate multiple perspectives, to evaluate and to actively use knowledge become more important. Task analysis from a constructivist point of view looks quite different from Instructional System Design. There is a concern to avoid over-narrow decompositions of learning activities. Tasks must remain embedded in the larger contexts that give them meaning.

The contrast with ISD is quite stark. ISD is in danger, to use Shakespeare's telling phrase, of 'murdering to dissect'. The skills and knowledge are so precisely decomposed and formalised as to become lifeless. Radical constructivism represents a swing to the opposite extreme. The skills and knowledge remain so embedded in life that it is hard to pin them down. The designer is presented with a series of principles, but no clear guidance on how to proceed. Moderate constructivists may link their approach to more explicitly stated criteria. The CTGV group, for example, link the goals of the Jasper tapes to the curriculum recommendations of the National Council of Teachers of Mathematics Curriculum Standards Group (1989).

One important feature of constructivism is to direct attention to the wider context in which multimedia artefacts are used. The analysis becomes directed at the whole context of teaching and learning practice. The multimedia artefact, often a tool rather than a complete system, becomes an enabling component within that context. The project by Goldman-Segall et al. (1994) is a good example of an intervention based on these wider contextual concerns. Research on modern software tools for learning has been strongly influenced by constructivist ideas (e.g. Linn 1996, Guzdial et al. 1996, Edelson et al. 1996). In these studies the tools are used for representation, communication and evaluation. These tools often give a 'value added' element to group problem solving.

Constructivism represents a valuable perspective in 'constructing' the types of problems we want to solve. In overall terms, however, it presents very little precise guidance for what is to be learned. Specific variants within constructivism can be more helpful. The general outcome is a set of principles for front end analysis with exhortation rather than precise guidance on how to proceed.

Instructional strategies and resources

Perkins delineates five primary facets of learning environments, and discusses the impact of constructivism in making choices on these components (Perkins 1991). The five components are:

- information banks
- symbol pads
- construction kits
- phenomenaria
- task managers.

Information banks are stores of information, such as textbooks, reference books or computer databases. Symbol pads are surfaces for the construction and manipulation of symbols, e.g. a writing pad or a word processor. Construction kits are sets of components which provide the raw materials for construction activities. This could be LegoTechnic or a computer based toolkit such as Logo. Phenomenaria are examples of the phenomena to be studied. The provision of old newsreels in a history class, or the objects in a computer microworld are examples. Finally task managers set the learning tasks, monitor progress, and assess the outcome. In the classroom this is normally the teacher. In traditional CAI and ITS systems the computer has a strong role as the task manager.

A traditional dry classroom gives primary emphasis to information banks (textbooks) and symbol pads (notebooks) with the teacher as task manager. In contrast, many constructivist learning environments give centre stage to phenomenaria and construction kits. The emphasis on 'situated learning' encourages placing children in authentic learning contexts. The computers are provided as tools for recording information, analysing information and communication to other groups. In the Virtual Clayoquot project children visit the forest and talk to the people involved. They use the computers as tools to record, analyse and communicate their interpretation of the information. The phenomena can be brought into the classroom, as in the Jasper tapes, to provide a resource for learning.

There is an emphasis on children building up their own information banks, and on moving responsibility for task management onto the learners. The Vanderbilt group, for example, emphasises that students use the Jasper tapes to set their own tasks and not just respond to the tasks set by the teacher. Group based project work is used encourage students to take responsibility for the organisation and monitoring of the problem solving process.

Treatment of assessment

Assessment reflects the goals identified for the system of intervention. Criteria for assessment will thus vary legitimately depending on the goals set. Two main demands may be placed on our method of assessment:

1. It evaluates whether the goals set have been attained.

2. It produces evidence which may be cross checked by independent interested parties.

As the constructivists emphasise the attainment of different goals from traditional instructional design, their approach to assessment also differs. The CTGV group discuss three different teaching models for using their Jasper tapes. They point out that different assessment criteria are relevant to the different models. They emphasise that assessment should be motivated from a theoretical perspective (CTGV 1993). Debate over assessment is thus intimately tied up with debate over learning goals. However, it should be pointed out that the goals and assessment should be acceptable to the wider community of interested parties – parents, teachers, and the public bodies who supply funds for education.

Cunningham (1991) provides a radical view on assessment. He rejects the idea of 'objective' evaluation applied as a separate measure of learning attainment. He describes it as 'a fiction' (p.15). He argues that assessment of learning is inherent in the successful completion of that task:

...when instruction is embedded in situations where students are involved in realistic or actual tasks, assessment arises naturally from those situations.

(Cunningham 1991, p. 15)

The judgement of successful completion should be made by the teacher, based on a consideration of all the evidence available. From a computer based learning perspective this tends to throw assessment 'off line' (Perkins 1991). However, it is possible to build learning environments where assessment is a natural part of the task. The business game simulation developed by Feifer and Allender (1994) uses success or failure in the game as the natural measure of attainment. This emphasis on assessment embedded in context is echoed by a number of constructivist writers (e.g. Jonassen et al. 1993, Perkins 1991).

A second problem in assessment arises from the emphasis of group work and collaborative problem solving. How do we assess successful learning when the tasks are carried out by a group? How do we know what the individual members of the group have learned? Cunningham, in the guise of his character Sagredo, admits that these are concerns which he shares and to which he has no completely satisfactory answers (Cunningham 1991).

The radical constructivists raise real concerns about assessment. Their arguments that important skills are not reflected in tests disembedded from the context of learning would find an echo among many teachers. Using exams to assess programming skill, for example, has always struck me as a rather peculiar activity. The search for better means of assessment is an important issue. However, the alternatives offered by the constructivists often sound rather imprecise. They need to be clearer, especially about issues such as assessing group performance. Alternative methods need to be shown to be 'valid', economical, and to meet the demands of different interested parties. One of the themes of the Teaching and Learning Technology Programme (TLTP) in Britain has been to try to find economical measures of assessment (HEFCE 1993a, 1993b). Radical constructivist approaches do not normally fall into this category. Managers in education and government agencies which supply the money often have rather different perspectives on assessment. The assessment methods must suit their requirements as well as those of workers on the ground.

6.4 Assessment of constructivism

Cunningham (1991) emphasises that constructivism provides a clear theory-based approach for design. However, this theoretical base reflects a mixture of influences. Can the main dimensions of variation be teased out so that an informed choice may be made as to which aspects of constructivism are most useful in design?

There are problematic aspects of constructivism. If these aspects are not clarified then the appeal of this approach will be markedly limited. These problems seem to emerge most sharply when the 'constructivist' design advocates diverge clearly from the psychological base of constructivist theory. The single most problematic point is the tendency towards extreme individualism, with the danger, as Cunningham (1991) admits, of collapsing into solipsism. Duffy and Jonassen (1991) argue that meaning is 'imposed' on the world rather than existing in the world independently of us. Jonassen et al. (1993, p.232) state:

The most important epistemological assumption of constructivism is that meaning is a function of how the individual creates meaning from his/her experiences. What we know is internally generated by the individual rather than received from any external source.

There is an assumption that the opposite of an external reality imposing its existence on us is for individuals to create their own reality. This is an over-simplistic opposition. The first great 'constructivist' psychologist was Piaget. His work had an immense influence in changing conceptions of learning and teaching that have deeply influenced school practice. Piaget's work also directly informed the design principles of Logo, which is probably the first major computer based constructivist learning environment.

Piaget's life's work focused on what he termed 'genetic epistemology'. Piaget believed that we all possess certain biological characteristics, and we all interact with an environment with certain invariant features. Piaget argued that there are certain biologically based invariants in how we interact with and 'assimilate' information about the world. There are certain invariant characteristics of the environment of interaction. Through interacting with the environment the child builds mental structures to make sense of that environment. The adequacy of that cognitive representation is tested in further interactions, and we refine and transform our mental structures in response to the feedback received. For Piaget constructivism means constructing **adapted** representations of reality. The representation is a product neither of the mind alone nor of 'reality' alone but the adapted interaction of the two. Because of invariant features in our biological makeup and the physical world we interact with, there is a basic universal pattern of cognitive development. This is what Piaget meant by 'genetic epistemology'. There are basic mental structures and modes of operation which we all share as human beings, and which define our common humanity as much as common physical characteristics. Variations operate upon this common base.

A major criticism of Piaget's theory is that he fails to take adequate account of the special nature of social interaction and the influence of cultural transmission mediated though these social interactions. The Russian psychologist, Lev Vygotsky, provides a 'complementary' view to Piaget's approach. Vygotsky believed that social interactions played a major role in intellectual development. He put forward the intriguing notion that functions which first appear as social phenomena later become internalised as psychological phenomena. For example, Vygotsky proposes that the origin of self-regulation is the social regulation of the child by the parents. The parents apply certain principles in regulating the behaviour of their children though social interaction. As the child develops language as a means of reflection these principles become internalised by the child as the principles guiding behaviour. Vygotsky's works are often quoted by modern constructivists as providing a basic framework for their work.

Vygotsky can be interpreted as challenging or as complementing Piaget's work. Since the two thinkers concentrated on different forms of interaction and the influence these had on mental development, there is much in the work that can be viewed as complementary. If we produce a pyramid we might place Piaget's biological perspective of constructive mental development on the base. Vygotsky's insistence of the formative role of culture as transmitted through social interaction provides a second powerful layer of interactions, and interactional influences on development (Figure 6.2). Both theorists emphasised the role of interaction and constructive development processes, though they focused on different forms of interaction. There is

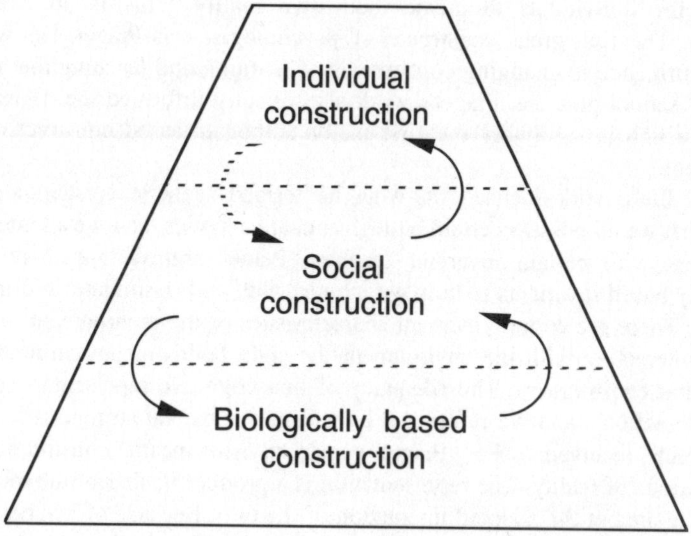

Figure 6.2 The constructivist pyramid

a further common feature – they both were concerned with 'common constructions' of the world. Vygotsky did not view culture primarily as a source of human difference, but as an influence which defines our common humanity which, in turn, underpins our ability to operate as co-operating social beings.

The modern constructivists have added a third layer to the pyramid, a strong emphasis on individual constructions of reality. This third layer, seen in context, is an important contribution. However, when expressed in terms which seem to deny the existence or importance of the other layers, it is a distortion which has potentially very damaging consequences. Constructivism, if it is to be widely successful, must be able to support a range of approaches. This is necessary if a constructivist approach is to be applicable across a wide range of disciplines in education. The emphasis in educational disciplines varies from individual interpretation and expression (e.g. literature, art) to consensual acceptance of rigorously tested theories. In order to make sense of life in all its diversity and adaptive demands we construct multiple forms of sense making. This essential point must be grasped if constructivism is to have universal appeal.

6.5 Summary

This chapter has discussed strategic approaches to the design of computer based learning environments. Traditional Instructional Design provides a systematic and formal set of guidelines for producing computer aided instruction systems. This approach has been strongly criticised. The theoretical basis of its propositions has been challenged as weak or outdated. The computer technology paradigm to which it seemed best suited has been bypassed. The prescriptions it proposes have become so detailed as to lead to complaints of 'analysis paralysis' (Booth et al. 1994). But Instructional Design does offer challenges to the multimedia designer. Its emphasis on a clear statement of objectives, clear thinking about choice of methods, and rigorous assessment remain important challenges.

Constructivism represents the dominant paradigm in educational multimedia design. It has a much stronger base in the psychology of learning and cognitive development. It provides a more 'liberating' view of the learner which fits well with the opportunities offered by hypermedia technology. Many of the tactics and principles discussed in subsequent chapters expand and exemplify this approach. There are, however, many strands within constructivism. This chapter has tried to provide a balanced view of common and individual factors. It is argued that constructivism must be seen in this wider, balanced sense if its full impact on multimedia design is to be achieved.

Chapter 7

Context and multimedia design

7.1 Introduction

Constructivism suggests a number of heuristics for IMLE design. These principles concern learning in general. They are not focused specifically on the design of computer based multimedia systems. These general heuristics are not sufficient to guide detailed design decisions. The present chapter concentrates on developing a systematic framework for understanding multimedia learning environment design. This conception provides the base for the detailed description of design options given in the final chapter of this part of the book.

The central argument proposed in this chapter is that 'context' provides a pivotal concept for understanding multimedia design. The importance of context is clarified by exploring three different approaches to this construct – from film theory, linguistics and psychology. The central leverage for developing a more formal framework for multimedia design arises from a synthesis of ideas derived from the first two disciplines. Hodges and Sasnett (1993) derive ideas from film theory which point to the central role of context in multimedia design. Their ideas have a productive correspondence to a theory developed for a different mode of communication – linguistic communication. The correspondence between the conceptual frameworks derived from visual and linguistic communication offers an emergent framework for conceptual design. In this discussion three macro-functions are delineated. It is proposed that these provide the main axes along which decisions about multimedia communication structure may be represented.

Multimedia learning environments add an extra layer of complexity to design. These environments must support performance that changes over time. Research in problem solving and cognitive development illustrates the crucial role that contextual variation plays in supporting these learning advances. The concept of context as a pivotal explanatory construct naturally extends from the communication disciplines to the study of learning. This clarification provides the background to the discussion of tactics in constructing multimedia learning contexts in the following chapter.

7.2 Context and macro-functions in multimedia design

7.2.1 Context and film theory

Hodges and Sasnett (1993) present a theoretical framework, derived from film analysis, which provides an initial pass over the problem of multimedia design. In film analysis, theorists traditionally divide their subject into two major components – mis-en-scène and montage. Mis-en-scène deals with the constructions of individual scenes – what objects are included and how they are framed and composed. Montage deals with the combination of scenes – selection, sequencing, and the handling of transitions. Hodges and Sasnett relate this to multimedia design as follows. There are parts of an interface that correspond roughly to the scene – 'these are groupings of information resources (text, graphics, video) and the controls needed to manipulate them' (Hodges and Sasnett 1993, p. 41). Configurations of this kind usually acts as independent units that appear and disappear together, e.g. media player or sound recorder in Windows. This groupings of objects and associated interactivity appears as a distinct 'context' to the user. They argue that in multimedia analysis the context is the equivalent of the scene in a film.

There are two major functions in the composition of a scene – to convey information, and to achieve an aesthetic effect. These two functions operate in parallel. The designer has to select which information to convey in a scene and design the aesthetic impact of the scene. Both these functions carry over to the concept of a multimedia context. The multimedia designer has to select which information to include in the context, and the aesthetic framing of that information. Ideas of information composition and visual composition derived from film analysis can provide guidance on these issues.

There is a third crucial aspect of a multimedia context which distinguishes it from a scene in a film. A film is essentially one-way communication. The viewer is placed in a comparatively passive role. In interactive multimedia, however, the user is an active participant. A context has an interaction aspect – 'a context is a set of information resources *and any control mechanisms associated with them*' (Hodges and Sasnett 1993, p. 42, my italics). Certain appropriate types of action may be carried out in a context. These actions are adaptively related to the content in the context. Context is a way of organising information and associated interactivity. Examples of context setting screens are provided in Figure 7.1 and Figure 7.2. In Figure 7.1 a contents screen from the CLEM system helps to establish an 'electronic book' context. A different type of context, an arcade game, is projected by the opening screen of the 'X' system (Figure 7.2).

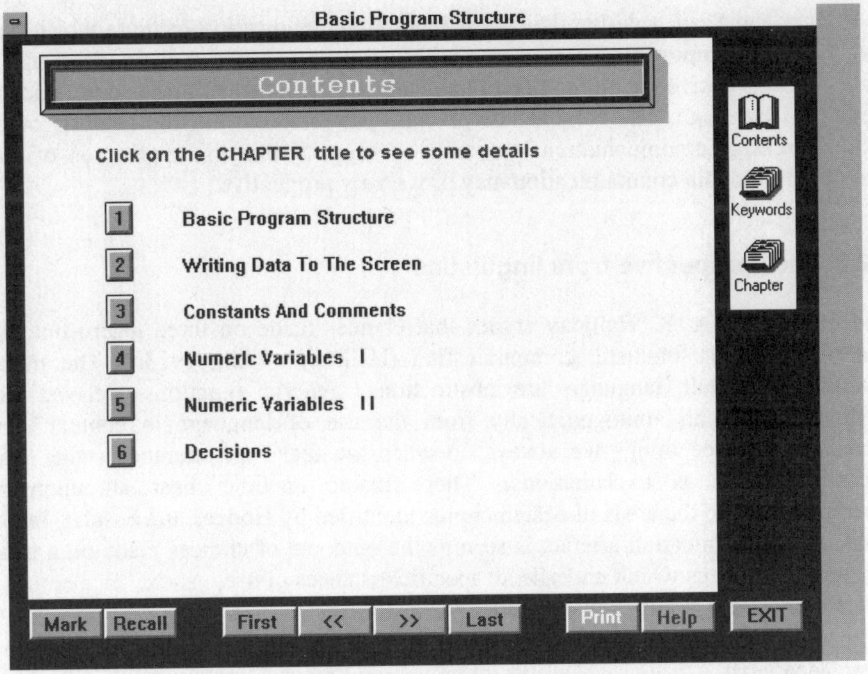

Figure 7.1 An electronic book context

Figure 7.2 An arcade game context: the opening screen from the 'X' system

Hodges and Sasnett derive their ideas from a communication medium which has a strong visual component. There is a marked similarity between their ideas and the main concepts derived from the functional analysis of another primary communication medium – language. The coincidence of concepts derived from the analysis of two distinct areas of communication is notable. It suggests that the application of these ideas to multimedia communication may prove very productive.

7.2.2 The perspective from linguistics

The linguist M. A. K. Halliday argues that choices made on three macro-functions underlie all adult linguistic communication (Halliday 1973a, 1973b). The macro-functions of adult language are abstractions, generic functions, derived both phylogenetically and ontogenetically from the use of language in context. They represent the three things we always do when we make an utterance (with a few exceptions such as exclamations). These macro-functions bear an interesting correspondence to the areas of design choice identified by Hodges and Sasnett. In both cases the communication artefact is seen as the outcome of choices made on a trinity of generic functions which underlie all specific instances of use.

Halliday labels his three macro-functions as follows:

- ideational
- interpersonal
- textual.

The ideational component is the function of conveying content. The interpersonal component involves controlling the interaction options open to the participants. The textual component is concerned with creating overall coherence in the communication. Halliday argues that the basic structure of grammar has been shaped to meet the need to express simultaneously these three macro-functions. We make choices on these three functional realms each time we utter a clause. These rather abstract points may be illustrated by quoting three simple clauses which represent different choices on the three macro-functions.

> 'The boy kicked the door.'
>
> 'Did the boy kick the door?'
>
> 'Did he do it?'

In the first sentence the basic ideational content is clear. There is an agent, an object and an action linking the two. The second sentence reflects a different choice made on the interpersonal component. In the second sentence the listener is defined as the primary transmitter of content. This contrasts with the first sentence. It is these contrastive possibilities that represent options in the underlying networks of choice. These underlying networks of choice are formalised in systemic grammar as 'systemic networks'. The third sentence reflects a variant choice on the textual function. Here anaphoric pronouns ('he') and ellipsis ('do it') are used to bind the individual utterance cohesively into the overall communication. The surface form reflects choices made about the nature of the context and the role of the utterance in that context.

There is an interesting correspondence between the three areas of choice identified by Hodges and Sasnett and the three macro-functions of linguistic communication. The first macro-function, the ideational, is similar to the 'content' area of Hodges and Sasnett. The second area of correspondence is between the 'interactional' function of Hodges and Sasnett and the 'interpersonal' function of Halliday. Both approaches emphasise that this macro-function is central. If we have a context then we have not only content but an appropriate set of options for action. Halliday emphasises that there is a third function in creating the fabric of communication. He calls this the 'textual' function. It is the function by which a whole coherent communication, a 'text', is created from its constituent parts. Choices on this macro-function are realised through a range of linguistic devices such as anaphoric pronouns and ellipsis. In the visual arts there is clearly a parallel function concerned with achieving an overall coherent effect. In multimedia design it seems best to label this third function the 'compositional' function. It involves parallel choices to the other two functions. It has the role of achieving an overall, satisfying coherence in the multimedia design.

The conjunction of ideas from two distinct areas of communication suggests a potential framework for making sense of multimedia design. It suggests that we should think of multimedia artefacts as contexts created by the designer for the user. It argues that there are (probably) three macro-functions in design – structuring content, providing interaction options, and achieving compositional coherence. The work in linguistics suggests that this knowledge may be formalised as networks of contrastive options. The construction of a multimedia artefact involves parallel choices in these three realms of meaning.

7.3 Relationships between contexts

The combination of contexts – how they share the screen, or how transitions are made from one to another – may be related to 'montage' in film theory (Hodges and Sasnett 1993). In a film a scene fills the communication space and scenes are linked in a temporal dimension. In multimedia design the situation is more complex. The range of possible links between multimedia contexts is rather greater than that between scenes in a film. Hodges and Sasnett pay particular attention to the problem of handling transitions between contexts. The primary aim is to maintain coherence so that the context switching does not confuse or disorientate the user. This is a potential problem of hypertext systems.

Sometimes explicit support has to be provided to help the user handle the transition between two contexts. Hodges and Sasnett quote an example of a multimedia introduction for visitors to CERN, the European particle physics centre. The introduction opens with a still picture of the complex taken from a helicopter. The visitor may click on a part of the complex to 'enter' that area and find out more information. The transition is handled by inserting a video window which shows an approach to the selected area shot from a helicopter. The area is then entered and the exploration begins. This choice of transition device helps maintain coherence for the user. The video is presented in a window set against the main picture to help the user make the transition. This also provides an aesthetic effect, balancing the visual impact of the video within the overall presentation.

A second example may illustrate the operation of the same technique, but with the use of rather different media. In the CLEM system (described in Chapter 5) one option for a user is to click on any fragment of code. This code is placed in the context of a fully working program and transferred to a commercial compiler environment where it may be compiled and executed. The compiler environment had a built-in editor. The problem was to transfer the code to this editor. The compiler system, however, was DOS based; the code would, therefore come up in a black DOS window on the screen over which we had comparatively little control. The jump from a fragment of code to a full program in a DOS window is potentially very disorienting to novice programmers. So context transition support is provided. This operates functionally in a very similar way to Hodges and Sasnett's system. When the learner clicks on the code fragment a 'Program Card' pops up which shows the code fragments within a full program (illustrated in Plate 2 of the colour insert). The original formatting and highlighting of the fragment is maintained within the program. The user can click back and forth between the 'page' and the card that sits on top of part of this page. The user can then choose to send the program to the compiler environment. This appears as a window on the top half of the screen with the original program card sitting beneath this window. The transition is thus handled in easy steps with the launch context still visible after the learner chooses to move to the new context.

Maintaining coherence as the learner moves across contexts, however, is not simply a matter of providing explicit transition support mechanisms. It depends on the conceptual structuring of the overall system. This depends on the hierarchical relationship between contexts built into the design. For example, the screen context the user sees may represent a page in an electronic book. If the book context has been clearly established as the overall context for the system, then transition between pages should be relatively straightforward. If all the pages are instances of the same context type ('a page') then the transitions are simple. However, there may be several variants in the page contexts. In the CLEM system there are different types of pages corresponding to different aspects of the CORE learning approach which underpins the system.

Figure. 7.3 and Plate 1 together illustrate how a specific page is context presented to the user. The outer blue panel acts as the 'control pad' for the book. The generic controls for the book are presented here. These controls are consistently present

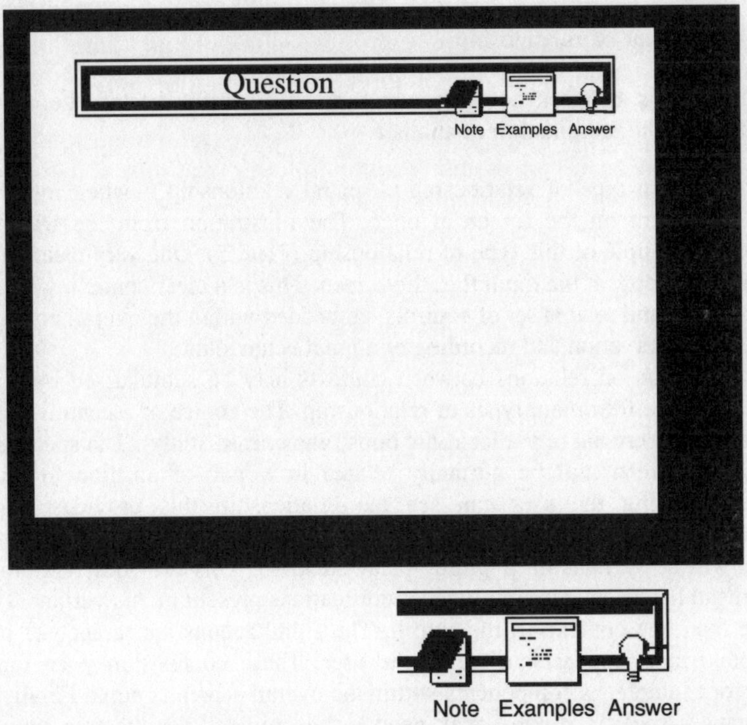

Figure 7.3 A variant on a 'page' context

throughout the system (with the single exception of on-line test sections where the controls are deliberately disabled). The central white panel represents the 'page' in the book. The pertinent information is presented here. The banner title signals the type of page, and attached to the banner are some icons. These represent the specific functionality associated with this type of page. The screen display thus clearly signals the overall context, the specific page context, and the functionality associated with each context layer. The basic pattern is followed in all chapters in the book.

This example illustrates two types of context relation. The first relationship is the hierarchical 'part-of' relationship – the page context is part of the book context. The second type is the 'is-a variant-of' type of relationship. The specific page type is one of a number of variants of the page context in the book. There is a default representation page, and then a series of variants supporting different phases in the learning process.

The context relationships discussed so far thus include:

- hierarchical 'part-of' relationship

- 'is-a variant-of' relationship
- transitions between contexts which are temporally related, i.e. one context follows the presentation of another.

There is a fourth type of relationship – spatial relationship – when more than one context is present on the screen at once. The illustration from the DOVE system provides an example of this type of relationship (Plate 5). One very clear sub-context is the video window at the top left of the screen. This is a clear context, with a specific type of content and related set of controls, embedded within the overall context (which involves the observation and recording of animal behaviour).

The discussion on relations between contexts may be summarised by stating that there seems to be four main types of relationship. The choice of a central context type for the system is crucial (e.g. electronic book, game, case study). The specific contexts signalled on screen will be normally related in a 'part-of' fashion to this overall context. Providing the user can see the relationship this provides a powerful, economical way to maintain coherence in moving between specific contexts. Some contexts will be variants on a 'prototypical' standard. This provides flexibility, while the overhead for the user is simply the modifications present in this variant. There may be more than one context on the screen. The simultaneous appearance of more than one context must appear sensible to the user. These contexts may be functionally related, for example, as components within the overall screen context. Finally, in some circumstances specific support may need to be provided for the transition between contexts when the jump might otherwise be disorienting for the user.

7.4 Context and learning

The discussion in this chapter has been concerned with the role of context in multimedia design. It has suggested a framework through which we may begin to think more systematically about the choices made in constructing multimedia contexts, and relations between contexts. There is a further challenge, however, in designing multimedia learning environments. Hodges and Sasnett, and Halliday, were concerned with the choices underlying communicative performance. However, IMLE design is dealing with performance that changes over time, i.e. learning. Crossing the landscape of learning may require the construction of transitional support contexts. The importance of context and transitional support mechanisms has been extensively explored in psychological research.

The crucial importance of context in learning is well illustrated by Margaret Donaldson's superb little book *Children's Minds* (Donaldson 1978). It is worth discussing one of her key examples in some detail as it captures a number of themes relevant to the design of multimedia learning environments. One of the central themes of the book is a critique of the concept of the egocentric child. Briefly, Piaget proposed that young children thought in a way which was qualitatively different from adults. In particular he argued that these children were egocentric. By this Piaget meant that they could not appreciate what the world looked like from the point of view of someone else. This is a cognitive egocentrism, an inability to decentre from one's own cognitive perspective, rather than an emotional egocentrism. A number of studies seemed to provide strong support for this idea. In one classic experiment children were shown a model of three mountains laid out on a table. They were asked to select a picture of what the scene looked like from the position of someone sitting opposite. The younger children inevitably choose the picture which showed the scene from where they were sitting. Piaget concluded that the children could not appreciate that the scene was different for someone else. This ability to decentre was only acquired, he argued, as the child approached eight years of age.

Donaldson quotes a number of beautifully designed studies which show that this cognitive limitation is strongly dependent on the contextual setting of the task. In one study carried out by Martin Hughes the children were given a task which demanded non-egocentric thinking. The major difference with Piaget's experiments was that considerable attention was given to making sure the context was meaningful to the children. The task was introduced as a naughty boy who was being chased by a policeman. The policeman and boy were represented by dolls, and the policeman doll was placed at the end of one wall in a model (Figure 7.4). The task for the children was to the hide the naughty boy so that the policeman could not see him. Ninety per cent of the children succeeded in the task. This was a striking disconfirmation of the absolute cognitive egocentrism proposed by Piaget.

A number of important points for designers of interactive learning environments flow from this study. The first is that if a learner is failing to perform effectively the first source for the failure should be sought not in the inadequacies of the learner but in the inadequacies of the learning environment. In particular the designer or teacher should ask – is there a way I could change the context of learning so that the learners will begin to succeed instead of fail?

There is a second point which flows from the first. It may seem a digression from the discussion of the role of context in learning but the insight is too important to ignore. Donaldson makes the point that it was not the children who were being egocentric – it was the adults. They failed to appreciate what the situation looked like from the children's point of view. The children behaved as they did in the three mountains task because an adult asked them to do a task which had no meaning for the child, and they obliged as best they could. This failure by an expert to adequately appreciate the perspective of learners seems to be replicated in many domains. This is illustrated nicely in a study by Segal and Amhad (1991). They studied the use of examples in programming. They found that the students paid their primary attention to the examples as a way of making sense of the language. The tutors, however, regarded the didactic expositions as the primary medium of communication. There was clearly a mismatch between the perspectives of the students and the tutors on the 'same' learning material. I have spoken to several designers of multimedia learning environments who made the 'surprising' discovery that the students did not have the same conception of the learning situation as they did as course tutors. It is often very difficult for experts

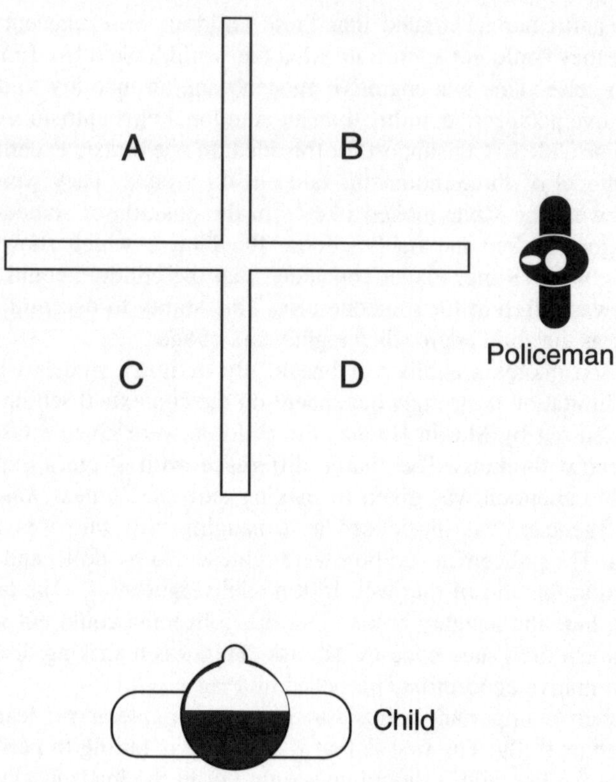

Figure 7.4 The policeman and boy set-up

to remember what it was like to be a novice. The designers of interactive learning environments have to make a conscious effort to overcome their own natural egocentrism. At the same time this attempt to be sensitive to the learner's perspective can yield great gains in fresh and productive ways of looking at design.

Donaldson not only revealed a series of provocative and productive insights, she also proposed a conceptual framework for recasting our understanding of the role of context in learning. She abstracted a general dimension relating learning and contextual support. She argued that cognitive skills are often initially acquired in a 'context embedded' fashion. For many of these skills, e.g. mathematics, this contextual support must later be removed so that the person can gain independent control. Donaldson thus proposed a general dimension in moving from context embedded to context disembedded cognitive skills. This may be extrapolated to suggest a dimension in IMLE design of providing levels of contextual support initially required by the learner, and then gradually removing this support to wean the learner towards full independence. Other researchers have referred to the provision of transitional support as 'scaffolding' (Bruner 1975).

A rather quaint example of the use of scaffolding is given by Tagg et al. (1995). A group of elementary school children using Logo had difficulty in working out left and right when using the screen turtle. The teacher helpfully provided some cardboard turtles with L and R marked on the front paws. As a transitional support mechanism the children could place the cardboard turtle over the screen turtle and read the direction from the marks. Rosson et al. (1990) report a more sophisticated use of scaffolding in a computer assisted learning environment for Smalltalk. The complexity of the user interface in Smalltalk is a significant learning challenge. The authors developed their own introductory tools with the provision of scaffolding for learning. For example, they replaced one Smalltalk interface tool with another that was identical in appearance and function but was simpler to operate. The wider list of features which the standard tool could access were filtered out. The replacement tool thus acted as a prop that significantly reduced the learning burden. At the same time the eventual transition to using the full tool was facilitated because of the similarity in appearance and functionality.

The theme of scaffolding has been emphasised strongly in a number of recent studies. Jackson et al. (1996) identify three 'key scaffolding strategies'. They illustrate the application of these strategies in a learner centred modelling tool called 'Model-It' which provides support to high-school children in modelling scientific problems.

The first scaffolding strategy is to ground the task in terms of familiar objects and relationships. For example, a photograph of the stream that the children studied is used as a background graphic in the tool environment. This 'personalised representation' grounds the learning in a familiar, supportive context. The students use English phrases, such as 'a lot', to construct expressions describing scientific relationships. These phrases are selected from lists provided in dialogue boxes. This is another example of grounding the learning in the familiar – in this case expressing ideas in the familiar terms of the English language.

This 'context embedding' of the task provides only the starting point. The children have to be helped to make the transition to new, more abstract forms of representation and understanding. The second scaffolding strategy supports 'bridging' between familiar and new forms of representation. The learners are exposed simultaneously to old and new representations of the 'same' information. For example, a graph is presented in parallel with the English statement 'stream quality decreases as phosphate is added'. The association of the new representation with the familiar base of experience aids the transition to understanding new, more mathematical means of representation.

A third technique is used to support the transition to new forms of understanding – immediate visual feedback contingent on the learner's actions. This falls into the traditional category of extrinsic feedback, i.e. feedback specifically added to help a learner master a task. This feedback allows students to test their hypotheses. Ideas can be adaptively changed and refined to fit the evidence from the situation itself. This echoes the strong visual feedback supplied in Turtle graphics.

Scaffolding plays a key role in the development of several 'learning environment architectures'. In this approach the learning task is broken down into a series of major activities. These activities are then provided with explicit scaffolding support. When applied systematically this technique provides a comprehensive support environment for learning. This approach is well illustrated in studies by Linn (1996) and Guzdial et al. (1996).

Linn uses an instructional framework called 'Scaffolded Knowledge Integration'. This was employed to construct a learning environment for 10–14 year old students to learn about science. The process of studying a scientific topic is broken down into a set of learner activities. These activities include:

- stating their initial position on the topic
- gathering evidence (from the Internet and other sources)
- reflecting on the evidence
- engaging in group discussions to clarify alternative positions and integrate the evidence to form a scientific argument.

Finally the students present their position in a class debate and field questions from other students.

These major activities are provided with explicit scaffolding support. Reflecting on the evidence, for example, is supported by a tool that provides prompts, hints and examples to help students think about the evidence and reflect on their own reasoning (Figure 7.5). The electronic group discussions were structured using a tool called SpeakEasy. This prompts students to indicate the function of their contribution to the discussion (e.g. does it support, extend or contradict a position already stated?), and to reflect on the function of other contributions (Figure 3.4).

Guzdial et al. (1996) use a similar approach to help engineering students learn about design. The aim of this study was to provide support for student performance and learning with complex problems. Authentic problems are often complex; if they are to be used effectively in learning, students must be supported in handling this complexity. This project developed a series of software supports to help students engage effectively in learning with authentic, complex design problems.

Software support was provided for three main types of activities:

- collaboration through electronic discussion groups
- expressing and visualising ideas
- access to problem solving resources.

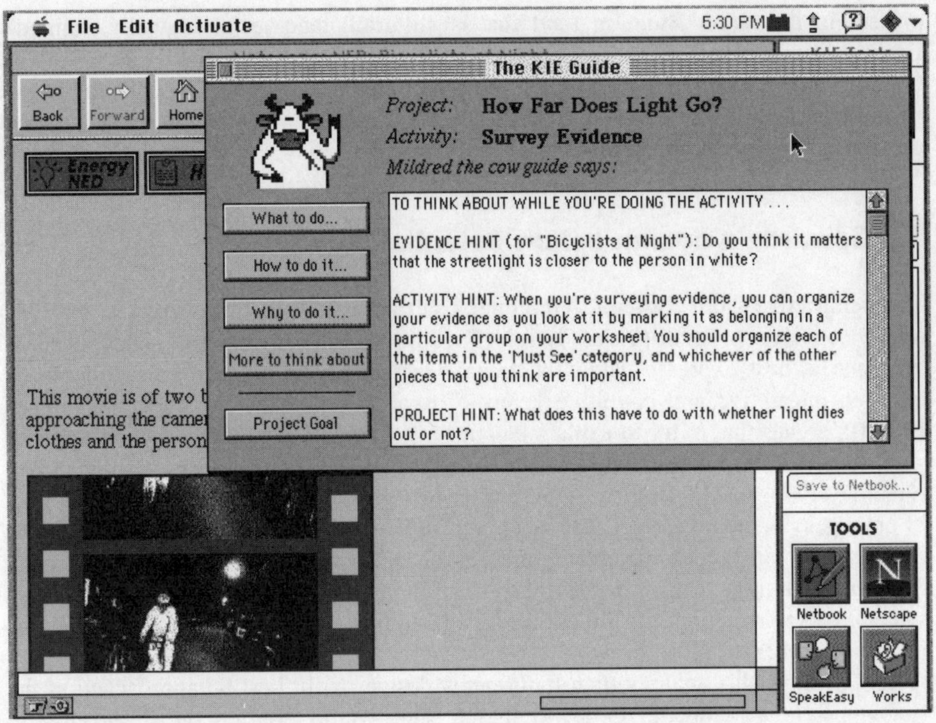

Figure 7.5 Scaffolding support for learning activities

Collaboration in electronic discussion groups was supported through the use of tools in a similar way to that of Linn (1996). The expression of ideas was supported by a specially designed graphical editor (called DEVICE) that supports student in visualising their ideas. A case library was provided to hold examples of the experiences and outcomes of others involved in similar problem solving situations. This facilitates students in discovering issues that need to be addressed, and provides suggestions about how to proceed. Guzdial et al. (1996) claim that the features of this environment to some extent emulate 'how a professional chemical engineer might support (scaffold) an apprentice or intern' (p. 45).

Before moving on it is important to qualify the conception of a simple transition from context embedded to context disembedded control. Experts in any domain rely on a number of contextual support features. Mathematicians, for example, could not function very effectively without contextual support such as pen and paper, or even computers. Without such external support their memory and processing capacity would become rapidly overloaded. The dimension is more precisely a move from extrinsic contextual support to intrinsic support only. Intrinsic support is that which is present in the target situation (and this is culturally and technologically defined). Extrinsic support is specifically supplied to help the learner and should be gradually removed as the learner moves towards the target attainment level. The construction of multimedia learning environments to provide and gradually remove extrinsic support provides an important lever in design.

7.5 Towards a design action potential

The perspective from Systemic Grammar contributes one further aspect to how we might conceive of multimedia design. Halliday (1975) argues that understanding language is best expressed at a functional level. This echoes the distinction made between interactive and cognitive layers of explanation made by Anderson (1990). Halliday argues that to try to explain language as a cognitive phenomenon, in terms of what goes on within someone's head, 'is merely adding an unnecessary unknown' (Halliday 1975, p. 21). Halliday seeks rather to represent the linguistic system as a set of options available to the speaker in a given situation. The options at this level can be expressed as an 'action potential', the set of options available to the participant. Systemic Grammar seeks to represent this action potential as systemic networks. Each systemic network represents the options available on one of the three macro-functions identified earlier.

If we follow this analogy then multimedia design might best be approached as the 'action potential' available to the designer. This would provide the designer with knowledge of what *can* be done, not what *should* be done. It would require a declarative expression of the options available on the three major axes of design choice. These might be organised, as in systemic networks, on a cline from general choices made at the beginning of the network to increasing finer distinctions as particular paths are followed.

This 'action potential' approach is quite different from a 'procedural ' approach which tries to specify what the designer should do. There are a number of advantages to this approach. First, it is simply a much more attainable objective given our state of knowledge. Secondly, it avoids the problem which worries many multimedia designers of the straitjacketing of design choice. This approach provides a method for formalising our scattered knowledge without constraining individual design decisions. The choice of the procedural activation of paths across the landscape of design options may be made idiosyncratically or according to some formalised method. This is a separate area of choice. There is a further advantage of this approach. When we come across an interesting new technique we do not ask the question – is it right or wrong? We ask the question – is it a productive alternative? If so, where could it be incorporated into the map of design options? The concept of elucidating design options as networks of choice is pursued in some depth in the following chapter.

7.6 Summary

The aim of this chapter has been to sketch an overall framework for making sense of IMLE design. The first step involved a synthesis of ideas derived from film theory and functional linguistics. This synthesis identifies context as the central construct for making sense of multimedia design. The use of the term 'context' has moved towards a more precise conception. Context is a construction placed upon the environment to make holistic sense of that environment. Halliday points out that context should not be conceived as a sort of vague social backdrop. It should be viewed as 'an abstract representation of the relevant environment' (Halliday 1975, p. 11). Decisions on the construction of the contexts may be formalised along three main functional axes. These three functions involve content structuring, interactivity and creating the compositional framework. It was suggested that choices made on these three areas might be represented by networks based on the model of Systemic grammar. These networks would represent the 'design action potential' available for IMLE development. The management of transitions between contexts was also discussed, and a number of design techniques were suggested.

Psychological research has demonstrated the crucial role of contextual variation in learning. A key dimension that emerges is that of 'scaffolding' – the provision and timely removal of extrinsic contextual support. This provides an important design lever in the construction of interactive learning environments. This dimension is particularly important in complex or abstract domains.

The following chapter moves from this base to develop a more systematic description of the design options open for the construction of multimedia learning environments.

Chapter 8

Design action potential

8.1 Introduction

A perspective on multimedia design has been developed in the previous chapter based on the idea of multimedia contexts and the macro-functions from which they are composed. This approach leads to the general concept of design action potential – a declarative expression of the set of options open to the designer in constructing multimedia contexts. The role of this chapter is to clarify the nature of this design action potential.

This chapter elucidates the options available for designing the learning context. These options are organised in three networks. These networks represent the principal options available in the three macro-functional domains – the content structuring, interactive and compositional functions. The design of a multimedia learning environment involves parallel choices in these three domains of meaning. Each network is a declarative expression of the action potential open to the designer (i.e. what the designer *can do*) in that domain.

The chapter is divided into four main parts. The first three sections develop in turn each of the three design action potential (DAP) networks. The aim of these networks is not to be definitive; it is to open up this area of analysis and representation. The first section discusses the structuring of content. It suggests that we need to do better than pure hypermedia for the structure of learning content. The second section discusses options for the structuring of learning interactions. The third section discusses compositional options for embedding all the elements in a coherent context. For each area an initial DAP network is developed to represent the action potential open to the designer in that domain. These networks are developed at the level of the primary choices made in creating a learning context. At this high level 'content structuring' parallels the traditional educational concern of curriculum development. The structuring of interactivity, in a similar way, corresponds to the concern of pedagogy – the structuring of learning interactions. Compositional structure does not have a simple correspondence in traditional educational theory.

The options for selecting and elaborating the learning context are a declarative expression of the options available to the designer. The designer may choose the path across these options or follow a 'method' which guides the selections to be made. The fourth section in the chapter discusses the issue of design 'methods' or 'tactics' and their relation to the DAP networks. These two sources of design guidance are not viewed as being in conflict. They are regarded as complementary resources for the designer.

8.2 The management of complexity: approaches to the structuring of content

The overall structuring of content for learning environments involves the creation of a curriculum. Many writers within the hypermedia traditions have deliberately underplayed this element. The careful structuring of content becomes increasingly important, however, as learning becomes more complex. This section reviews several options in content structuring. An important theme in the discussion is how these options contribute to dealing with the problem of complexity in learning.

One approach to structuring content is a formal analysis of the required domain, followed by a systematic structuring of the curriculum to ensure that this content is covered. This is a highly disciplined approach to design (Gagné and Briggs 1979). You first analyse the target behaviour to systematically decompose it into its constituent parts (Figure 8.1). This decomposition is used to derive a curriculum sequence. Simpler skills are practised and mastered before more complex skills. This systematic structuring of the curriculum is usually matched by a pedagogy where the emphasis is on systematic instruction and practice. It is an extremely precise model of the instructional domain.

During the eighties self-instructional materials were developed to meet the needs of the vastly expanded user base of microcomputer software. These materials were influenced by the systems approach to instructional design. Carroll (1990) argues that serious limitations in this approach were revealed in a series of empirical studies. These standard self-instructional techniques seemed to conflict with the learning styles and strategies that people adopted spontaneously. Drill and practice in a formally derived curriculum did not work well. Users expressed a preference for getting started on meaningful tasks that could be accomplished quickly. The learners were too busy making sense of the situation to follow a rigid series of steps. As Carroll (1990) puts it, 'They were too busy learning to make much sense of the instructions' (p. 74).

The information revealed by these early studies led Carroll and his co-workers to develop a radically different approach to the construction of learning materials called the 'Minimalist' approach. The domain considered was mainly text based learning

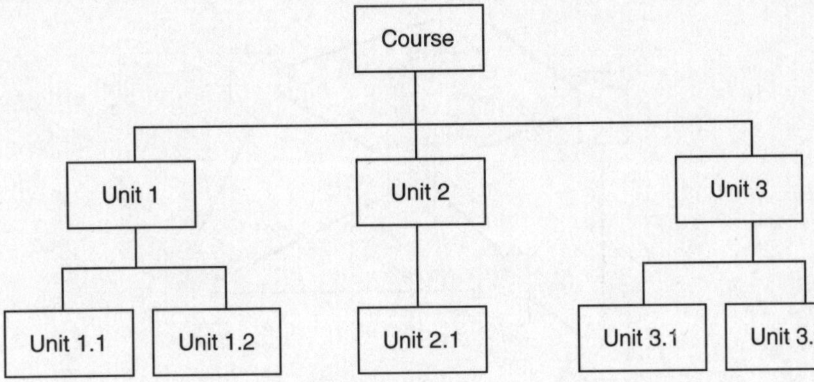

Figure 8.1 Curriculum structure based on a formal hierarchical analysis of the domain

material for information technology skills. The name was chosen to reflect the primary aim of supporting the natural strategies of learners, and to minimise the impact of intrusive instructional materials.

Minimalism represents a functional as opposed to a formal approach to constructing a curriculum for learning. It is the learners' strategies and preferences that drive the selection and structuring of the content. The curriculum is structured around getting the learners started quickly on real tasks. Meaningful tasks in real contexts take precedence over any systematic curriculum. Content is structured in a highly modular way as a network of small self-contained units (Figure 8.2). Learners thus do not have to follow a rigid predefined sequence. They can construct the sequence that best matches their needs and personal agendas. Incomplete materials are used to encourage the active completion by the learners through reasoning, improvising and experimenting. The nature and sequencing of the content of learning is thus highly user centred. The freedom from predefined sequences reflects a similar emphasis in hypertext and hypermedia systems. The set of principles developed within the Minimalist tradition thus supplies a useful set of heuristics for the design of hyperstructured learning environments.

The studies on which the Minimalist principles were developed concerned professional people working on acquiring IT skills such as word processing. These were people who already knew what they wanted to do; they were trying to acquire skill in computer based tools for carrying out these familiar tasks. The findings from this type of setting may not generalise to other users with different types of tasks. One type of domain is particularly challenging for curriculum structuring. What happen when you have to deal with complex, highly structured knowledge, as in mathematics or programming?

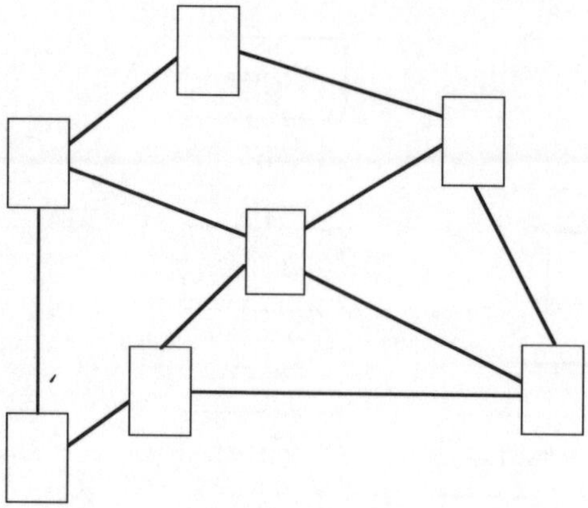

Figure 8.2 Network structured content

If we follow the theme of programming we come to another approach that emphasises a functional approach to curriculum structuring. The CORE approach was developed as a student centred, guided discovery approach to acquiring programming skills. This emphasises a competence based approach to structuring the curriculum. Textbooks on programming usually structure the content on a formal model of the language to be learned. The CORE approach aims to structure the curriculum based on sensitivity to the process of learning. There is a similar emphasis on a functional as opposed to formal approach to the curriculum as found in the Minimalist tradition. The CORE approach, however, was developed to deal with a complex skill domain. The guidance on how to structure the domain content is thus perhaps more specific.

The CORE approach divides the curriculum into a series on competence based blocks. Each block is introduced by a 'Context' program which demonstrates the new competence to be acquired. At the end of the block the learner writes a program that requires a demonstration of the new competence. The selection of content within the block is driven by the competence. Only those forms that are relevant to the competence are introduced. This means that new language forms are not introduced unless the learner can quickly use them in building programs that work.

This approach contrast markedly with standard textbook approaches. It is quite normal for textbooks to introduce language forms and distinctions that the learner cannot use at that stage of learning. For example, all the basic data types that a language can handle are usually introduced together (e.g. characters, various types of numbers and Boolean variables). They are introduced together because formally they go together as basic data types. But there is no way the learner can use this knowledge at this stage. The knowledge is both complex and functionally incomplete. Without knowing other parts of the language you cannot write a program that utilises this

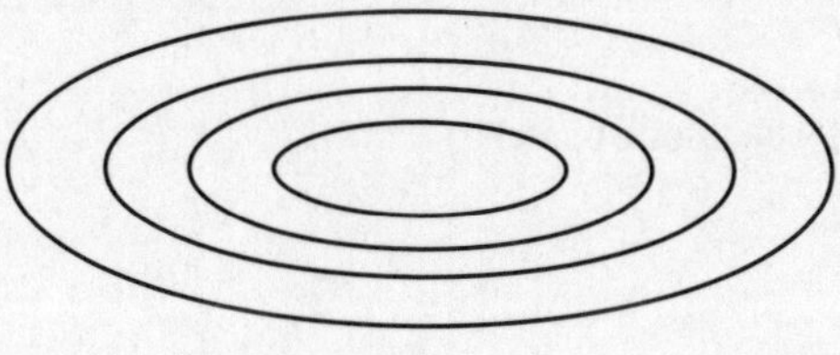

Figure 8.3 Rings of competence (from Boyle and Margetts 1991)

knowledge. A competence based approach structures together those constructs, and *only* those constructs required to achieve a specific achievement. Form is introduced in the service of functional achievement.

At a simple level this competence based approach can be diagrammatically represented as a series of circles (Figure 8.3). The inner circle represents the first competence that the learner acquires. In programming this is to write a simple complete program. The competence is complete in itself. It also provides the base on which the next competence can be built. The curriculum is thus constructed on a series of competence 'rings' which build upon each other. The learner could stop at any level and still have complete competence at that level of skill.

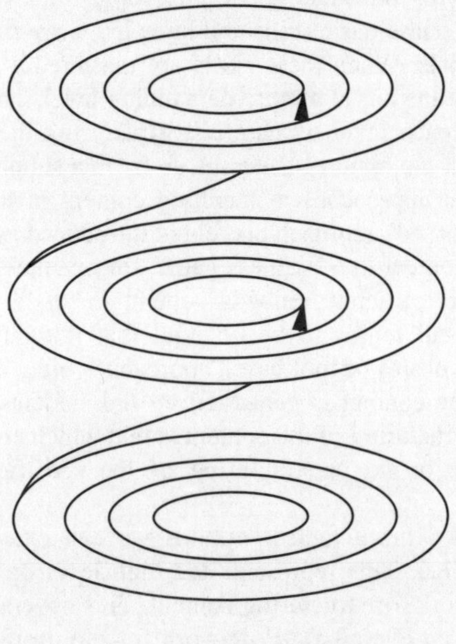

Figure 8.4 The spiral curriculum

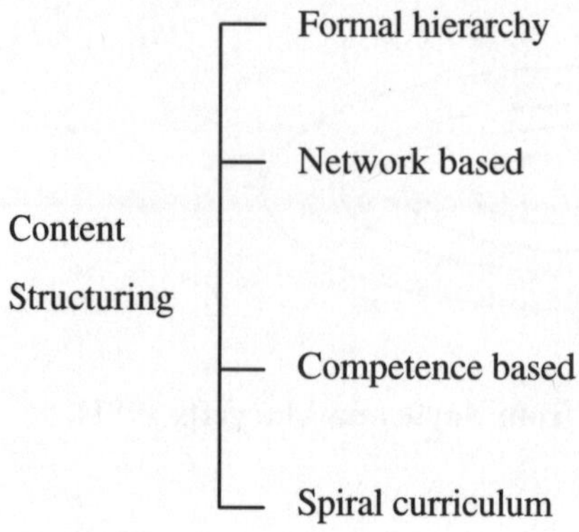

Figure 8.5 An initial outline of the content structuring options

This approach can be extended to lead to a 'spiral curriculum'. Rosson et al. (1990) ran into a problem when they applied the Minimalist approach to develop a computer based learning environment for the programming language Smalltalk. They had to revise the approach of structuring content as small independent blocks. In order to deal with complex skills you need to build up basic skills first. Their answer to this problem was the 'spiral curriculum' (Figure 8.4). The spiral curriculum deals with the problem of complexity by introducing complex topics in several phases that build on each other. In the first phase basic skills and knowledge are introduced so that the user can achieve certain goals. When these skills are mastered a second phase covers the same skills and knowledge but at a more demanding level. This approach supports the user in succeeding at each level by carefully structuring the curriculum to build on itself. We can represent the options discussed so far in a simple diagram (Figure 8.5).

There are two other approaches to handling content in this field that need to be mentioned. In a 'case based' approach content is introduced as part of the theme of the unfolding story. The content in a business game, for example, emerges as the game is played. This 'thematic' structure embeds content in an 'authentic' task. This may enable certain skills and topics to be covered that it would be difficult to cover otherwise. Finally, advocates of tool based approaches often downplay the role of any formal curriculum. The content is generated by the students as they use the tool to solve problems. The structuring of the content is that which emerges from the learner's efforts. There is little or no prestructuring of the specific content domain to be covered.

If we add these two more radical options we can extend the options to those represented in Figure 8.6. This represents the high level options in a 'design action potential' (DAP) network for structuring content. This covers the first macro-function in the construction of an overall DAP network for the design of interactive learning environments.

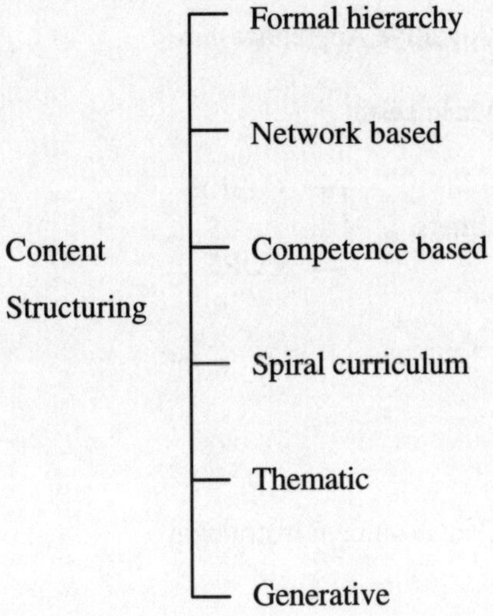

Figure 8.6 DAP network for structuring content

8.3 Options for the structuring of learning interactions

The second macro-function in the design of the learning context involves the structuring of learning interactions. The basic options in this area may be derived from the studies reviewed in the first two parts of the book. These options are set out in Figure 8.7. The options represented in this network inform design choice in the realm of pedagogy.

The three major options are constructivism, instruction based methods and free access/browsing. It may be questioned whether free access amounts to a clear pedagogical option. However, 'resource based' learning has been a popular area given the nature of hypermedia technology. By stating it as an option we can examine its strengths and weaknesses.

Instructivist approaches were dominant for a long period of time in computer aided instruction (CAI). These approaches vary from programmed learning through to sophisticated cognitive based approaches. In these approaches the computer is viewed primarily as a teaching machine. Traditional ITS systems are based on this framework. They represent technological variants within this tradition. Laurillard (1993) criticises traditional CAI and proposes an alternative approach based on 'instructional conversations'. The tutor controls the main purpose and framework of the

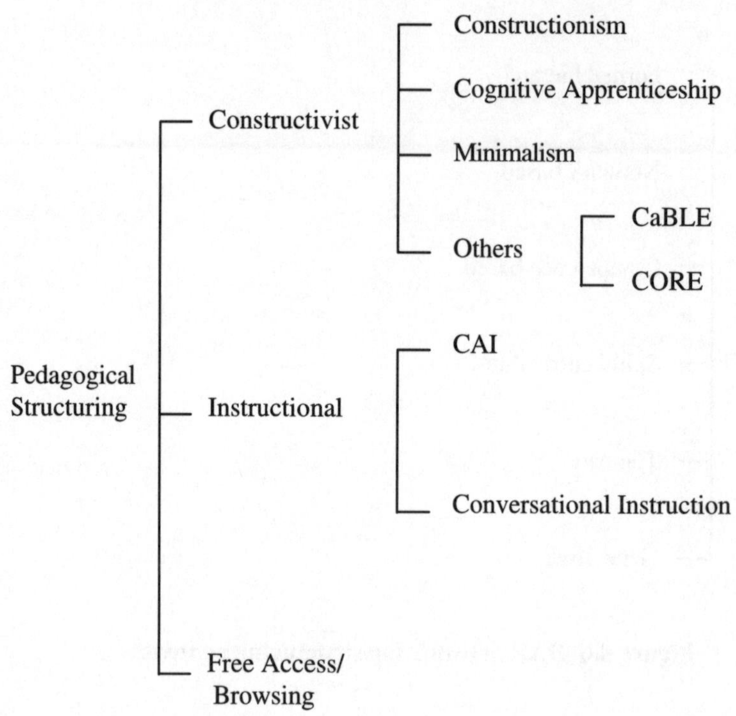

Figure 8.7 An initial DAP for pedagogical design

conversation but there is considerable dynamism within the discussion. Laurillard sees ITS technology as providing the best implementation of this approach.

Constructivism represents the dominant intellectual trend in modern IMLE design. This approach focuses on learning rather than teaching as the central issue. Based on solid psychological research, learners are viewed as constructing their knowledge. The role of computer based systems is to assist this constructive process. There are several variants within this approach. Some of the main strands are listed in Figure 8.7. Construct*ionism* places a particular emphasis on learning through the construction of artefacts (Papert 1993, Harel and Papert 1991). Cognitive Apprenticeship uses the model of traditional apprenticeship to structure learning environments. Minimalism provides an educational perspective which fits well with hypermedia technology. The CaBLE and CORE approaches have been placed at a lower level of delicacy of choice because they seem more focused.

The further one goes in the network of choice the more specific is the guidance provided. The options can be specialised further. At a sufficient level of specialisation this brings us to specific products. The HeRMiT system, for example, represents a specialisation within the CaBLE approach (Feifer and Allender 1994 – reviewed in Chapter 4). CLEM is a specialisation with the CORE approach (Boyle et al. 1994 – reviewed in Chapter 5). In the case of CLEM, tool support has been developed to support the development of systems using this format. These products, however, embody choices from all three functional areas (content structure, interaction and composition). The distinctive pedagogical features exemplified in these systems need to be separately identified.

Figure 8.7 is not meant to be a definitive summary of the high level pedagogic options open to the designer. It is rather an initial sketch. It provides a useful function in summarising some of the principal options. The area of interactive multimedia education is developing in a very dynamic way. As the area develops our knowledge representation need to be adapted to capture these changes.

8.4 Towards a more formal representation of pedagogical options

The descriptions given in Figure 8.7 present options to inform practical design. However, there are clearly both productive overlaps and tensions across these pedagogical approaches. A useful conceptual exercise is to analyse these similarities and differences. This process helps clarify the strengths and weaknesses of the various approaches. It also provides the basis for creating new syntheses. A network constructed for this purpose requires a more analytic set of options. The procedural approaches listed in Figure 8.7 then become mappings of choices across these analytic categories.

An initial representation for a more analytic framework is presented in Figure 8.8. The initial sub-division gives three main functions that should all be considered. The various pedagogical approaches presented in Figure 8.7 can be analysed in terms of how they deal with each of these functions. This provides a basis for comparison and contrast. This information, in turn, provides the basis for generating new, more powerful approaches.

The first node in the network in Figure 8.8 may be expanded to illustrate some of the comparisons that emerge (Figure 8.9). The three options for providing orientation are well illustrated by work in the field. Laurillard (1993) regards the function 'state objectives' to be of central importance. She gives detailed advice on how to expand and implement this choice. The second option 'model target competence' is preferred in the CORE approach. Here the competence to be acquired by the student is demonstrated to the student at the beginning of a learning block. This option gives greater scope for multimedia implementation. This option may be combined with stating objectives. The statement of objectives is then usually kept very brief.

The third main option is to set a task. This immediately divides into setting a structured task or an open task. 'Set a task' is often linked with the compositional option 'simulation'. There are two broad categories of simulations. There are

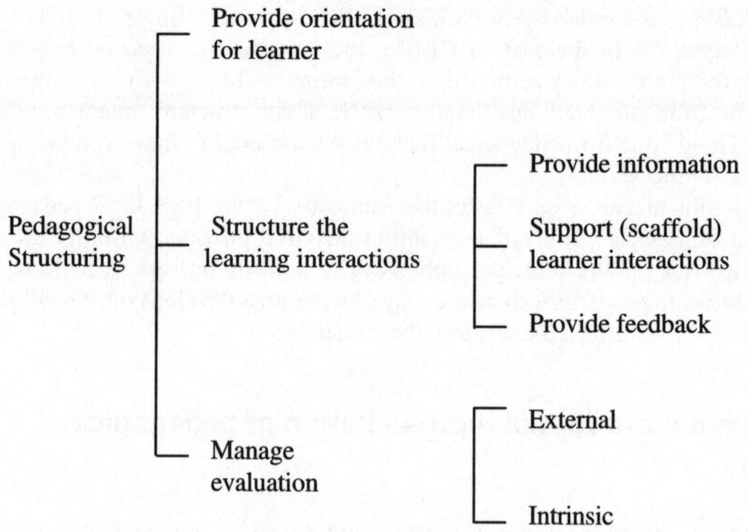

Figure 8.8 An initial analytic framework for pedagogical decisions

structured task based simulation as in Murder One or the HeRMiT system. The alternative is unstructured simulation, such as visit a 'Quartier' in Paris. Open tasks are often emphasised in using hypermedia, or in the constructionism approach advocated by Papert. The analytic categories used in this network can be used to map the options in specific functional areas advocated by different pedagogies. This enables us to break down the structure of choices enshrined in set approaches. This exercise provides insights for creating new, more powerful approaches.

An expansion of the 'provide information' function is presented in Figure 8.10. There is an initial division into providing explicit or implicit access to target knowledge. Traditional CAI gave *explicit* didactic expression of the knowledge to be learned. Constructivist approaches emphasise providing learners with the resources to construct their own understanding. Perkins (1991) refers to a further division between BIG and WIG constructivist approaches. In a BIG approach (Beyond the Information Given) the learners are supplied with direct information for their knowledge construction. The phrase is from the title of a book on educational psychology by Jerome Bruner. Cognitive Apprenticeship, for example, emphasises making the expert knowledge available to learners through the use of protocols. The teacher talks through explicitly the expert's way of tackling the problem. The alternative approach is to present the learners with the *implicit* resources to construct their own understanding. The CORE approach, for example, emphasises the use of examples from the domain

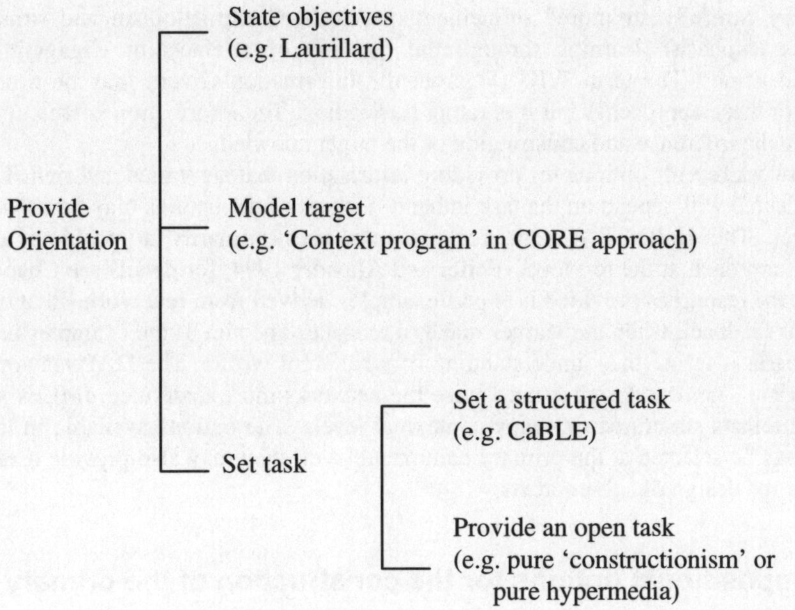

Figure 8.9 An elaboration of the 'provide orientation' function

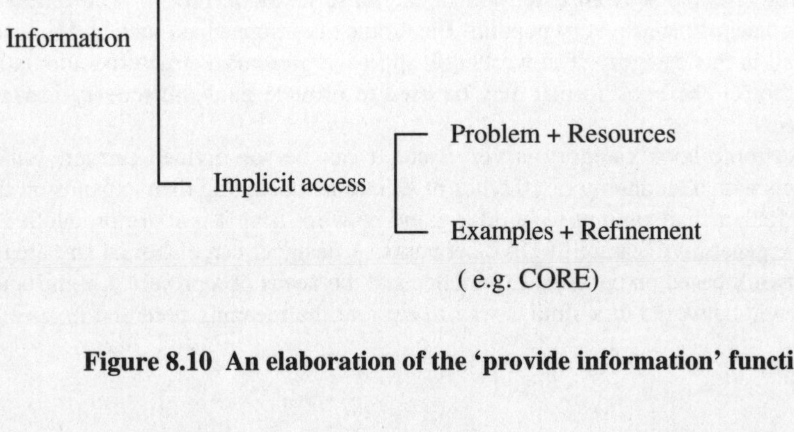

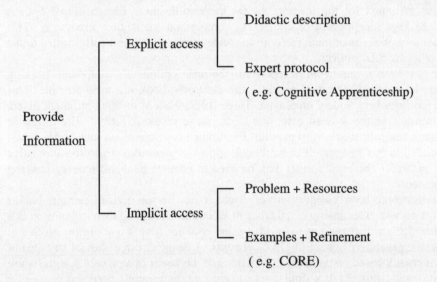

Figure 8.10 An elaboration of the 'provide information' function

followed by carefully structured refinement questions. Constructionism and similar approaches emphasise learning through the building of artefacts or engaging in educational games. The term WIG (Without the Information Given) may be a neat acronym for these approaches but it is rather misleading. The information is structured to facilitate the inference and construction of the target knowledge.

The network reveals options for providing information that are varied and rich. The options selected will depend on the task in hand. Several of the options may be used in one project. The HeRMiT system, for example, uses primarily a 'problem and resources' approach at the top level (Feifer and Allender 1994, for details see Chapter 4). One of the resources provided is expert examples derived from real work situations provided as feedback when the learner makes a mistake. The aim of the examples is to help the learners refine their understanding of what went wrong. The DAP networks are 're-entrant', i.e. the designer may reuse the networks more than once. IMLEs are complex artefacts structured on many contextual levels. The options available in this network may be selected at the primary contextual level; they may also provide useful options for the design of sub-contexts.

8.5 Compositional options for the construction of the primary context

This is the primary 'context forming' function We may delineate the main compositional options from the studies reviewed in the book. The resulting network is presented in Figure 8.11. These options describe a range of ways in which we can compose a context for the learner. As far as possible these compositional options should be kept independent of choices in content and interaction structuring. This provides us with the maximum freedom to create learning environments adapted to the needs of a particular project.

The first level in the network represents the main options for composing learning artefacts in the field. The first option – the electronic book – is very flexible. This option has been very widely employed. Three specialisations of this option are given. The electronic textbook is an extension of the basic textbook format. The reference hyperbook category is also very popular. Electronic encyclopaedias, such as Microsoft Encarta, fall in this category. The workbook approach presents a structured alternative to the textbook. The book format may be used to provide guided-discovery learning environments.

The electronic book category is very rich. It can be sub-divided further. Barker (1995) starts with a taxonomy of 10 types of electronic book, and then expands on this grouping. Rather than attempt to build a grand network here it is more productive to point to the generative feature of DAP networks. A designer can elaborate any area of a DAP network based on personal experience and the needs of a project. Linguists use local systemic networks in a similar way to explore the meaning potential in specific contexts.

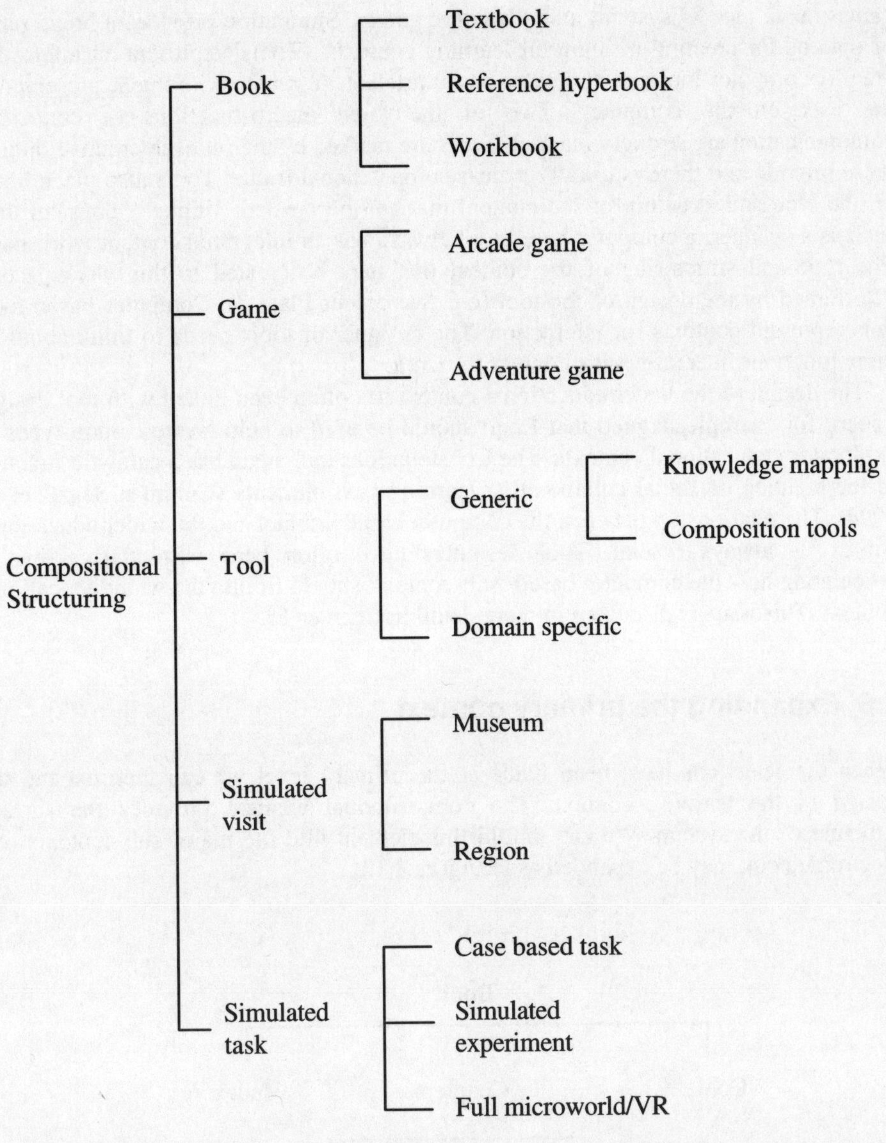

Figure 8.11 Composition action potential for the selection of the primary learning context

The network in Figure 8.11 lists the other primary compositional options. Electronic games provide an attractive format that can be sub-divided into arcade games (as in the 'X' system) and adventure games. Simulation provides a broad range of options for creating meaningful learning contexts. 'Tools' represent an interesting area. A computer tool is a computer based artefact. It is an environment presented to the user on the computer. Two of the three macro-functions of contextual communication are strongly marked. Tools are marked by the set of interactive options these provide and there is usually a clear compositional frame. Tools also place limits on the type and structure of the content that can be created. Unlike a physical tool, such as a spanner, a computer based tool always has an integrated content workspace. The type and structuring of the content that may be created in this workspace is determined by the design of the tool (e.g. see colour Plate 7). Computer based tools thus represent contexts for interaction. The designer of tools needs to think about all three functions in creating this context for work.

The design of the wider educational context has often been linked with tool design. Papert, for example, argued that Logo should be used to help create certain types of exploratory educational contexts. The Constellations tool again has a catalytic function in the creation of social collaborative learning environments (Goldman-Segall et al. 1994). The relationship between the computer based artefact and the wider educational context is always crucial. Tool designers have often been particularly clear in articulating how the computer based 'sub-context' should fit into the wider educational context. This issue is discussed in more detail in Chapter 15.

8.6 Expanding the primary context

When the selections have been made at the primary level we can then expand the design of the learning context. The compositional element provides the surface structure of the system. We can unfold this element into the major sub-contexts. An electronic book may be expanded as in Figure 8.12.

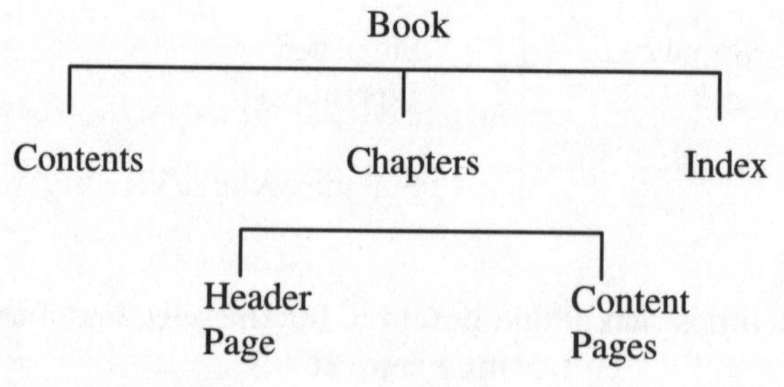

Figure 8.12 Expansion of the electronic book context

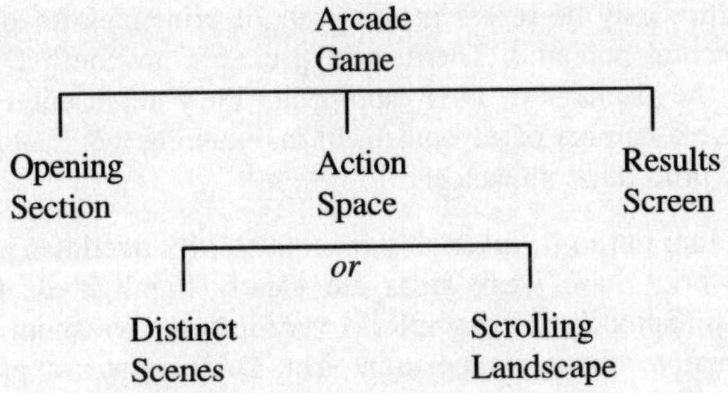

Figure 8.13 Expansion of an arcade game context

The book is broken down into three main components – contents section, chapters and an index or indexes. Each chapter is broken down into a header page and contents pages. The three macro-functions are reapplied at each significant sub-context. An initial expansion for an arcade game context is given in Figure 8.13

These expansion networks are 'part-of' networks. They break down the primary context into the parts from which it is formed. The main levels of decomposition reveal components which are significant sub-contexts. The choice of context, interactivity and composition need to be mapped for each of these sub-contexts. For example, if an electronic book context is chosen this naturally breaks down into chapter units. The units of curriculum structure chosen must map onto these compositional units. If competence based curriculum is chosen each competence ring should map onto one chapter. The pedagogical framework must also map onto the chapter units. If a Cognitive Apprenticeship approach is chosen, for example, each of the six main pedagogical events might be mapped onto functional sections within a chapter. A learning structure is created that reflects a particular mapping of pedagogy, content structuring and compositional choice.

8.7 Further thoughts on the separation of design potential and prescriptive guidance

The DAP networks capture design potential – what we *can* do. The second major source of design guidance is more prescriptive. This consists of 'methods' or guidelines for what we *should* do. Several approaches have been reviewed in this book, e.g. Cognitive Apprenticeship, Minimalism and CORE. Many of these approaches fall under the strategic umbrella of constructivism. The advice provided is usually not sufficiently precise (often deliberately) for the approaches to be labelled 'methods'. The term 'design tactics' seems to capture the level at which they operate to provide prescriptive guidance for the design of IMLEs.

These design tactics may be represented as sets of principles for making choices across the design action potential. There is in principle no conflict between these design tactics and the declarative DAP approach. They represent complementary knowledge. There are a number of advantages of maintaining this dual perspective on design potential and procedural guidance:

1. Design tactics turn out to be invariably incomplete. By overlaying the guidelines on DAP networks these weak areas are clearly highlighted. The Cognitive Apprenticeship approach, for example, is very informative about pedagogy and very uninformative about composition. The DAP networks provide sets of choices that the designer can use to move forward with system design.

2. Design tactics become viewed in a different light. The design guidelines become resources for the designer rather than prescriptive straitjackets. These tactics are not candidates for the 'true path' to multimedia design. They are tactics for making adaptive choice. Different tactics may be suitable for different circumstances.

3. Since these frameworks concern adaptive choice the designer may adapt them to suit project needs. By viewing the design tactics against the network of potentiality the designer has a principled basis on which to make these adaptations.

The argument presented here is that we should separate prescriptive guidance and design potential. This articulation provides two sets of complementary resources. These represent the potential available for design (DAP knowledge) and tactical guidelines for exploiting this potential. These representations are dynamic and evolving. Our knowledge of design potential and tactics will continue to grow as the field expands.

Different tactics often focus on different aspects of the meaning potential. Certain tactics emphasise the compositional component. Barker, for example, has explored in some depth the potential of electronic books as a basis for the design of multimedia learning environments (Barker 1990, 1995). By contrast, pure hypermedia places almost sole emphasis on the networked structuring of content. Other approaches emphasise the pedagogical area – e.g. Cognitive Apprenticeship and CORE. Some approaches emphasise a combination of elements. The CaBLE approach, for example, emphasises a specific composition method (task based simulation) along with a pedagogical emphasis on guided discovery learning (Williamson 1994). By analysing the 'tactics' in this way we can reveal their strengths and weaknesses. It also opens up discussion of their potential for expansion. Many tactics have overlaps and complementary features. More advanced tactical frameworks may be developed through a synthesis based on the critical comparison of present methods.

There is a final point about the usefulness of DAP networks. In linguistics systemic networks are applied to the question of representing general linguistic knowledge.

They are also used to articulate the 'meaning potential' of particular communication contexts. These networks are richer and more local in orientation. In a similar way a local DAP network may be constructed to elucidate the design potential for a particular project. This clarifies the options available before the inevitable prescriptive choices are made There is a general technique in problem solving that lateral thinking should precede vertical (or convergent) thinking. In lateral thinking we think around a problem and clarify the various ways that it might be tackled. DAP networks represent a useful tool for lateral thinking in design. The various options available may be clarified before the process of vertical prescriptive choice. Since IMLE design is a highly iterative process the lateral representation provides a continuous resource for vertical design decisions.

The purpose of this chapter has not been to provide a complete declarative map. That would be premature. The aim has been to illustrate the generative and integrative power of this approach. The further development of this approach points to an elaboration of the networks and to the development of computer based representation of this knowledge. This would provide the knowledge base to underpin powerful decision support systems for multimedia design.

8.8 Conceptual design: overall summary

The first chapter in this part of the book reviewed strategic approaches to conceptual design. The main strategic approaches are instructionism and constructivism. Constructivism represents the dominant intellectual trend in modern IMLE design. The main tenets of constructivism were examined and clarified. There are many variants possible within a constructivist approach. The need for a broad view of constructivism, in line with its base in psychological theory, was emphasised.

There is a marked gap between general cognitive claims and the specific decisions made in constructing learning environments. The second chapter advanced 'context' as the central holistic concept for IMLE design. In designing multimedia learning environments we design contexts for learning. Based on a synthesis of ideas from linguistics and film theory it was argued that there are three macro-functions in designing contextual artefacts – the content structuring, interactive and compositional functions. The decisions to be made in these three functional domains may be operationalised in design action potential (DAP) networks. The ideas of Donaldson and her colleagues were used to illustrate the importance of context in learning. The provision and removal of scaffolding was explored as a significant dimension for structuring transitional contexts of learning.

The present chapter has used DAP networks to organise and represent significant options for conceptual design. The networks for content structuring, interactivity and composition represent three parallel areas of choice. Options from each area must be chosen in the construction of multimedia learning environments. An overall representation of design action potential is achieved by combining the three parallel networks of choice.

The aim of this part of the book has been to clarify conceptual design. Having clarified issues at this layer the next significant problem is how to give life to these concepts as fully realised multimedia systems. This is the concern of the next topic in the book – presentation design.

Part Three

Presentation design

Chapter 9

A holistic perspective on presentation design

9.1 Introduction

The purpose of this part of the book is to discuss and elucidate presentation design. In presentation design we map the abstractions of conceptual design onto a real multimedia environment. Presentation design has its own problem space. This problem space involves the holistic framing of the multimedia artefact and the design and integration of the individual media.

The first chapter (Chapter 9) deals with holistic aspects of presentation design. Key features of human perception are reviewed. These highlight the nature of perception as a highly active, constructive process. Composition principles are discussed that take advantage of the selective, constructive nature of perception.

Multimedia artefacts are created using a range of specialist tools. Chapter 10 reviews the multimedia toolset. These tools are organised in a hierarchy from multimedia platform to high level authoring tools. As specific tool details can change very rapidly this chapter emphasises a framework for understanding the types of tools available.

The remaining chapters deal with the specific media types. Chapter 11 deals with text and still graphics – the basic elements of a multimedia system. Chapter 12 deals with the dynamic media of sound, animation and video. These chapters describe the technical issues involved in the capture and editing of the media components. They review principles for the design of each media type, and consider the integration of the individual components into a full multimedia system.

9.2 Characteristics of human perception

It was difficult for Europeans to see sunspots at all because Aristotle had said that celestial bodies were perfect and without blemish...

(Tufte 1990, p. 18)

This section outlines salient features of human perception that inform the process of presentation design. Perception is not a passive process of reflecting the external world. It is highly active and constructive process. It involves the interaction of two sources of information: information from our senses, and accumulated knowledge stored in memory. The process of perception relates the information from our senses to our established experience in some meaningful way. The central design features of human perception may be summarised under the acronym PASS. Perception is a:

PATTERNED

ACTIVE

SELECTIVE

SYSTEM

Presentation design can be informed by an understanding of how this active constructive process works. The following sections discuss in turn key features of human perception.

A major influence on perception is expectancy:

People often see
what they expect to
to see in everday life.

The quotation above has a mistake. Can you see what it is? I have shown similar examples to many classes of students. The great majority do not perceive any error. It is only on repeated viewing that the error is noticed (a word is repeated). We tend to notice features like the influence of expectancy when they go wrong. However, it is exactly these features that make perception a powerful, adaptive system. A key theme is to design the activity and context to tune in with these selective processes and so enhance performance. We should design activities so that the users can deduce patterns that enable them to form accurate expectations. The compositional option chosen at the conceptual layer should provide a clear cognitive framework. Presentation design needs to clearly convey this contextual patterning. This supports the user in forming expectations that guide accurate perception.

Perception is strongly orientated to the perception of patterns. The Gestalt

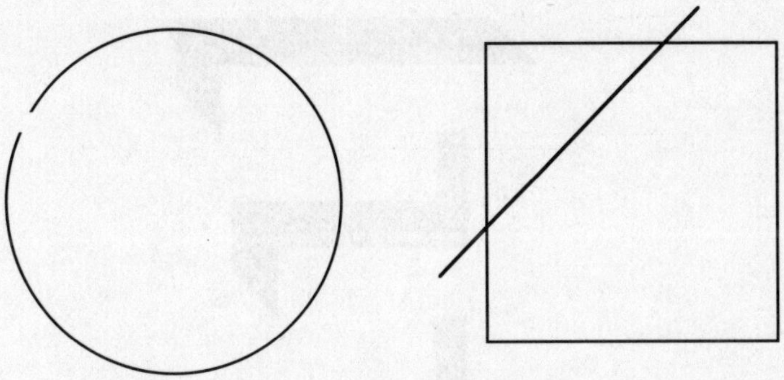

Figure 9.1 Simple example of Gestalt perception

psychologists identified many pattern-based phenomena. Their primary insight is summarised in the phrase:

The whole is greater than the sum of the parts.

This is an important insight for interface design. Portraying a coherent context on the screen is one way to utilise this selective pattern based nature of perception.

Some of these pattern based effects are very easy to demonstrate. What are the shapes in Figure 9.1? When I show these to students they respond readily: they are a circle and a square. However, the shape on the left is not a circle. There is a gap and no closure is made. The figure on the right tends to be perceived as a square with a line through it.

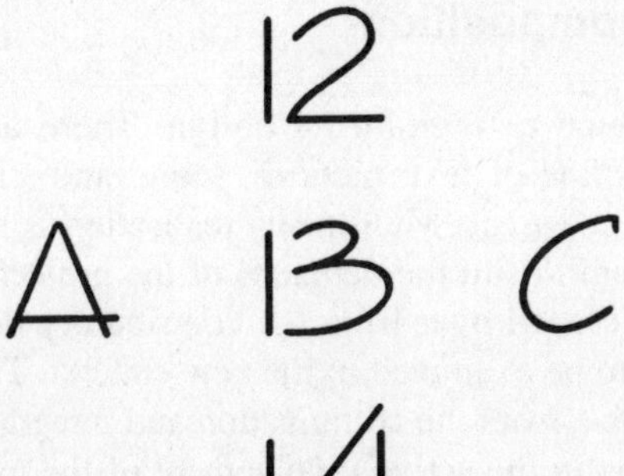

Figure 9.2 The influence of expectation on perception

Figure 9.3 Perception as a constructive process

Expectancy and pattern recognition operate together to produce highly selective perception. In Figure 9.2 the central shape is perceived as a 'B' when it is presented in the alphabetic list. When it is presented in the numeric list it is perceived as a '13'. In Figure 9.3 the figure is perceived as a block shaped 'E' even though the letter is not actually drawn. The role of the designer is to create interfaces that support effective perception by tuning in with these natural constructive processes. Screens with clear patterns that are consistently used enable us to perceive effectively quite complex information.

9.3 Principles of composition

Many disciplines contribute to multimedia design. There are established traditions dealing with the composition of text, pictures, sound and animation. No one person can be an expert in all these areas. Multimedia realisation is naturally a team process. We need to select the team to suit the demands of the project. For multimedia design some techniques can be carried over from the contributory disciplines. Each of these design guidelines needs to be examined in the new context. There are also completely new design issues that arise from the combination and integration of the media. There is a whole new dimension in the active involvement of the participant. The design of activity as well as appearance is central to the new Gestalt. The aesthetic is found as much in the choreography of action as in the appearance of the system.

There is considerable guidance in the literature on the shaping and realisation of the individual media. There is less clarity about the holistic aspects of design – how to create an overall coherent multimedia artefact. The ideas of Hodges and Sasnett have already been introduced in this book as a contribution to a framework for conceptual design. At the heart of this framework is the idea that multimedia design creates interactive *contexts*. This notion was extended, and formalised to some extent, through contributions from linguistics. Hodges and Sasnett, however, come from a visual design tradition. Their ideas are aimed not just at the abstract conception but also at the physical realisation of the system. If we follow these ideas through then presentation design deals with the realisation of multimedia contexts. We need to project the design image clearly to the user. This involves portraying the primary context and the sub-contexts and objects from which it is composed. Each context involves the projection of the three functional domains: information, interaction and compositional framework. The last function provides the foundation for the aesthetic framing of the system.

9.3.1 Unity, harmony, balance and visual flow

Unity and *visual balance* are desirable features of multimedia composition. Unity refers to the wholeness of the experience; all the elements forming the experience should belong together (Schwier and Misanchuk 1993). The perception of unity derives from the conceptual design of the system. The various components are perceived as belonging together because they have roles in the context. Sub-contexts can be incorporated because they have clear functions within the overall context. The recording sheet and the video observation panel in DOVE are examples of sub-contexts embedded within an overall coherent context (Figure 9.6). The unity of the display is grounded in clear conceptual design.

Harmony refers to how all the parts of the system fit together. Harmony is closely tied in with building and maintaining expectancies. The basic layout of the main components should be consistent across screens. The deeper basis for this consistency is conceptual design. The transition mechanisms discussed in Chapter 7 are relevant to maintaining harmony. Many transitions across screens are fairly effortless because they follow a pattern expected by the user. The pattern is expected because the users know what type of context they are in, e.g. turning pages in an electronic book. Visual consistency in the framing of the screens also needs to be constructed and maintained. This principle of consistency in layout has been strongly advocated in the HCI (Human Computer Interaction) literature (e.g. Preece 1993, Johnston 1992, Newman and Lamming 1995). A consistent pattern of screen elements – e.g. screen banners, information areas and tool bars – helps the learner navigate efficiently through a computer based system.

Balance is concerned with the visual 'weight' given to each component and the distribution of these objects on the screen (Hodges and Sasnett 1993). A simple example is presented in Figure 9.4 of balanced and unbalanced screen layouts. The layout on the left is the basic screen structure used by Tway in 'The Colour Book' (Tway 1992). The top element in the display is a banner headline indicating the screen

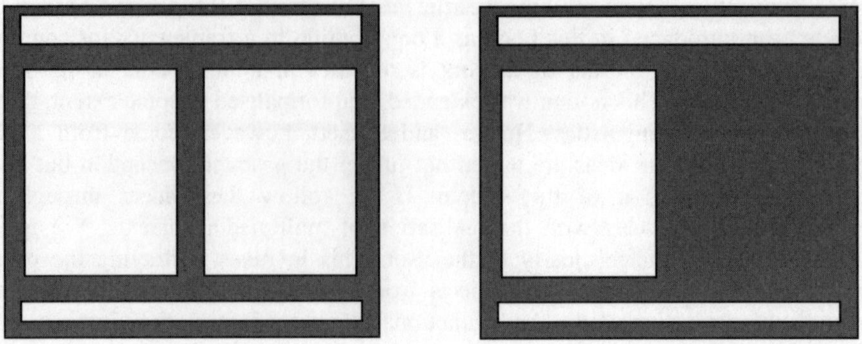

Figure 9.4 Visual balance and imbalance

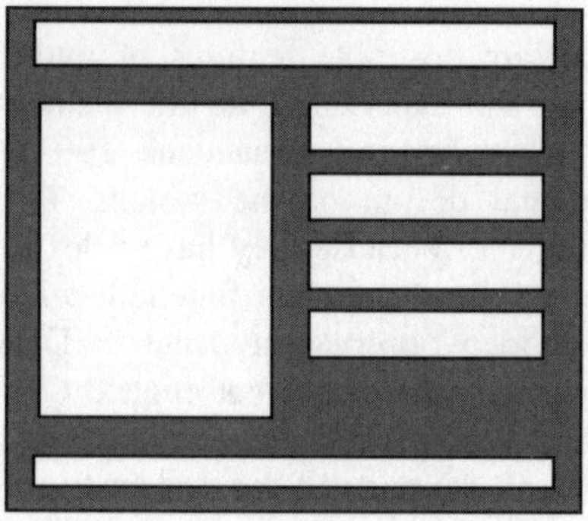

Figure 9.5 Variation in achieving visual balance

topic. The bottom element is a panel containing navigation controls. The middle two elements normally consist of a text box on the left and a graphic illustration on the right. The two elements visually balance each other. When one is removed the imbalance becomes clear. Visual balance can be achieved by using a number of smaller objects to balance a larger one. Figure 9.5 shows a variation used by Tway. Each of the boxes on the right displays a different colour. The text box on the left contains relevant information.

Imbalance can occur because an underlying template is used for a series of screens. Earlier screens may have a blank area because this area is required for use in later screens. This problem occurs in the ToolBook 3 on-line tutorial. The tutorial uses a left/right screen division. The left panel gives information and instructions: the right panel is used for illustrations and practice (Figure 11.1). However, on some screens

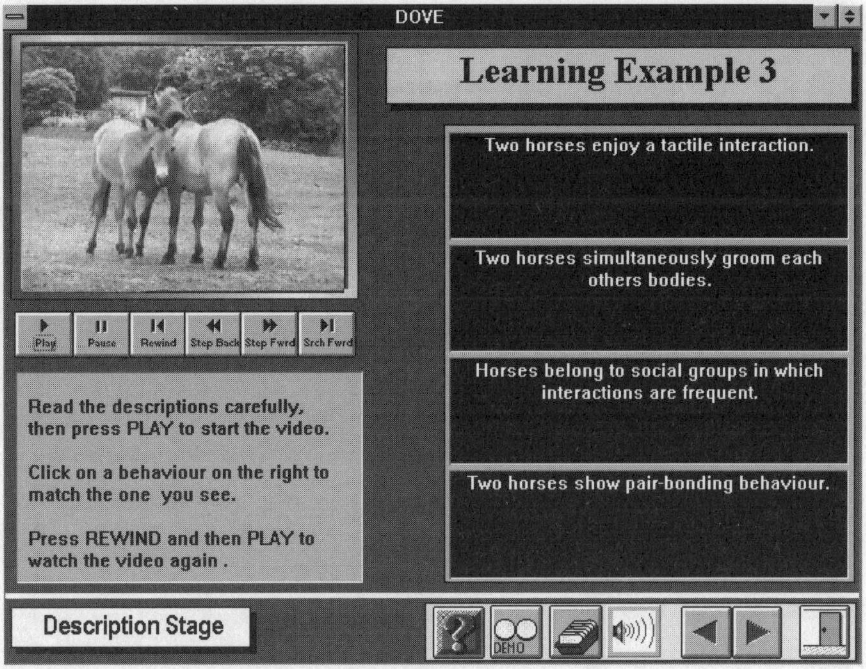

Figure 9.6 Visual flow: a screen from the DOVE system

there are no relevant illustrations or practice sessions. The designers fill the gap by putting general illustrations on the right hand panel. These have no informational content. They achieve an aesthetic effect of balancing the screen and keeping the sequence of screens in visual harmony. Novice designers sometimes fail to keep this need for balance and harmony in mind.

There is a further, dynamic aspect to visual composition. When a screen is displayed the user's attention should be attracted to the focal object. Attention should then be drawn round the objects on the screen in a way that reveals the relationship between the elements. The problem with achieving this effect increases with the number of objects on the screen. The DOVE system, for example, requires a number of different objects on the screen at once (Figure 9.6). When the user moves to the screen the first frame of the video is loaded. This action attracts the user's eye to the top left quarter of the screen. The gaze then falls to the instruction box below the video. When this column of information is completed the user's view switches to the interactive panel on the right. The user can then play the video and make the recordings. Feedback on user choice is provided in a pop-up box with a drop shadow that sits over the instruction box (Plate 5).

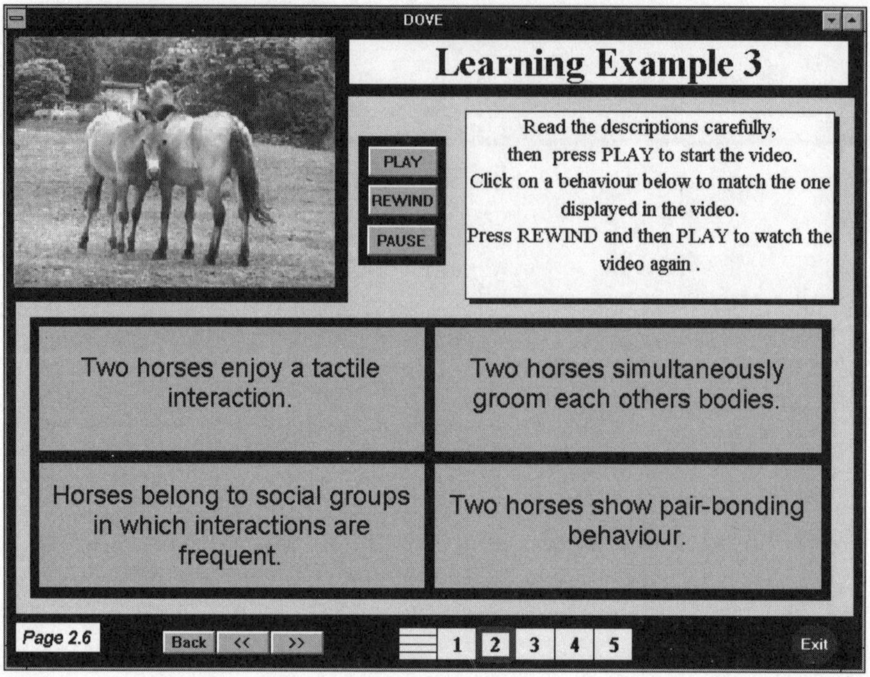

Figure 9.7 Screen from an earlier prototype of the DOVE system

This screen layout divides the screen into two parts: the left part dealing with observation, the right part with the main user actions. Feedback from formative evaluation indicates that this approach worked well. A presentation of an earlier prototype is given in Figure 9.7. This prototype divides the screen into top and bottom halves. The information box is placed adjacent to the video screen at the top right of the page. This seemed an intuitive design choice. The information requires early attention, and it thus seemed better to place it at the top of the screen. This earlier prototype, however, was rejected in favour of the layout in Figure 9.6. One of the reasons was judgement based on the visual prototypes created. The visual flow of attention through the later prototype seemed to be superior. There was a second important reason. The recording charts become more complex on later screens. The right hand panel becomes divided into two columns for user response and expert feedback. To maintain harmony and consistency across the screens it is important that all the screens follow the same basic pattern. This pattern is then elaborated in the later blocks. These elaborations deal with greater information demands, while providing some aesthetic variation on the basic screen structure.

9.4 Resources for composition

Multimedia composition is not an abstract art. Composition principles are mapped using a set of tools onto the materials available. There are a number of resources that may contribute to the dynamic process of multimedia composition. These resources include:

- conceptual design structures
- composition principles
- specific guidelines
- good examples
- tools and associated libraries
- experimentation and visualisation.

The first two types of resources have already been discussed. Many of the problems in presentation design can only be resolved effectively if a correct base in conceptual design has been established. There should be a clear set of principles that guide the mapping from conceptual to presentation design. The earlier part of this chapter has discussed principles to guide composition. Style guidelines usually operate at a more specific level. These guidelines are often associated with particular graphical user interface (GUI) systems. Style guidelines for their respective interface systems have been issued by Apple Computers and Microsoft (Apple 1992, Microsoft 1995). These style guides promote some general principles and global rules applying to the user interface. The bulk of the documents, however, involve specific guidelines and directions for constructing GUI components.

A very useful source for design decisions is a store of good examples. These provide concrete exemplification of design principles in practice. They also provide integrated, complete systems. Composition principles may seem too abstract or fragmented unless backed up by a store of concrete images. There is a useful interplay between good examples and composition principles. The examples make the principles more concrete and accessible. The principles in turn support us in analysing the examples and identifying why they are good. This provides a stronger base for generalising to the design of new systems. Samples of many educational systems are provided on ‘free’ CD ROMs supplied with magazines or can be accessed over the Internet.

It may seem strange to refer to tools as a resource for presentation design decisions. However, most tools have two features that influence design decisions. The first feature is the encapsulated design ideas built into the tool. In ToolBook, for example, it is very easy to create an ‘electronic book’ with a set of standard paging buttons.

These buttons include – 'page forward', 'page back', 'contents' and 'backtrack' controls. Numerous physical design solutions are incorporated in multimedia authoring tools, e.g. navigation buttons, scrolling text boxes, and 'stages' to display graphics and video. Presentation involves mapping ideas onto the realisation options available. It is natural to use the prefabricated realisation options offered by the tool. It can be objected that the nature of the tool may unduly shape the design decisions. It is thus best to have knowledge of a number of tools. You may then select the tool that best fits the project requirements.

The use of multimedia tools as a design resource is made explicit through the provision of component libraries. These components may include screen templates, widgets and clip art. Widgets are objects with attached functionality, e.g. a video stage with an attached set of controls. There is a CBT version of ToolBook, for example, that includes an extensive library of components for building multimedia learning environments. This version of ToolBook includes presentation design 'specialists'. These operate like the 'wizards' in word processors such as Microsoft Word. The specialist engages in an interactive dialogue with the user. On the basis of the user's responses the specialist builds an application template of screen layouts with the necessary controls. This highly structured support may be very helpful to those beginning multimedia design.

There is thus a range of resources at different levels of specialisation. Some resources operate at the level of general principles of visual composition. At the other end of the spectrum are concrete templates. The preferred choice of resources varies with the nature of the project and the experience of the designer. Experienced designers, for example, tend to find global templates to be too rigid. However, they often provide an attractive resource to people entering into multimedia design.

The final resource mentioned is visualisation through experimentation. Each project seems to throw up unique challenges. We may conceive of a possible presentation format, but we may be simply unsure whether it will work. A prototype in an authoring tool allows us to see or hear the proposed solution. This prototype then provides a basis for interactive refinement. In the Braque system, for example, colour coding is used to indicate the level of decomposition of sub-goals in a design. When this was suggested it seemed a good idea. Design examples, such as the London underground map, suggested that this solution would be a significant help in distinguishing sub-patterns within a complex structure. However, it was unclear how it would look. Would it seem too garish? Would a multitude of colours interfere with perception of patterns rather than support it? A visual prototype of the idea showed that it worked very well (Plate 7).

We often cannot solve presentation problems on the basis of principles alone. We need to invent, represent, experiment and refine. This can often be a fun part of multimedia development. The experimentation is often done on a team basis. One person may suggest an idea. The graphic artist or programmer may then produce a physical expression of the idea. This provides the basis for focused group discussion and decision making. The phrase 'invention and test' captures nicely this dynamic process in multimedia development.

9.5 Summary

Presentation design is grounded in conceptual design, but it in turn has its own problem space. A crucial task is the holistic design of the presentation. Human perception is a highly active and constructive process. Expectancy and pattern recognition enable us to see 'more than the sum of the parts'. Presentation design should exploit these features to achieve the powerful effects of perceptual clarity and simplicity.

Principles of composition help to guide the decisions about holistic aspects of the presentation. Unity and harmony emphasise the wholeness of the experience. A clear conceptual framework mapped onto consistent screens helps to maintain this sense of harmony and unity. Principles of visual balance and flow structure the media elements and guide the eye through the significant components of the display.

A range of resources may be used in presentation design. Masterful examples provide ideas on holistic aspects of design, such as system structure and screen layout. Specific guidelines may help to solve particular interface problems. Tools and libraries provide a range of physical resources that help shape the realisation of the system. Experimentation and visualisation allow one to see and judge possible presentation structures. There should always be some clear high-level principles that guide the shaping of a coherent attractive system. The particular selection and combination of resources will then depend on the type of project and preferences of the designer.

Chapter 10

The multimedia toolset

10.1 Introduction

Presentation design involves the use of tools to translate ideas into physical systems. The multimedia toolset has developed quite dramatically in this decade, and information on this topic can date quite rapidly. Knowledge of these tools, however, is essential for designers. The aim of this chapter is to provide an overview of the multimedia toolset. This should provide guidance for the selection of appropriate tools, and a base for further development of knowledge in this area.

A range of tools is used in constructing multimedia systems. These tools may be organised into a simple hierarchy (Figure 10.1). At the top of the hierarchy are powerful multimedia authoring tools, such as ToolBook, Authorware and Director. These provide a number of features for media integration, and facilities for creating a variety of end user interactions. Crucially, they also support the use of a wide range of media imported from specialist editors for graphics, animation and sound. These high level tools act as the 'glue' which holds everything together. Knowledge of the construction power and limitations of these tools is important to the designer.

The second layer contains specialist tools for the creation and editing of specific media. These programs greatly expand the capabilities of the high level authoring systems. They support the creation or capture of specific media types and their manipulation in a way that is not supported by the multimedia authoring tools. This layering of media manipulation tools provides a flexible way to manage the creation and integration of a comprehensive range of media.

At the base of the hierarchy is the computer hardware. This provides the basic platform for developing and delivering multimedia systems. For the PC these have been clearly specified in the MPC (Multimedia Personal Computer) standards. These provide a set of specifications for the hardware required for a given level of multimedia

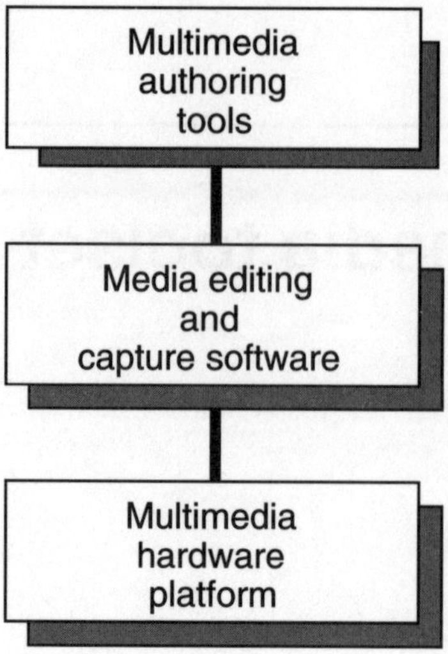

Figure 10.1 Overview of the multimedia toolset

machine. These standards provide the framework for developing systems that have a guaranteed delivery platform.

This chapter reviews each of the layers in the multimedia toolset. It deals first with the base layer of the hierarchy – the multimedia hardware. This section outlines the MPC standards which provide clear specifications for multimedia hardware. Software tools for media capture and editing are then discussed. This review provides an overview of the range of tools and facilities available. Detailed discussion about software for specific media domains is left to the succeeding chapters. The selection of the central multimedia authoring tool is then considered. A set of criteria is presented for evaluating multimedia authoring tools. Two popular tools that represent distinct authoring paradigms are then discussed in some detail. The chapter concludes by summarising the principal points about the selection and configuration of the multimedia toolset.

10.2 Multimedia hardware

10.2.1 The basic multimedia platform

The two most common platforms for multimedia development and delivery have been the Macintosh and Windows based PC. The evolution of these two systems has been rather different. The Macintosh was launched in 1984 with a graphical user interface

(GUI). This interface was based on the pioneering work carried out at the Xerox PARC research centre in the seventies (Smith et al. 1982). The Macintosh was the first machine with a GUI interface to be a commercial success. This interface provided the base for a series of innovative developments. The release of HyperCard in 1987 was an important landmark. This provided a sophisticated tool for handling multiple media in a flexible, hypermedia-style format. Multimedia hardware and software evolved rapidly in this supportive environment.

The release of Windows 3 for IBM compatible PCs in 1990 provided the first standard GUI environment for the PC. Microsoft provided multimedia extensions for Windows 3. These utilities were bundled in with the release of Windows 3.1. Multimedia support was further significantly enhanced in Windows 95. Standards are very important in the computer industry. They provide the basis for a market where products can be developed and delivered within a common, agreed framework. The Windows environment has provide the de facto standard for GUI developments in the PC environment. Explicit standards for multimedia personal computers based on this platform have been agreed and promulgated by the Multimedia PC Marketing Council. This consists of a number of the principal hardware and software producers in the PC market. This council has specified two main standard levels – MPC (Multimedia PC) level 1 and MPC level 2.

MPC level 1

The level 1 MPC standard provided the basis for the development of a market in multimedia CD ROMs. The specification, which was released in 1991, is now looking increasingly dated. The minimum specification involves:

- 386 sx processor
- 2 megabytes of RAM
- 30 megabyte hard disk
- CD ROM drive with a transfer speed of 150 kilobits per second.

The minimum video specification is the VGA standard which provides a resolution of 640 x 480 pixels with sixteen colours. The sound card is based on eight bit sampling. The memory specifications for this standard now look ridiculous. This specification illustrates how rapidly multimedia equipment has developed in the first half of the decade.

MPC level 2

The MPC level 2 specification was released in 1993. Table 10.1 provides a summary of the principal features. This specification is really aimed at a delivery rather than a development platform. The minimum processor specified is a 486 sx. Many modern

Table 10.1 Summary of key features of the MPC level 2 specification

Component	*Specification*
Processor	486 sx at 25 MHz
RAM	4 meg. (8 meg. recommended)
Hard Drive	160 meg.
CD ROM	Transfer at 300 kilobits per sec.
Video card + display	640 × 480 with 64k colours
Audio card	16 bit sound, MIDI support

authoring systems require a minimum of 8 megabyte of RAM rather than the 4 indicated. A dual speed CD ROM is specified as the minimum standard. This supports the playback of KODAK photo CDs. The material on these CDs may be read onto the disk on several recording sessions. The level 2 standard thus requires CD players that can deal with these multi-session disks.

The hard disk standard is clearly a minimum. For development purposes the size of the hard disk becomes crucial. The required disk size depends upon the media types used. Text and some types of graphics are reasonably compact. Sound and especially video are very demanding on disk space. If the system is to be developed for a full CD ROM a minimum disk size of one gigabyte (1000 megabytes) is recommended.

The video standard requires colour sampling at 64k (65,536 colours). This provides a much superior basis for development and delivery. A sophisticated range of facilities is specified for audio. Considerable support is provided for the three main types of sound file: normal CD Audio, MIDI and digitised sound. The specification requires digital sound capture using 16 bit samples. This greatly improves the quality of digital sound. The details of audio sampling are dealt with in Chapter 12.

Standards are important because they provide a clear framework for development and delivery. The development machine may be much more powerful than the delivery machine. A development machine will probably have a much more powerful processor, more RAM and a very large hard disk. There may also be hardware peripherals required for the development machine, such as a video capture card. It is important, however, to keep in mind the difference between development and delivery platforms. It is possible to build in a series of delivery problems if one is not careful.

Some people prefer to use a development platform that is close to the delivery specification. It is then easier to see at each stage how the delivered product will perform.

The MPC level 3 specification

In early 1995 the Software Publishers Association absorbed the MPC Marketing Council, and changed its name to the MPC Working Group. Microsoft, one of the key founders of the MPC standards, withdrew from the alliance. The MPC Working Group issued a new standard – MPC level 3. This standard requires personal computers running Windows 3.11 or above, a Pentium processor, 8 megabytes of RAM, MPEG-1 video, sophisticated audio and a quad speed (600 bits per second) CD ROM (*CD ROM Magazine,* August 1995). The most significant new development is a specification for video based upon industry standard MPEG-1.

The split with Microsoft has confused the picture. Microsoft has set up its own de facto standard with the release of Windows 95. This specification is set at a lower level – 66 MHz 486 processor, 8 megabytes of RAM, and dual speed CD ROM. There is no specific requirement for MPEG although Windows 95 does support MPEG. A key issue for standards is to set an agreed framework for delivery. The developer must be clear about the specification of the delivery platform. When there is a potential for confusion the designer should specify the characteristics of the delivery machine. These requirements should be communicated clearly to the users of the system.

10.2.2 Hardware peripherals

The multimedia development computer may be enhanced by the addition of hardware peripherals. These peripherals may be classified into two main groups:

- media input device
- output and delivery devices.

External support may also be provided for file storage and archiving.

The peripherals for the capture of specific media types are discussed in the relevant chapters. These include scanners, special still cameras, audio-tape players and VCRs. There are some general peripherals that enhance the computer system. The storage and transfer of multimedia files can produce some problems as these files can be very large. There are a number of possibilities for dealing with this problem:

- portable hard disk drives
- tape streamers
- re-writeable optical disks

- writeable CD ROMs.

Portable hard disks provide a reasonably secure method for storing and transporting multimedia files. When attached to a computer the files can be read in the same way as from an internal hard disk. Tape streamers provide a back-up mechanism that provides an important insurance against accidents such a hard disk crash. Re-writeable optical disks may also be used for back-up. As these disks are re-writeable the same disk may be used more than once. Large multimedia systems may be backed up onto writeable CD ROMs. The price of CD ROM writers has dropped sharply over the last few years. A good CD writer will support multi-session writing, i.e. the CD ROM may be used more than once until its capacity is exhausted. Computer and Multimedia magazines provide a useful source of current information on prices of these various options.

10.2.3 Cross platform standards

The World Wide Web provides a potential base for delivering educational multimedia that is not tied to a specific delivery platform. The growth of the Web has been phenomenal. It must seriously be considered as a delivery platform for educational multimedia. The Web was originally developed to provide hyperlinking across static documents. These documents consisted mainly of text with some pictures. The Web has been rapidly extended so that in principle almost any multimedia system could be delivered. There are significant problems in delivering multimedia systems given the bandwidth restrictions. Given the enormous effort put into the Web and the expansion of fibre optic networks these restrictions may be markedly reduced in the future. However, there is a second significant problem. The multimedia helper applications and plug-ins to Web browsers are often hardware dependent. The universality of the Web as a delivery medium is weakened. The designer thus must ensure that the user has access to the full range of helper applications (for sound, video and animation) required to run the multimedia system. This configuration may well mean that the delivery is limited to certain types of hardware.

Neuwirth (1996) has pointed out that Web applications are not limited to new systems built using Web oriented tools. Many old systems can be fired off from Web browsers and delivered on the Web given the appropriate helper application or plug-in software. There are significant delivery problems as indicated above. However, the ability to deliver systems in stand-alone mode or over the Web makes the transfer into a future of network based delivery easier. The Web sites for the main multimedia tool developers carry the latest information on developments in this area (Appendix 1).

10.3 Media capture and editing

The second layer in Figure 10.1 relates to software tools for the capture and editing of specific media. The media types are: text, graphics, animation, sound and video.

Software programs control the hardware capture devices. This software allows one to select options that affect the quality and size of the capture file. These decisions are important in order to obtain suitable playback of the media. Standard capture tools in the Windows environment include Sound Recorder for audio and Video for Windows for video capture, control and editing. Discussion of these tools and other utilities is provided in the following chapters.

Sophisticated editors for individual media types may be installed. These editors extend the functionality of the main multimedia authoring tool. Examples include Corel Draw for graphics and Adobe Premiere for video. The output from the editor is saved as a file. This file may then be imported into the main authoring environment where it is treated as one of a number of media objects. The media object may then be integrated into the multimedia system being developed. Each editor may have its own specific file format. It is important to check which file formats may be imported by the main authoring system. This information is clearly given in the documentation for the multimedia authoring tools. In certain cases files may be converted before importation. A graphic file in the wrong format, for example, may be converted to an appropriate format by using a utility such as Paint Shop Pro.

The specialist editors provide a significant enhancement to the power of the multimedia tool set. Balanced against this consideration are the cost and learning overheads associated with each tool. The configuration selected should be the one that best suits the requirements of the project and the talents available in the development team.

10.4 Multimedia authoring tools

Multimedia authoring tools are the central integrative tools. They combine all the media resources within a structured framework. This section considers factors influencing the choice of multimedia tool.

10.4.1 Choice of authoring tool

It is important to select an authoring tool that best suits project needs. There are a number of factors that will narrow the range of choice. These factors include:

- the hardware available for development and delivery
- the nature of the multimedia project
- price
- the market penetration of the tool.

The hardware platform is the first constraint on choice. We need to match the authoring tool to the *delivery* platform. The Macintosh and the MPC are the two main platforms. A wide range of multimedia authoring tools is available for both platforms. Other hardware platforms have their own multimedia tools, e.g. Genesis for the Archimedes. The range of tools in these cases is more limited. A number of tools were originally developed for the Macintosh and then ported to the MPC, for example, Authorware Professional and Macromedia Director. It is possible to develop a system using these tools on one platform and port it to the other.

The proposed multimedia system may have a natural structure. It will ease development effort if the natural 'grain' of the tool and product are in harmony. If the product is an electronic book, for example, then Authorware Professional may not be the best choice. HyperCard and SuperCard on the Macintosh would support this format better. ToolBook would be a better option for the MPC. This choice, however, tends to be strongly influenced by the expertise available in the development team. It is quite feasible to develop electronic books in Authorware. If there is an experienced Authorware programmer in the group this may swing the balance of the decision. Another issue that may influence choice is the price of the authoring tool. When several copies of a tool are needed this may become a significant factor.

It is very important to consider the degree of support provided. This is related to the market penetration of the tool. If the tool is widely used it is likely the manufacturer will continue to support the tool through new releases. There will also be a number of people using the tool and it is likely there will be national user groups that provide a support forum. This is, of course, a conservative strategy. Newer tools with little market penetration may have useful features. But you need to be aware that support will be weaker, and you may be in the exposed position of being a pioneer with the new tool.

There are two further general factors to be considered in the choice of authoring tool:

- ease of use
- expressive power.

How easy will the tool be to learn and to use? The usability of the authoring tool will depend on the match between the facilities it provides and experience in the team. Relevant experience includes both ways of thinking about design and technical experience. Authoring tools present different authoring interfaces to the user. A tool may be chosen that presents its facilities in a manner that suits the group's needs and background. Programmers usually prefer tools that offer a scripting language. Educational teams from a non-programming background may prefer a tool such as Authorware that avoids the need for a scripting language.

A key general consideration is the expressive power of the tool. There is no multimedia tool that offers the full range of potential expressive power. One approach is to have a set of authoring tools and to select the tool that matches a particular task.

However, this approach may appeal only to groups heavily engaged in multimedia development. Many individuals or groups may want to specialise in one authoring system. The problem then is to choose the system which will best meet short term and longer term needs. There are several dimensions along which we may evaluate the expressive power of a multimedia authoring tool. These are:

- how the components of the system are constructed
- how these components are linked
- support for the individual media types
- libraries of components supplied.

The last two factors influence the richness of the tool. The first two issues provide a useful way of comparing the strategies adopted in different authoring tools. These issues are discussed in the following section.

10.5 Types of authoring tools

Authoring tools may be divided into groups depending on their basic conceptual framework. The main types of authoring systems are:

- page and object based
- flow line and icon based
- time and script based
- pure hypertext or hypermedia.

Two of the most common authoring tools for the MPC are Authorware Professional and ToolBook. These represent two contrasting approaches to authoring – icon based and object based respectively. These two tools are discussed in some detail to give a feel for these contrasting approaches. Time based and pure hypertext alternatives are then reviewed more briefly.

10.5.1 Icon based systems: Authorware Professional

Authorware Professional is an icon based authoring tool produced by Macromedia. It is available for both Macintosh and Windows based PCs. It is a powerful system that has been widely used in educational multimedia development. The development and presentation sides of the system are well integrated. It is easy to switch from developer to user mode and vice versa during development of an application. The developer can thus easily check what the application looks like from a user's point of view

An application is constructed by dragging icons from a palette onto a flow line. Figure 10.2 represents a development screen for an Authorware program. Icons have been dragged from the icon palette on the left to the flow lines. The flow lines specify the order in which elements are to be executed. The top window represents the top level of the Authorware application. The final icon in this window has been selected (it is highlighted). The contents of this 'map' icon are then expanded in the lower window. Multiple windows may be used in this way to express the structure of the program at increasing levels of detail.

There are a number of icon types. The first icon is a 'presentation' icon which is used to construct text and graphic displays. When this icon is selected a presentation window opens which displays the current contents of the icon. A graphics toolbox is displayed sitting on top of the window. The toolbox gives access to a set of tools for creating and editing text and graphic objects. When a particular tool is selected the cursor changes shape. You then move the cursor to the appropriate part of the screen and use the tool. For example, to draw a rectangle you click on the rectangle icon, move to the selected part of the screen and draw a rectangle with the mouse. The tools cover text and basic graphic shapes. Various effects are controlled through menu selection. These include the colour of object frames and fills, effects when objects are overlapping, and screen fade in and fade out.

Authorware provides a set of icons to cover the functionality required for full multimedia systems. As well as the basic icons for presentation, sequencing and selection control there are separate icons for integrating animation, sound and interactive video. Icons are simply picked up with the mouse, dragged to the selected part of the flow line and released. The content or action of the selected icon is specified largely through direct manipulation, as in the presentation icon described above, or through specifying option in dialogue boxes. This powerful authoring interface is easy to learn and use.

A wide range of file types can be imported and integrated into Authorware presentations. For more advanced graphics the objects can be developed in a specialised graphics package and imported into the Authorware environment. This feature is illustrated in the tutorial which comes with Authorware. A detailed drawing of a camera is supplied as a separate file which is imported into the tutorial. Once imported the graphic can be moved to the chosen position on the screen and linked with other text and graphic objects. Authorware will also import animation files created by Macromedia Director or Autodesk Animator. Sound files and video files are controlled through separate icons with their own dialogue control boxes.

Comments on Authorware Professional

The expressive power of Authorware and its usability may be examined in terms of the three main features set out above – how the components of the system are constructed, how they are linked, and how processes of change are dealt with.

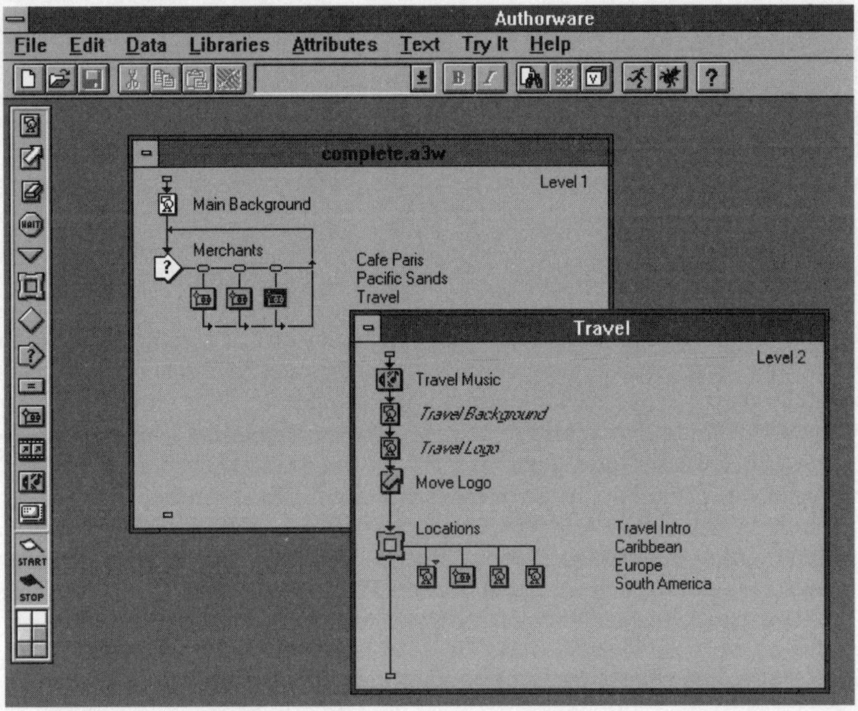

Figure 10.2 Example of an Authorware development screen

The individual components of the system are the contents of the icons. Authorware Professional supports a full range of multimedia components. Some of these components are constructed internally in the Authorware development environment as described previously. Others have to be created in external specialist packages and imported into Authorware. Certain levels of control are provided over these imported objects through specialist dialogue boxes. The display of imported animation sequences, for example, can be controlled through variables which specify the frames to be played. Authorware aims to provide an environmental 'glue' through which all these components can be combined.

The overall structure of an application is specified thorough the flow line which links the various types of icon. It uses a 'visual programming' approach. The application is constructed through linking icons and specifying the content of those icons. The appearance and behaviour of these items are specified through direct manipulation, menu selection and filling in dialogue boxes. Authorware is not based on a scripting language. It thus provides a powerful range of effects that require minimal authoring effort. The manual emphasises that this is an approach suitable for non-programmers. However, the structuring provided by the flow line is similar to that of a traditional imperative programming language.

The structuring of applications and the handling of structural change in Authorware are based on a traditional flow of control approach. If the applications fit naturally with this approach, Authorware can be used to built very impressive applications very quickly. Authorware is very good at building interactive simulations where the simulation is expanded in a forward direction. For more flexible movement it may be best to build the application as a series of small files. Flexible movement can be achieved by jumping between files. Authorware was not constructed as a hypertext or hypermedia authoring tools. If you want highly flexible movement between nodes of information you may find a 'data' based approach such as that used in ToolBook to be more suitable. Macromedia, the producers of Authorware, have sought to address this problem by adding a ‘hyperlinking’ icon to Authorware.

The sets of files that comprise the Authorware application are 'packaged' for delivery. This creates a stand alone 'exe' file, or one 'exe' file' with a number of files controlled by it. The user only has to select the 'exe' file to start the application. At the simplest level these files can be compressed using a utility such as pkzip and distributed on a number of floppy disks. Using appropriate plug-in software Authorware programs can be accessed over the World Wide Web. The performance of the program may be markedly limited, however, by the network bandwidth available.

10.5.2 Page and object based approaches: ToolBook

In Authorware the overall structure of an application is organised through the procedural flow of control on the flow line. ToolBook uses a different approach to building an application. This is described as an ‘object oriented’ approach. The object oriented approach to software construction focuses on the objects from which an application is constructed. Objects are set up with properties and behaviour; program control is achieved by these objects passing messages to each other. Using this approach it is much easier to author the highly flexible navigation we may want in a multimedia learning environment.

ToolBook uses the overall metaphor of a book, which is basically a collection of pages, as a standard organisational structure for building applications. The objects are organised into a series of layers. At the top layer is the 'book'. This consists of a collection of the objects from the next layer. In ToolBook the next layer consists of page backgrounds. The next layer consists of pages, and below that are the basic multimedia objects that may appear on a screen. These may consist of text, graphics, movies and control objects such as page turning buttons. An example of a ToolBook development page is given in Figure 10.3

Following the division set out earlier ToolBook may be examined in terms of how individual objects are created, and how overall structures are created from these objects. ToolBook provides a tool palette for the creation of objects on a page. The tool palette is the leftmost object in Figure 10.3; it is also illustrated in Figure 11.1. Objects are selected from the palette and positioned on the screen using intuitive

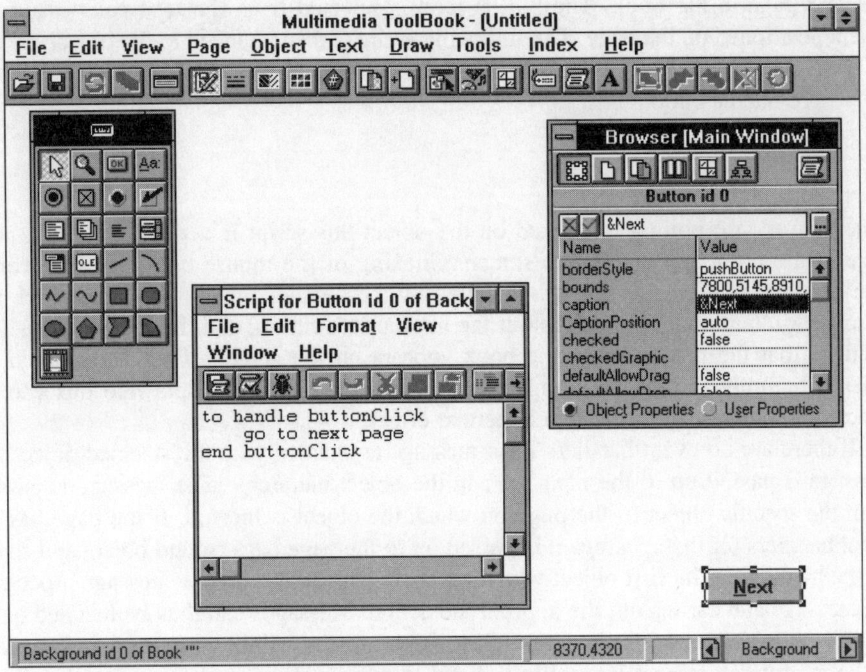

Figure 10.3 Multimedia ToolBook

mouse actions similar to those used with the graphics toolbox in Authorware.

Objects have default behaviour that can be modified or extended. You select the object from the tool palette, e.g. an ellipse, and then choose options to modify the appearance and behaviour of the selected object. Each type of object has as series of properties that can be set. When an object is selected using the mouse cursor it becomes the active object. The pull-down menu options are automatically configured for that type of object. The properties of objects can be set by making menu choices and selecting options in dialogue boxes. Alternatively the values of properties may be changed directly in the browser (Figure 10.3). The style of the authoring interface at this level is similar to that used in Authorware. In ToolBook, however, scripts may be attached to objects to specify their behaviour. It is these scripts rather than an overall flow line that control the behaviour of the system.

Objects can respond to events such a mouse click on the object. This 'event' is handled by a set of event handlers attached to the object. These event handler instructions are written in OpenScript, the scripting language that comes with Toolbook. For example, you may wish to create a button to act as a control for paging forward. When the user clicks the mouse pointer on this button the system will move to the next page in the book. The button icon is selected from the tool palette and the object positioned on the page. The following script is then attached to the object:

```
To handle buttonClick
        go to next page
end buttonClick
```

When the mouse pointer is clicked on the object this script is activated and the next page in the book appears on the screen. Clicking of the mouse button is an 'event'. The message sent by this event is handled by the handler script. This recognises the action, e.g. 'buttonClick', carries out the appropriate action, and then terminates. The result is that the next page in the book appears on the screen. This script could be amended simply to create a jump to any page in the book. Scripts like this can be attached to hotwords to achieve a hypertext effect.

If there are no event handlers for a message associated with the selected object the message is passed up to the next layer in the object hierarchy. The message is passed from the specific object to the page on which the object is located. If the page has no event handlers for that message it is passed on to the page background object and so on up the hierarchy. The first object which has an event handler for the message processes the message and carries out the appropriate action. Messages can thus be handled quite flexibly. A message such as a mouse click on the screen will be picked up and handled at the appropriate object layer. Illustrations of screens developed using ToolBook are given in Plate 5 (the DOVE system) and Figures 12.1 and 12.2 (the VirCom system).

Comments on ToolBook

The structural architecture of a ToolBook system is quite different from the approach adopted in Authorware. In Authorware there is explicit procedural control for linking and sequencing icons on the flow line. In the object oriented approach adopted in ToolBook control depends on the message passing between objects. Any object may process a message as an instruction to jump to a particular page. This supports the construction of very flexible interaction architectures. It provides better support for the construction of the flexible navigation that may be required in hypermedia systems. At the same time standard interaction architectures, such as page-turning electronic books, can be built very easily. ToolBook allows easy switching between authoring and reader levels during development. This supports the developer in viewing and debugging the application as it develops. Good debugging support is provided. When an error is found in a script the debugger window will display the script highlighting the portion where the fault was found.

Toolbook handles a wide range of multimedia data types within a framework which is flexible. The basic electronic book metaphor supports the rapid development of standard applications, but will also support the construction of flexible network structures. The basic node in these networks is the page. There are good tutorials for introducing the main features of ToolBook and the OpenScript language. OpenScript is a powerful language. This is an appealing feature for those with a programming background, but may provide a barrier to those not familiar with programming. The language has been made as English like as possible to aid rapid learning. Asymetrix, the producers of Multimedia ToolBook, have released a CBT version. This includes libraries of page templates and widgets (pre-scripted objects). It also includes 'specialist' programs. A user may invoke a 'specialist' and answer the questions asked. The specialist will then build a functioning screen template that meets the user's request. A ToolBook application is packaged with certain support files for delivery. The system may then be run without the support of the development environment. As with Authorware, ToolBook systems can be run over the World Wide Web by using appropriate viewer software. Information on these resources is provided on the Asymetrix Web site (Appendix 1). There are also variant of ToolBook for directly creating Web applications.

10.5.3 Wider approaches to multimedia authoring

Two multimedia authoring tools have been reviewed in some detail to illustrate the range of facilities that may be expected. Each of these tools represents a distinct authoring paradigm. There are, at least, two other authoring paradigms that may be followed – time based, and pure hypertext. Macromedia Director, a popular authoring tool, follows a time based approach. The analogy of a stage production is used. A 'cast' is created that details the elements in the system. These objects are arranged into a score for the production (Figure 10.4). This tool is oriented to producing powerful presentations. Animation files produced using Director can be imported into other authoring systems, e.g. Authorware and ToolBook, and run from Web browsers using the Shockwave software. However, the built-in scripting language, Lingo, is very powerful. Flexible options can be built in to provide rich interactive effects. A number of applications have been developed using Director, including the Broderbund Living Books series.

The most salient example of a pure hypertext approach is HTML (HyperText Mark-up Language). This approach provides the base for applications developed for the World Wide Web. HTML has the advantage of being easy to use – it involves adding mark-up tags to a text file. It also opens up the vast distribution base. The 'documents' may be placed on a Web server. They can then be accessed by millions of net users across the world. The document can contain tag 'anchors' that provide links to other documents on the Web. This is a very popular area, and there are numerous books that provide an introduction to HTML (e.g. Ford 1995). Wilson (1995) provides a good introduction to designing and authoring systems based on HTML.

The advantages of HTML are clear – comparative ease of authoring and a massive distribution platform. However, compared to tools such as Authorware and ToolBook, HTML seems to provide very low level authoring facilities. The most frequent products are 'annotated text'. However, the power of authoring for network delivery is striking. Increasingly, more powerful facilities are being built to support distributed multimedia authoring. Java, a language developed by Sun Microsystems, supports the

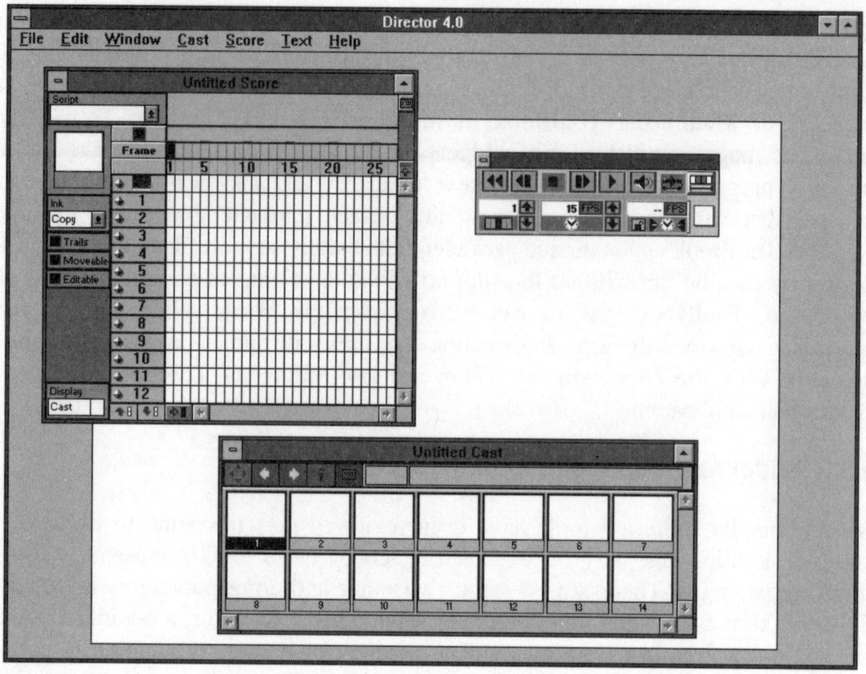

Figure 10.4 The opening screen of Macromedia Director

delivery of more powerful interactive effects on the Web (Van Hoff et al. 1995, Lemay and Perkins 1996). Java 'applets' (small programs) may be downloaded and executed within HTML documents. This greatly extends the interactive power of Web based authoring. Java, however, looks rather similar to programming languages like C++. It requires programming expertise to develop these applets. The influence of the Web means that increasingly powerful tools will be developed with high level authoring interfaces. Given the market imperative traditional authoring tools are developing increasing support for embedding Web links.

10.6 Summary

Multimedia designers need to have a good knowledge of the available toolset. A range of tools is used in constructing multimedia systems. These may be organised in a simple hierarchy. At the base is the multimedia hardware. Standards for multimedia hardware have been specified as in the MPC levels. This provides a clear indication of the target delivery platform. The second layer in the hierarchy consists of specialist media editing tools. These are discussed in more detail in the following chapters. At the pinnacle of the hierarchy are the high level multimedia authoring tools. These tools fall into different groups of authoring paradigms. Two tools were reviewed in some detail to provide a description of the typical range of facilities. Authoring for network delivery is a major growth area. Future developments should see an increasing synthesis of the powerful facilities provided by traditional tools and the flexibility of network delivery based on standard protocols.

The primary thrust of the book is to elucidate design principles that have a deep, long lasting relevance. Specific tool features can change very rapidly. It is crucial, however, to have knowledge of multimedia tools as they provide the principal mechanisms for realising design ideas. This chapter has presented a framework for understanding the main types of tools, and the opportunities they offer to the designer.

Chapter 11

Text and graphics

11.1 Introduction

Text and graphics are the basic components of multimedia systems. Text may be regarded as the Cinderella of the new systems. Text, however, can be one of the most effective components in multimedia. Negroponte (1995b) comments that the power of the word is extraordinary. When the word is embodied as text that too is powerful, whether expressed on paper or a computer screen. Multimedia provides the opportunities to extend the traditional power of text by linking it to other media in new and exciting ways. Pictures and illustrations catch the eye. They enhance the attractiveness of the system and deepen the information channel. When hot spots are added they become rich interactive objects. Colour infuses life and aesthetic impact to the presentation. It can also signal screen composition, and code and separate blocks of information. This chapter deals with these important contributions to multimedia composition.

11.2 Text

You are light as dreams,
Tough as oak,
Precious as gold

'Words' Edward Thomas

11.2.1 The use of text in a multimedia system

The type of system determines the way text is used. In a hypertext system the text predominates. Other media elements, e.g. pictures, may provide annotations to the narrative structure provided by the text. This is the most common format on the World Wide Web. In comparison with traditional narrative structures, the text is divided into smaller chunks that provide the nodes in a flexible network of choice. Other media elements provide expansions on the material presented in these nodes. In a full multimedia system text plays a complementary role to the other media components of the scene. The text may be creatively incomplete: it may point to other media elements in the context to complete the message. In a hypermedia system these elements are linked in a network that may be traversed in a highly flexible manner. A hypermedia system requires a communication system that can be broken up into these distinct multimedia nodes. This is suitable for some forms of communication, e.g. electronic encyclopaedias.

There are many forms of multimedia and hypermedia systems. The conceptual design determines the architecture of the system, and hence the role of text within that architecture. For clear presentation the position and appearance of text on the screen must then be planned, the individual message must be composed, and this message must be legible and aesthetically pleasing. These three issues are now discussed in turn.

11.2.2 The position and appearance of text messages

There are a number of emergent conventions for the positioning and appearance of text. A text message is often presented in a rectangular block on the screen. If this block of text is substantial, a left–right division is often used in screen design. This division corresponds roughly to the left and right pages in a book. The text block is normally placed on the left 'page' or panel of the screen. The graphic animation or work area is then presented on the right 'page'. This approach is used in the on-line tutorial for the ToolBook authoring system. In the tutorial for ToolBook version 1.53 this page division is very clearly marked. In the main tutorial for ToolBook 3 this division is perceptually softened. The left and right 'pages' are replaced by two slightly overlapping grey panels positioned on a reddish brown background (Figure 11.1).

This scheme often implements a 'tell and show' approach. The text provides the basic information; this may be supported by a relevant illustration placed in the right hand panel. This presentation scheme may be expanded to a 'tell, show and do' approach. In this case the learner can act directly on the right hand area to mimic or carry out the action described. In the ToolBook tutorials, for example, a live ToolBook application may be loaded in the right panel. The learner can then practise the skills described in the accompanying text. There are a number of variants of this scheme. One variant is provided, for example, in the on-line tutorial for Windows 3.1. In this case there is no explicit division into left and right panels. The text and graphics are presented as moveable objects on top of a blank desk top. The text is presented in a box on the left hand side of the screen; the graphic work area is on the right hand side. The text box moves position as the learner steps through the system. Sometimes it

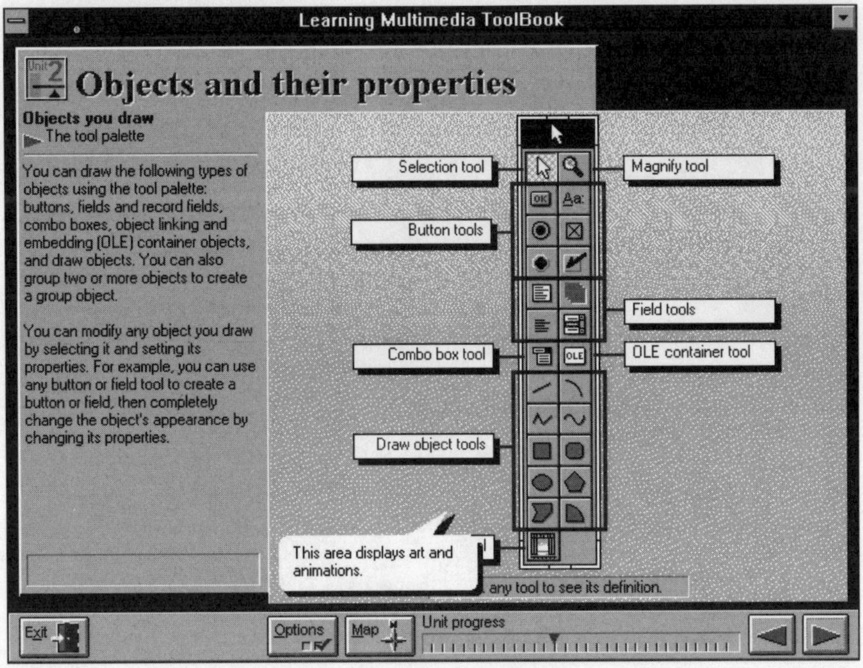

Figure 11.1 The ToolBook 3 tutorial screen layout

partially overlaps the graphic, but it never moves to the right of the screen.

This left–right division is also used to organise the screens in the DOVE system (Plate 5). There are a number of objects that need to be presented on a DOVE screen. This produces a problem in how to manage the presentation of this material. The left half of the screen is used for objects the learner needs to observe or read. The right half is used for the interactive recording charts. The evaluation indicated that this broad division seemed to work well. This example illustrates how standard (perhaps even clichéd) schemes can be adapted to solve problems in new circumstances.

A second presentation device is to overlay text on top of the main screen. This device may be used in a number of ways. A constant overlay display tends to play a central role in a structured presentation schemes. 'Pop-up' text tends to provide more flexible functions. The provision of feedback is a central function in learning environments. Pop-up text boxes are often used to provide feedback to the user. The learner is given information, carries out some action, and is given feedback in an pop-up text box (e.g. Plate 5). The Windows 3.1 tutorial uses this approach. The use of pop-up text panels to provide feedback is generally applicable within a wide variety of presentation schemes.

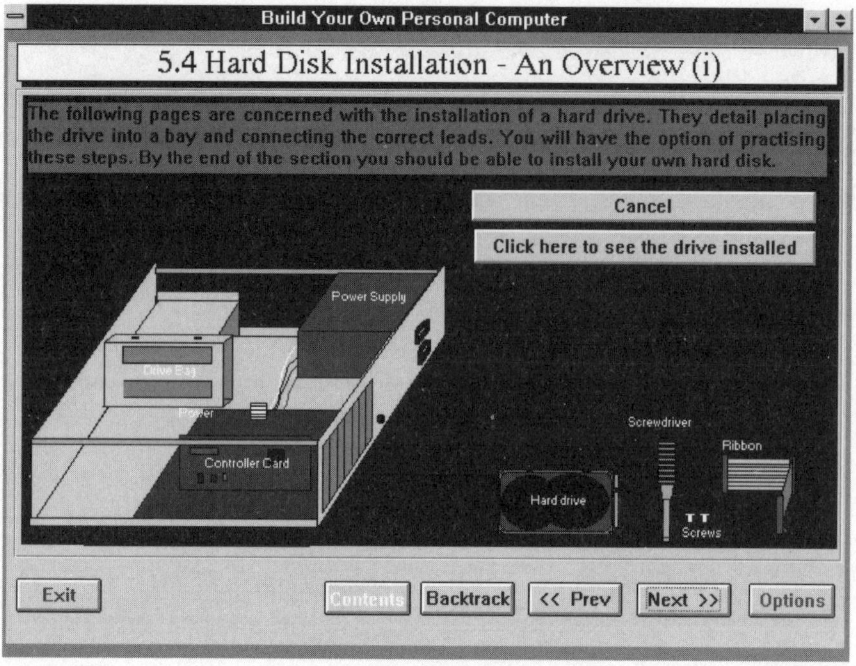

Figure 11.2 Text labelling in VirCom

A second function for pop-up text is to provide selected annotation. This device reduces screen clutter and provides extra information or selective help on demand. Pop-up text boxes may be used to annotate words, pictures or controls. Pop-up text is often used to provide further information about a target word or phrase. Overlay text may also be used to annotate graphics. In the VirCom system, for example, users may select a 'label' button. Labels for the significant components in the display then appear on the screen (Figure 11.2). The word on the label button is changed to 'cancel' while the labels are displayed. These labels have a 'transparent' background. They thus appear as words overlaid on the graphic. Pop-up text may also be used to provide selective help about controls. The 'bubble help' on the Macintosh is a good example. When this facility is selected a help bubble appears when the cursor is moved over an object.

11.2.3 Composing the message

A clear message often has to be conveyed in a limited space. This requires skill in conveying the message clearly and precisely. Advice on prose writing has been given by a number of writers; this may be may be summarised as a series of guidelines (Orwell 1945, Quiller-Couch 1916).

1. Choose a suitable compositional structure and keep to it.

2. Make each paragraph deal with one central idea or event.

3. Use definite, concrete language.

4. Never use a long word where a short one will do.

5. If it is possible to omit a word always cut it out.

6. Use plain words in preference to jargon.

7. Break any of these rules rather than write clumsy text.

The advice is to aim for simplicity and clarity in communication.

Be specific, definite, concrete and precise.

The choice of style must be related to the context of use. In formal and scientific writing, for example, passive sentences are frequently used (something frowned on in many style guides). This use conforms to the conventions for this type of text. The guidelines in the list above, however, seem to produce good advice for writing text for learning environments. The application of this advice in specific systems is the decision of the designer. It is important to remember one over-riding principle – make the text fit its purpose.

11.2.4 Legibility and aesthetic effect

Selecting Fonts

A typeface is a collection of characters with a distinctive shape. The characters forming the main text of this book belong to one typeface. Within a typeface there are different styles. Bold and italic represent different styles within one typeface. Strictly speaking a 'font' is a particular style of a typeface, e.g. Arial italic or Arial bold. In computer circles, however, font is generally used as a synonym for typeface. Figure 11.3 gives examples of some different fonts.

Fonts are divided into two broad families: serif and sanserif. The text you are reading is a serif font. The serifs are the small decorations added to the ends of the letters. The difference between serif and sanserif is illustrated in Figure 11.4. The

Times New Roman

Arial

Courier New

ALGERIAN

Figure 11.3 Examples of different fonts

capital letter 'F' is shown in Times New Roman (a serif font) and MS Dialog (a sanserif font).

In printed material a serif is usually used for the main text. The reason is that the serifs help the eye flow along the line of the text. Headings may use serif or sanserif characters. If you scan through a number of books you will notice the different choices made for headings. A good example of a variety of fonts is found on cereal packets!

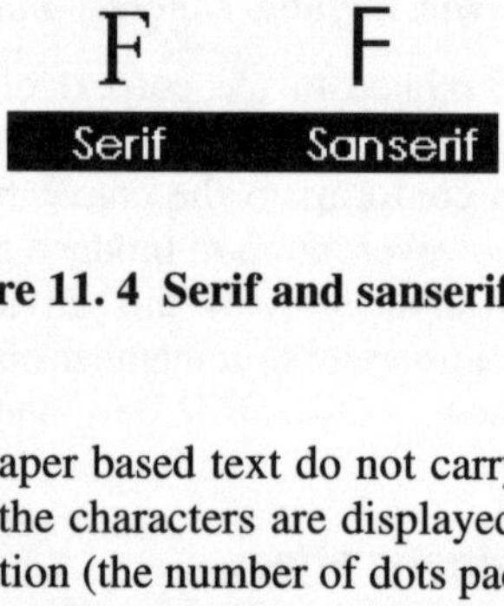

Figure 11. 4 Serif and sanserif fonts

The conventions used for paper based text do not carry over to a computer screen. The physical media on which the characters are displayed is quite different in at least two major respects. The resolution (the number of dots packed per centimetre) is much poorer than ink on paper. A small serif font on a screen can look crowded. Visual resolution of the individual characters can strain the eyes. The second characteristic of computer screens – that light is projected rather than reflected – exacerbates the problem. A sanserif font is thus often used for blocks of text. For headings, by contrast, a serif font may be used to create a decorative effect (see Figure 11.2).

Size

Schwier and Misanchuk (1993) provide the homely and practical advice that characters should be large enough to be read comfortably, but not so large as to interfere. For blocks of text they recommend twelve to fourteen text size. This recommendation needs to be checked for the specific fonts on the computer you are using. Vaughan (1994) points out that characters identified as the same font and size may not appear the same physical size on Macintosh and Microsoft Windows systems.

A suitable size for text depends upon the context for use. It is the interplay of these local factors, together with general considerations of legibility, that shape the choice of text size. If you examine the examples of multimedia screens shown in the book you can discern the influence of local factors. The final decision is – does it look right and perform its function?

11.3 Graphics

There are two basic types of still graphics used in multimedia systems:

- bitmaps or paint graphics
- vector or draw graphics.

Each type of graphic has its own characteristics and satisfies different needs and composition. The essential difference between these graphic types is that bitmaps are stored in the computer's memory as an image of what appears on the screen. Each dot on the screen (pixel) is stored as a number in a matrix. Draw graphics, by contrast, are stored as sets of instructions for how to create the image. These methods of storage place different demands on the memory and processor of the computer.

11.3.1 Bitmaps

A bitmap is represented as an array of numbers in the computer's memory. Each number codes information about one pixel. If only one binary digit is used then two colour values (0,1) can be stored – black and white. If more memory is allocated then more precise information can be stored about each pixel. If four binary digits (bits) are used then sixteen colour values can be stored. The relationship of memory allocation to *colour depth* is presented in Table 11.1. The degree of colour depth we can achieve depends upon the computer hardware. The MPC level 1 standard specifies a standard of 256 colours at a screen resolution of 640 by 480 pixels. This has provided a standard for the development of many multimedia systems. The MPC level 2 standard specifies 16 bit colour giving over 65,000 colours.

Bitmaps provide a basis for incorporating material from a variety of sources. The major sources of bitmap art work are:

1. Pictures created in special Paint programs
2. Photographs
3. Scanned images

4. Screen dumps.

Pictures can be created in Paint programs. These images can then be transferred to the main multimedia authoring environment. Once in this environment they can be treated as objects that can be manipulated to fit into the multimedia layout. In this way the Paint program can be used to augment the power of the multimedia authoring tool. Photographs can be captured directly onto the computer and stored as a file. The image can then be directly imported into the multimedia authoring environment. The image may need to be retouched and enhanced in packages such Adobe Photoshop before transfer into the main authoring environment.

There are two broad methods for capturing photographs directly onto the computer. These methods differ in ease of use and the quality of the images produced. Special cameras, such as the Cannon Ion camera, capture photographs directly onto small floppy disks on the camera. These photographs can be downloaded from the camera to the computer over a cable. This method is very fast. Pictures can be taken, downloaded and displayed on the computer in a few minutes. This is very useful for rapid prototyping. The resolution of many of these cameras, however, is limited. Depending on the application the pictures may be retained or replaced in later prototypes by pictures taken using the second method. More expensive cameras can produce very high resolution pictures, e.g. the Illumina Leaf camera.

The second approach produces high quality pictures very cheaply. The Kodak Photo CD system accepts photographs taken with normal cameras, digitises them, and stores them in CD ROM. Either slides or negatives can be taken to a standard processing shop for transfer onto CD. The CD ROM can hold about 100 photographs, and it can be used more than once. The quality of the resulting pictures is extremely good. The pictures can be read from the CD ROM into the computer's memory and incorporated into the multimedia system.

Table 11.1 Relationship of memory allocation to colour depth

Memory in bits	*No. of colours*
1	2
4	16
8	256
16	64k
24	over 16 million

* 'k' indicates a binary thousand, which is 1024 in decimal terms

Images may be captured from three other sources. Images can be scanned into a computer. This provides access to a wide range of source material. However, copyright considerations must be kept in mind. Images can also be captured as 'screen dumps' directly from the computer screen. Packages such as Photoshop and Paint Shop Pro allow you capture specified parts of the screen. This is a powerful utility, but again copyright considerations need to be kept in mind. Finally, there are clip art collections on CD ROM. These libraries can provide a useful source of material.

11.3.2 Vector or 'draw' graphics

Vector or draw graphics represent an object by the minimum information required to draw the object. A rectangle, for example, can be defined by the co-ordinates of the top left hand corner and the bottom right hand corner. Further information can be added to indicate the colour of the line used to draw the rectangle and the colour of the 'fill' area enclosed by the rectangle, e.g. '100, 100, 500, 300, green'. The software in the computer uses this information to draw and fill in the shape.

Most multimedia authoring tools provide a good set of draw commands. These are usually accessed through options on a tool palette. Figures 10.3 and 11.1 illustrate the tool palette in the ToolBook authoring system. To draw a rectangle, for example, you select the appropriate option and then simply draw the rectangle on the screen. Outline and fill colours can be separately selected. The outline colour is used to draw the shape; the fill colour 'fills' the area inside the shape. These draw tools are an integral part of many multimedia authoring systems. These tools can be used to create a variety of graphic shapes. The direct manipulation style of interaction makes them very easy to use.

11.3.3 Integrating graphics into the multimedia system

A visual composition for the screens in a multimedia system needs to be established. This issue has been discussed in Chapter 9. This composition may be represented on outline storyboards. Figures 9.4 and 9.5 illustrate the outline form normally used for storyboards. Textual annotations are usually added to indicate the functions of the various components. These storyboards provide the overall framing of the screen. They ensure harmony between the different screens in a system. As graphics are created and imported they may be placed into these 'holding' slots. The visualisation produced may lead to further enhancements and modifications. For example, highly detailed pictures may not be easily readable in the space allocated. We found this problem when we initially tried to import photographs of computer hardware components into the VirCom system. Some pictures were far too detailed for the space allocated. In this sort of situation several options are open, i.e. replace the graphic, allocate more space on the screen, or use a 'hypermedia' jump from a small representation to the full graphic. These choices form part of the iterative refinement of the system. The choice taken will depend upon many factors: time factors, the importance of the picture, and side effects on other parts of the system.

11.4 Colour

...at every screen are two powerful information-processing capabilities, human and computer. Yet all communication between the two must pass through the low-resolution, narrow-band video display terminal...

(Tufte 1990, p.89)

11.4.1 Technical considerations in the use of colour

The aim of the multimedia designer is to use colour to create effective and pleasing displays. Some technical information about the two information processors, human and machine, helps to illuminate why some choices work better than others. The human eye contains two main types of light receptors – rods and cones. The rods react to light intensity; colour processing is carried out by the cones. There are three types of cones. These respond maximally to the wave lengths of red, green and blue respectively. The red and green cones are most numerous in the eye's central focusing area. There are less blue cones but they are distributed more evenly over the central and peripheral regions of the eye. The three colours have different focal lengths. The three different focal distances mean that blue tends to be seen as further away and red as closer. Green is intermediate between the two. This effect can lead to colour stereopsis. The impressionist painters used this phenomenon to create depth effects based upon colour alone.

There are many ways to represent colour. Most of these use a trichromatic scheme, i.e. they use three dimensions. Colours may be coded on a colour cube of red, green and blue. All other colours can be obtained by mixing these three colours. Another popular classification scheme is Munsell's hue, saturation and value. Hue refers to the place of the colour on the spectrum from red to violet. Saturation is the density of the colour. Brightness or value classifies the colour on a scale from light to dark. Tools for manipulating colour on a computer are often based on these schemes. PalEdit in Windows, for example, has distinct sets of controls (Plate 8). The user can use either the RGB (Red, Green, Blue) or the Munsell method to manipulate colour. The effects are displayed in a small window. When a target effect is achieved this may be saved on a colour palette.

Computers vary in their power in processing colour and this directly affects the design process. The CLEM system, for example, was originally developed for delivery on computers with VGA graphics cards. This limited the colour selection to 16 colours. The MPC level 1 standard requires a super VGA graphics card that will handle 256 colours. The 256 'colours' refers to 256 samples of colour. These samples are biased towards the nature of the objects displayed. If the display, for example, consists mainly of green fields and a blue sky the sampling will be strongly biased in the blue-green area. This palette will support more subtle representations of various shades of green and blue. If a picture of, say, a red car is then shown, the phenomenon of ‘palette flash’ occurs. The computer has to change the colour palette and this change is signalled by a flash on the screen. This looks rather like the colour equivalent of flashing to a negative version of a black and white image.

Palette flashing may be a problem for multimedia systems. There are a number of possible ways of dealing with this:

1. Tolerate it

2. Create a common system palette

3. Fade to black between screens with conflicting palettes

4. Use delivery hardware that supports higher levels of colour representation.

A common system palette may be created by finding a set of 256 colours that is the best sample for the multimedia system. Software tools will assist in creating a common palette. The achievements of a high quality effect may be very time consuming. Stewart McEwan, in answering a question on the Musical Instruments project, said it took three months to develop a common palette for this system (McEwan 1993).

There are two more economical approaches. You may decide to tolerate the effect. The decision depends upon the nature of the system and the intended audience. One of my colleagues working with special needs children found that some of them liked the palette flash effect. Alternatively you can fade the first screen to black before loading the next screen. Most authoring tools will support this transition effect between screens. The aesthetic effect needs to be judged in the context of the project. The palette problem arises from the limitations of the computer hardware. When more powerful machines become commonplace the problem will eventually disappear.

There is an associated problem with palette limitations – ‘dithering’. Dithering refers to the process where the colour values of pixels are changed to match the closest equivalent on a target colour palette. Kodak Photo CD images, for example, are captured with very detailed colour information. This sampling, which may be over 16 million colours, may have to be reduced to fit the target system. If an image is going to be dithered to a lower colour depth the original photograph has to be taken with care. Unwanted gradations, such as light gradients across an object, should be avoided. ‘Noise’ variations may lead the dithering process, which is based on a mathematical algorithm, to be less effective.

11.4.2 Guidelines for colour composition

An immediate question that arises in the choice of colour composition is the choice of the background colour. In some respects white has many advantages. This leaves maximum freedom for the selection of colours for foreground objects. Large areas of white, however, can create screen glare. Light is projected from a monitor, not reflected as on white paper. The resulting effect may cause eye strain. An alternative to white is the use of grey. The degree of glare is reduced while retaining the freedom for foreground colour choice. Grey backgrounds are quite widely used. The on-line tutorial for ToolBook 3, for example, makes extensive use of grey backgrounds.

There are a number of other possibilities for background colour choice. Many people regard grey as rather dull. In the VirCom system many of the foreground objects are greyish in tone (e.g. various computer components). The main background colour selected here was blue. Blue is a 'retreating' colour; the distribution of cones in the eyes also makes peripheral vision of blue over large areas quite effective. Blue, set at the right level of saturation and brightness, can be a very effective background colour.

The choice of colour depends, as always, on the specific nature of the project. The project will entail certain types of objects being presented on the foreground. The background colour must be selected to fit with the colour of these objects. Connotations associated with the system may also influence the choice of colour. The main background colour for the DOVE system is green (Plate 5). This fits in with virtual field trip connotations. Whatever colour is chosen, the background colour should be soft on the eye and non-intrusive.

The colour choice of foreground objects may be affected by a number of considerations:

- realistic portrayal of objects
- aesthetic effect
- to convey colour coded information
- to conform to standards.

The realistic portrayal of objects places constraints on the colour scheme which we may use. Colour may also be used to aid the perception of relevant information. The banners for the overlay cards in CLEM are all colour coded (Plate 2). This makes the card easy to 'pick up' when it sits in the background behind the main book. Colour schemes may also be chosen to conform to standards such as the default colour scheme for the windows environment. There is a fair amount of subjective judgement in achieving a pleasant aesthetic effect. The first principle expounded by Tufte is *'Above all, do no harm'* (Tufte 1990, p. 81, writer's italics). Most writers propose restraint in the use of colour. Avoid using too many colours and avoid abrupt changes in hue in adjacent highly saturated colours (Marcus 1992). Using a blend of tones of one colour can help create a harmonious colour scheme.

Whatever colour scheme is chosen some users may have different preferences. It may be feasible to let the users chose the colour scheme. Figure 11.5 shows a screen

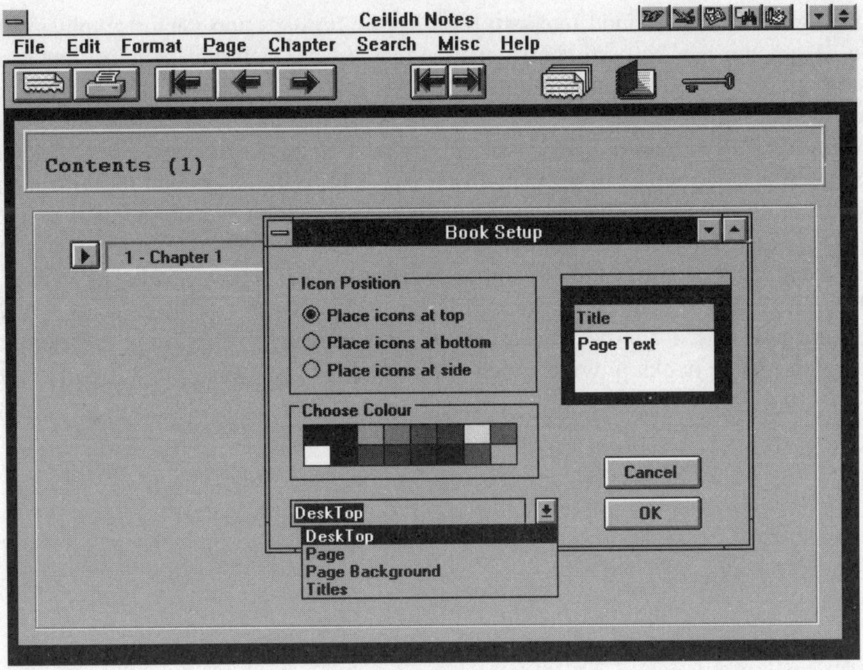

Figure 11.5 User selection of colour scheme in the Ceilidh Notes Shell

from the Ceilidh Notes Shell. This shell provides an authoring and delivery environment for instructional material. The students can chose their own colour schemes by selecting from the options provided. This echoes the ability of users to choose their own colour schemes in Windows.

11.5 Summary

Text, graphics and colour are the basic elements of multimedia systems. Knowledge from the traditional media based disciplines contributes to multimedia design. The contribution of each media form must be reconsidered in terms of the interactive multimedia context. The position and deployment of text must be planned to enhance and complement the contributions of the other media. The messages have to be succinct and clear. This requires skill in verbal composition. The text should be legible and aesthetically effective. A useful source for further reading on the design of instructional text is Hartley (1994). This discusses in some depth the design of text for computer based learning environments.

Still graphics are divided into two basic types: bitmaps and vector graphics. Each type of graphic has its own characteristics that satisfy different composition needs. Vector graphics require small amounts of memory. They can usually be produced easily within high level multimedia tools. The small memory requirement makes them a useful base for animations (discussed in the next chapter). Bitmaps can be captured from a variety of sources to provide a rich visual impact and deepen the information channel of the system. The choice of colour composition has immediate aesthetic impact. It also aids the separation, grouping and presentation of information. For further reading a detailed guide to computer based colour is provided by Jackson et al. (1994). This covers both technical and design issues. Tufte (1990) presents a highly rated example based approach to effective graphic design. This book is beautifully illustrated. These books provide a rich exploration of the use of graphics and colour for effective communication.

Chapter 12

Animation, sound and video

12.1 Introduction

These are dynamic time based media. They contribute a dramatic, attention grabbing dimension to multimedia. Used effectively they contribute enormously to the impact of the learning environment. But their very power (and time based nature) can produce problems. The challenge is to integrate these media elements as components within an integrated multimedia experience.

The chapter begins by discussing the various types and uses of animation. There is a rich diversity in this area. When these animation effects are placed under user control this draws the user into new powerful forms of expression. Full frame based animations use techniques that overlap with those used for video. This section discusses the options available in this area for enhancing learning environments.

The effective use of sound requires some technical knowledge, and ideas for the effective incorporation of sound into the system. The use of speech, in particular, provides a powerful resource for IMLEs. Good design requires careful thought on how speech and sound effects are to be used. The discussion covers both technical issues of sound capture and guidelines on use.

Video is the most dramatic medium. It provides a rich resource for portraying authentic learning situations. Video is a time based multimedia phenomenon in its own right. This poses a significant challenge for multimedia design. The discussion explores the possibilities of moving video towards being a flexible resource integrated into the overall multimedia system.

12.2 Animation and special effects

Animation adds impact to a presentation. The visual impact of animation should be harnessed to serve the learning objectives. There are a variety of forms of animation that can be used to enhance learning. In this section four types of animation will be discussed:

1. Moving objects across the screen
2. User controlled movement of objects
3. Bitmap flipping
4. Full animation files.

The first two forms of animation usually involve draw objects, though the techniques can also be applied to small bitmaps. Authoring tools, such as ToolBook and Authorware, provide techniques that make it easy to move objects on the screen. This facility is very useful for demonstrating processes to a learner. Each block in the VirCom system begins with an animated demonstration. This demonstration provides an overview of the skill to be learned, e.g. installing a hard disk on a computer. Animated demonstrations are also used within the learning blocks to illustrate individual steps in the assembly process (Figures 12.1(a) and 12.1(b)). Animated demonstration is useful for any learning task that involves the assembly of objects or arrangement of abstract categories.

Animations may also be used to enliven a message. In the DOVE system, for example, animation is used to introduce the navigation controls for the system. The controls are initially presented in the middle of the screen. As each control button is described it floats down to its proper position on the tool bar at the bottom of the screen. Animation may also be used for entertainment. The letters of a heading may move into position accompanied by a musical flourish. The problem with this effect is that it can rapidly become tiresome on repeated use of the system. There is a general principle here: unnecessary time based effects should not be imposed on the user. If effects like this are used there should be a by-pass mechanism.

A significant step forward in terms of learning design is to let the learner control the movement of objects. This facility may be used in conjunction with demonstrations to create a 'show and practise' learning dialogue. In VirCom after each demonstration the users are asked to practise the skills. The learner carries out a virtual assembly operation by moving and positioning objects with the mouse. This process culminates at the end of a learning block when the user carries out a full virtual assembly of the component. The user picks up each object in turn with the mouse and assembles it in the right position. Figure 12.2 illustrates two stages in a user's virtual assembly of a hard disk drive. In the first screen the hard disk is sitting to one side of the computer casing. In the second screen the user has dragged the hard disk unit across and installed it in the bay.

A different form of animation may be achieved by flipping bitmap pictures. This techniques works effectively with small pictures. Multimedia authoring tools allow objects to be stacked on top of each other. If all the objects are the same size only the

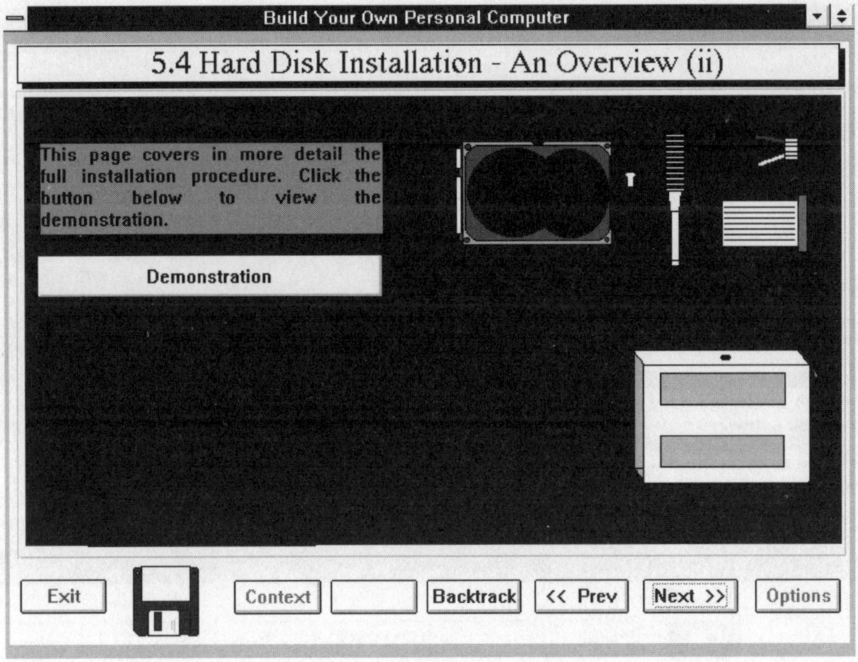

Figure 12.1(a) Demonstration by moving objects

top object will be visible on the screen. An animation effect can be created by displaying a picture briefly then moving it to the bottom of the stack. If each card shows a state from a sequence of actions then this animation will be perceived by the user.

Flipping pictures to create an animation effect is very inefficient in computer resources. The whole image has to be rebuilt for each display. One of my undergraduate students was asked to convert an application from one multimedia tool to another. His first approach was to capture each complete screen in the original and paste these bitmaps into the new tool. He came to me to complain that the computer was very slow! On the second attempt the various objects in the original were captured as separate bitmaps. Many of these were placed on the background that does not change between screens. The computer only had to write the new objects on any screen. The performance quickly reached an acceptable level.

Special animation file formats have been developed to deal with this problem. They reduce the information that has to be held by removing redundant information (the information that remains the same across several pictures in the sequence). This leads to more efficient execution. These files are created by special animation tools such as Animator Pro for the PC. These tools support the creation of a wide range of

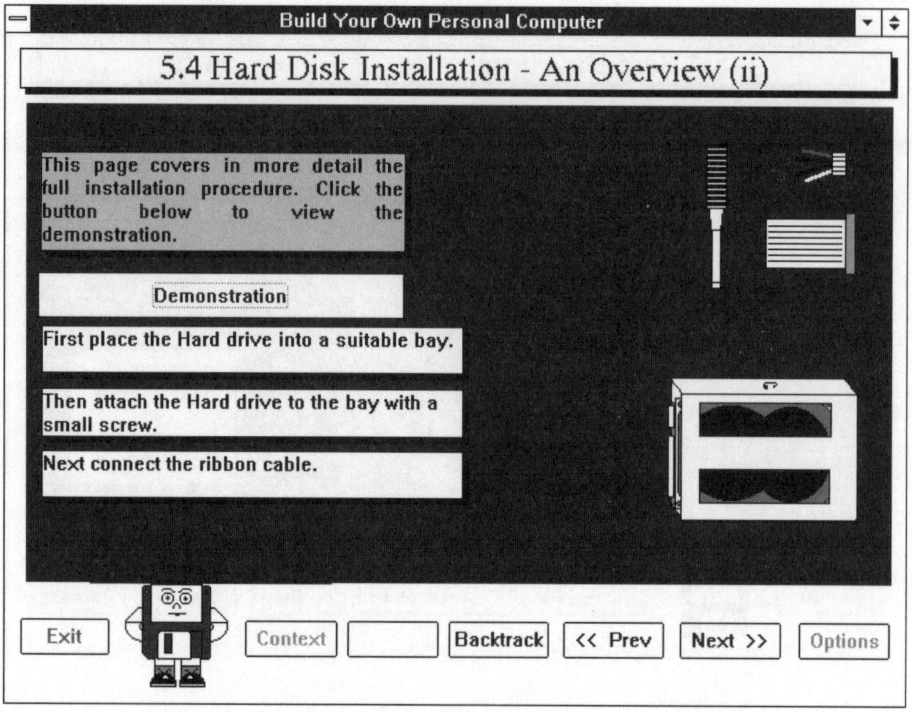

Figure 12.1(b) Demonstration by moving objects

animation. The files can then be imported and used as 'objects' within the main multimedia authoring tool. Macromedia Director is a multimedia authoring tool that is particularly well adapted to producing animations. It has been used, for example, to produce the animated demonstration introducing Microsoft's Windows for Workgroups. It was also used to produce the Broderbund Living Books. Files from Director or Animator Pro can be imported into a number of multimedia authoring tools, and used as components within the wider application.

Animation files consist of a series of frames. These files can be controlled in a similar way to digital video. Plate 6 shows an animated display of information on the menstrual cycle from the Cytofocus system. By moving the lever on the screen the user can view how the graphs change over the monthly cycle.

There are different forms of animation. These provide a variety of resources to achieve eye catching effects. An animation that looks good certainly impresses. The primary function, however, must be to support effective learning. The selection and use of animation techniques should be determined primarily by its function in the learning context.

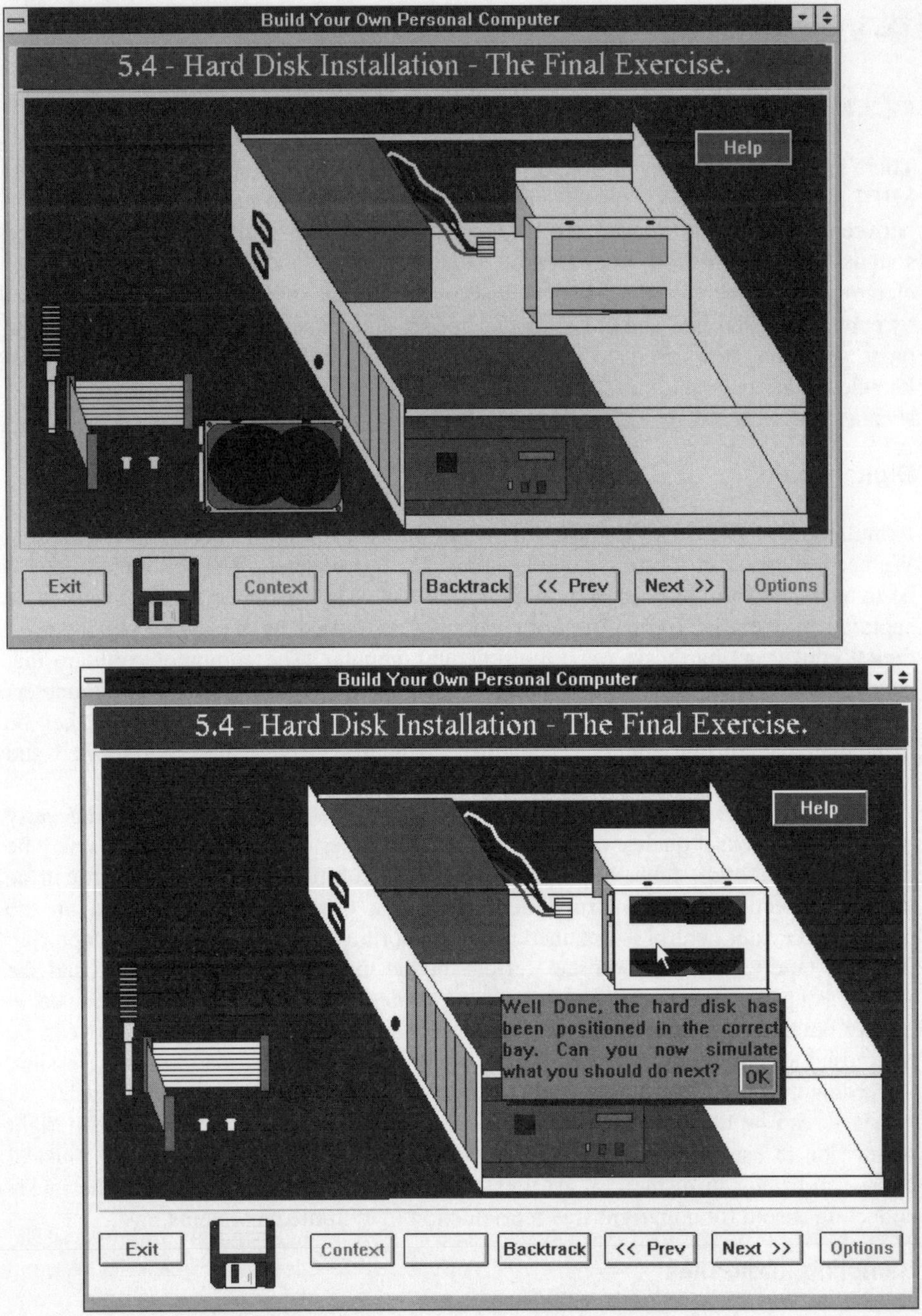

Figure 12.2 User controlled animation

12.3 Sound

12.3.1 Understanding digital sound: a brief overview

There are two basic types of sound files used as components of multimedia systems: MIDI and digital audio. The difference between these files parallels the distinction between vector drawn images and bitmaps. MIDI files store instructions for creating sounds. These instructions are based on a standard developed for sending messages to electronic instruments – the **M**usical **I**nstrument **D**igital **I**nterface. Digital audio files by contrast are digitised samples of actual speech and music. Digital audio files are the most common type used in multimedia systems. MIDI files require specialist knowledge to create and modify. Digital audio files can be captured from any source, such as tape recorded speech, and are much easier to manipulate.

Digital audio

A multimedia system may require the use of speech, music or special sound effects. We need to create or locate a suitable source for this material. The source is likely to be in analogue form, e.g. speech on a cassette tape. This analogue source needs to be captured in a digital form. The conversion is performed by the ADC (analogue to digital convertor) hardware on a multimedia computer. The computer software that controls the capture process allows us to set several parameters. These parameters affect the quality and size of the digital sample. The captured sound file may then be manipulated in special editors. The edited sound file may finally be imported and integrated into the multimedia system.

The first stage is the creation or location of the source material. During early prototyping the exact quality of the source may not be crucial. Speech samples may be gathered to prototype how they may used in the multimedia system. Speech can be recorded directly from a microphone linked by a cable to the sound card on the computer. Greater control is obtained by first recording on the tape and then capturing from the tape recorder. When the 'script' for the multimedia system is finalised the speech samples can be recorded in a more professional manner. The difference in quality obtained by using a professional presenter is quite marked. The cost can be minimised by presenting a script that can possibly be recorded in one session. Recording the whole script in one session also produces a consistent quality level.

Music can be captured from many sources. The key issue is to ensure copyright permission to use the music. There are also CD ROMs with copyright free musical clips – an extension of the clip art idea. You need to check carefully that the music collection is sold for copyright free reproduction in multimedia systems.

Sampling audio files

A multimedia computer has the hardware and software required for digital sampling of analogue sound. On the basic multimedia PC, for example, the sound recorder package is supplied. More sophisticated software programs are usually included with the sound card supplied with the computer or upgrade kit. Sound varies on two major parameters: frequency and amplitude. The quality of the digital sound sample depends upon the precision of the measurement on these two dimensions. *Sampling rate* is the frequency with which the samples are taken. The precision of the measurement taken for each sample is called *sample size*. Sample precision might be a more accurate term.

Figure 12.3 illustrates the concept of sampling frequency. The two 'rulers' on the baseline indicate different sampling frequencies. Each line on a 'ruler' indicates when a sample is taken. Precision of information is lost when a lower sampling frequency is used. This loss of information is especially noticeable with the high frequency notes, which are produced by high frequency vibration.

Sample size is illustrated in Figure 12.4. The two curved lines represent two sound waves that are being sampled. The sampling size indicated on the right distinguishes between the two waves. The sampling size on the left, however, would give both samples the same value.

The quality of the digital recording improves with increases in the frequency and precision of the measurements taken. These sampling parameters may be adjusted on control panels supplied with the audio capture software. CD quality sound is obtained by a sampling rate of 44.1 kHz (kilohertz) and a sampling size of 16 bits. The sound is

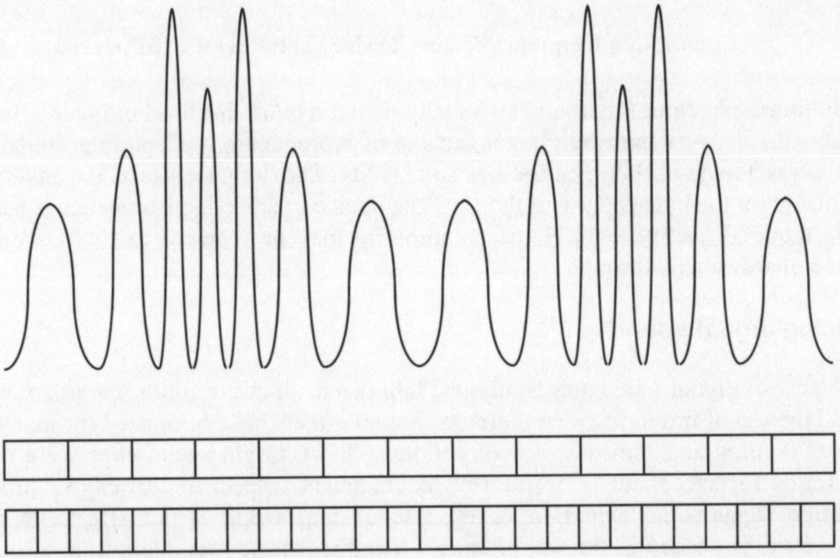

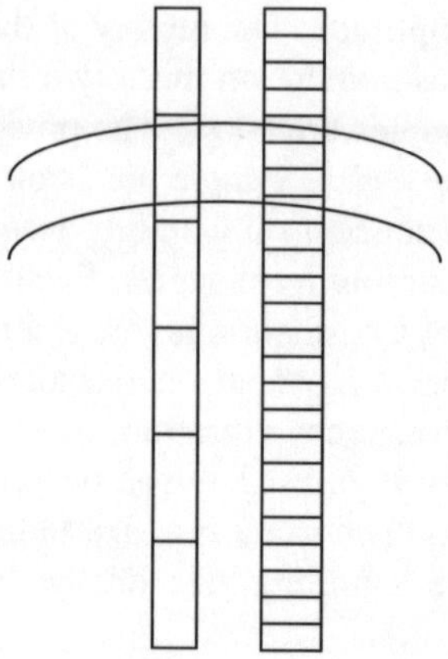

Figure 12.4 Sample size: precision of sampling from an analogue source

recorded on two channels to achieve a stereo effect. The problem of high quality sound is that it produces very large files. One second of CD quality sound takes over 176,000 bytes of data. This is calculated by the formula:

sampling frequency × sample size (in bytes) × 2 (for stereo)

Multimedia learning environments usually do not require this level of quality. In many cases the delivery hardware is not capable of reproducing it. Capturing digital audio involves a trade-off between file size and quality. The designer selects the quality level suitable for the intended use of the file. The choice of sampling parameters is based on the required quality level. Some compromise may be required to fit files onto the target hardware platform.

Using digital sound

The use of digital sound may be divided into two distinct categories: the use of speech, and the use of music and sound effects. Sound effects have been used for many years in CAL programs aimed at school children. Short, bright sound clips were used as rewards for successful answers. The 'edutainment' aspect of learning environment design suggests an extension of the use of music and sound effects. Restraint, however, is needed in the use of sound. Swelling music may seem fine on our first introduction to an IMLE. With repeated use of the system it can rapidly become irritating.

In some systems music is not an embellishment but the central topic. The thrust of interactive multimedia has been to provide *interactive* access to the music. Particular parts of a composition may be accessed and linked to other sources of information, such as musical scores or comments by critics. Interactive access is provided in this way in works such as the Multimedia Beethoven CD ROM. The 'Carnival des Animaux' CD ROM goes one step further (Heppel 1993). In this system children can create their own collection of resources, including sound clips they have selected from the musical piece.

Speech

The integration of speech into multimedia learning environments can be a demanding task. In normal use speech is integrated in complex ways with on-going interaction. Initially speech is likely to be used in much simpler ways in IMLEs, but there is considerable scope for the continuing development of this resource.

The first issue is to establish the function of speech in the system. Having established the role of speech we then need to integrate speech with the other multimedia elements. There are some general guidelines for this process. The speech segments should be generally:

- short
- manageable
- integrated
- complementary to text.

Long monologues are not very attractive in interactive multimedia. The attention of the learner soon wanders. Speech is more effective if delivered in conversation size bites and short descriptions. Longer messages may be broken up and distributed, or expressed through text rather than speech.

As a general principle the user should have as much control as possible over the audio. The range of controls may include: initiate, pause, repeat, and interrupt. An important feature is the ability to interrupt the speech. This is especially important for longer speech sequences. The learner should not be 'time-tied', required to wait until the announcement is complete. If the user leaves the scene, for example, by clicking a paging button the sound should stop automatically. Authoring tools provide standard commands for controlling sound output in this way.

Speech output should be integrated with the other media in the system. One approach to integration is to create a character who acts as a source for speech commentary. This technique is used very effectively on a CD ROM used to promote Intel products. A cartoon character acts as a guide to the system. As 'it' speaks it often turns to look and point at the topic. The speech is, of course, interruptable. There is a unity to the system built around this speaking guide. Speech from other sources, e.g. video clips, fits naturally into this overall context.

There are situation where the use of speech is particularly advantageous. A classic example is an animated demonstration. If the user's visual attention is attracted to a demonstration it may not be a good idea to distract it with text descriptions. A good example is the interface 'guru' in the MoleHill system (described in Chapter 5). The guru explains interface features of the Smalltalk environment by providing animated demonstrations. During these demonstrations the guru provides commentary and explanations. While the demonstration shows actions, such as cursor movements and menu selections, the guru explains the meaning of what is happening. The commentary is used to enrich the learner's understanding of the demonstration. There is a powerful complementarity of speech and action. Used together they achieve what neither could easily achieve alone. The Smalltalk guru system is discussed in Chapter 5. A screen dump showing the interface guru is given in Figure 5.6.

Multimedia learning environments produce a particular problem in the relationship between text and speech. There are no definitive guidelines on how this relationship should be managed. Where speech and text overlap the speech may be used to give a brief description of the key points. The text may then provide more detail that the learner may choose to read. The needs of hearing impaired learners must also be kept in mind. Multimedia should not be used to shut off learning opportunities. Text can also provide a more permanent record. The user may initially pay attention to the speech message, for example, during an animated demonstration. A text message may provide a more permanent record of the important points being conveyed.

12.4 Digital video

Analogue video disks have been available as a resource for computer based learning for over a decade. This technology, however, had a limited impact. Video disk players are fairly large, the disks are expensive and the forms of integration with the computer are limited. There has been a major commercial thrust to produce commercial video on CD ROMs. Once video is digitised it can also be delivered on demand over high speed networks. Educational courseware can benefit from these significant commercial developments.

The desktop education market has benefited from a number of significant developments in technology. The development of CD ROMs provides a large capacity storage medium. Faster, more powerful computers have made the delivery of video on CD ROM a feasible proposition. Software tools for capturing and editing digital video are readily available, e.g. QuickTime and Video for Windows. There is a choice of hardware capture cards from the comparatively cheap through to expensive, high quality systems. Once captured, video clips can be imported into multimedia authoring tools. Each new release of these systems provides more sophisticated controls for managing and using video.

12.4.1 Digital video capture and integration

In order to incorporate digital video into a multimedia learning environment four steps are involved:

1. Create or locate the source material
2. Capture the video in the digital form
3. Edit the video (optional)
4. Integrate the video into a multimedia authoring environment.

Video source material is normally in analogue form. It needs to be converted to a digital format in order to be used as part of an interactive multimedia system. The quality of the digital end product will depend upon the quality of the source material. There are some technical issues that have a direct bearing on quality. Two basic issues are:

- the format of the analogue source material
- the conditions of shooting.

The conditions of the original recording determine the quality of the analogue source and hence the eventual digital quality. What is acceptable quality depends upon the intended audience and delivery conditions. The basic question is – will the video meet an educational need? If the delivery platform supports software only playback there is a limit to the quality which can be achieved.

The format of the analogue recording affects the quality. VHS is the standard for most home video recorders. This is generally not regarded as a good base for video capture. The minimum recommended standard is SVHS. This is particularly important if editing of the analogue tape is made. Analogue editing involves making a new copy of the tape. Quality in VHS systems drops markedly when copies are made. If higher quality tapes are required then industry standard systems such as Betacam SP should be used.

To capture the source video, special capture hardware is required for the computer. The video source (for example a VCR) is attached to the computer by a cable. The hardware on the card will capture the video source and save it as a digital file on the hard disk. A good capture card will compress the video as it is captured. The alternative is to capture the video directly and compress the file later. This is a longer and messier operation.

Digital video files have to be stored in a compressed format if they are to be useable. A raw video file contains so much information that the computer could not transfer it from the storage device to the screen quickly enough. For example, a standard computer screen at 640 × 480 resolution and 8 bit colour might need to be rewritten at up to thirty times per second. The resulting transfer of raw data would be enormous. It requires

$$640 \times 480 \times 8 \times 30 \text{ bits of information per second}$$

This amounts to over 70 megabits of information per second. With true 24 bit colour the number is increased threefold. The data transfer standard for a single speed CD ROM is 150 kilobits per seconds. Even by quadrupling transfer speeds, and quadrupling speeds again, the machine cannot read the data quickly enough to refresh the screen.

The answer to this problem is to compress the video file to a size that can be handled within the time constraints. A major effort has been put into finding suitable data compression methods. Different systems for compression have been developed. The choice between these systems depends upon a trade-off between quality and price. The option chosen depends upon the project budget and the target delivery situation. Two major systems that represent clear alternatives in price are:

- Indeo
- MPEG.

Indeo is a proprietory system developed by Intel. Capture cards such as the Intel Smart Video Recorder are reasonably priced. The price range is a few hundred dollars or pounds. The capture process may be controlled through the standard Video for Windows interface. This produces a standard file format that can be handled by multimedia authoring systems. Decompression and playback is software controlled. There is no need for any special playback hardware in any of the delivery computers. The software will also scale the quality of the playback to the capacity of the delivery computer. This makes the system quite flexible. If the system requires video in a window to be delivered on standard computers (i.e. with no special playback hardware) Indeo is a useful option to consider. The video sequences in the DOVE system are based on Indeo compression (Plate 5).

MPEG 1 is an industry wide standard. MPEG stands for Motion Pictures Expert Group. This group produced a standard for the compression and decompression of video under the aegis of the International Standards Organisation (ISO). This standard, MPEG 1, provides the basis for White Book Video CDs. This is the international standard for producing commercial film to be delivered on CDs. The quality of MPEG video is very good. Full screen, full motion video can be produced; the quality of the video is similar to, or better than, that produced by VHS tape. MPEG represents a high quality standard for digitised video.

To get the full benefit from MPEG compression the delivery machines require special playback hardware. This is normally in the form of a card that can be added to the computer. Digital video is a major area of commercial activity. There have been very rapid developments and progress will continue. To get the best price/quality trade-off it is necessary to keep up-to-date with developments. There is now a variety of magazines dealing with CD ROM and multimedia. These provide a good source for up-to-date information.

Setting parameters for digital video capture

The aim in capturing video is to achieve the best balance of file size (and hence performance) and image quality. This is achieved by setting the three parameters given in Table 12.1. These three sampling parameters are:

- sampling rate
- image depth
- frame size

The first two parameters are similar to the parameters for digital sound capture. They refer to how often a sample is taken and the precision of the measurement. For video, sampling rate is measured in frames per second. Sample precision is usually set at 8, 16 or 24 bit colour. The third parameter, frame size, refers to the size of the capture window.

NTSC, the American television standard, specifies a frame rate of 30 frames per second. The PAL standard used in most of Europe specifies 25 frames per second. At these frame rates we see full motion video. In order to produce an acceptable file size it may be necessary to reduce this sampling parameter. A rate of 15 frames per second is often adequate to obtain the effect of full motion. The exact choice of frame rate is affected by the video content. Video sequences involving fast movement require higher sampling rates than those involving slow movement or static scenes.

Table 12.1 Parameters for the digital capture of video

Frame rate	NTSC	PAL	Other
	30 fps	25 fps	<15 fps

Capture size	1/16 screen	1/4 screen	Full screen
	160 × 120 pixels	320 × 240 pixels	640 × 480 pixels

Image depth	8 bit	16 bit	24 bit
	256 colours	64 k colours	over 16 million

The image depth affects the clarity or resolution of the pictures. The selection here will be influenced by the quality of the delivery computers. There is no point selecting 24 bit colour if the delivery computer uses 8 bit colour. It is also possible to experiment. For small sample clips this variable can be changed and the effect on video quality can be observed. If there is little or no noticeable difference on the delivery computer there is no point in selecting a higher image resolution.

Frame size refers to the size of the capture window. In most multimedia learning environments video will be delivered in a window. As a general rule match the size of the capture window to the projected delivery window. There does not need to be an exact match. After capture the video frame size can be altered. Providing the alteration is not too large there will probably be no noticeable effect on image quality.

The capture process for digital video may be controlled through standard software utilities, such as QuickTime and Video for Windows. QuickTime was developed by Apple Computers as a standard utility for Macintosh computers. It was then ported to the PC. Video for Windows is supplied by Microsoft. The VidCap facility in this system provides an interface for digital video capture. These utilities allow one to select values on the parameters described in Table 12.1.

Multimedia authoring tools provide a range of facilities for managing video. The sophistication of these facilities can jump markedly with new system releases. It is always best to get the most recent version of the multimedia tool. ToolBook 3, for example, provided a marked improvement in video handling over ToolBook 1.53. These improvements included a simplified command set, a 'stage' object for displaying videos, and a management system for video clips and other media resources. Improved tools lead to a marked reduction in authoring time. There are also specialist video software editing programs, such as Adobe Premier and Digital Video Producer (Figure 12.5). These provide a range of video editing facilities.

12.4.2 Incorporating video into the multimedia system

Video provides a very powerful resource for learning. However, that very power can induce a comparatively passive mode of viewing. To obtain the full benefits of video for learning the video should be used as an active resource. The learners should not just view the video, they should *use* it. The use of video needs to be functionally integrated into the overall learning context. This integration should be realised by a screen layout that balances the impact on video with other objects on the screen.

Constructivists have argued strongly for the need for authentic learning experiences. Video clips can greatly enhance the authenticity of a computer based learning environment. This experience may be the central focus of the system, e.g. animal observation in DOVE. It may be an important additional resource that students cannot normally access. The CTGV group at Vanderbilt used video as a resource for embedding mathematical problems in real life situations. This technique could be further amplified within a computer based learning environment.

Video is a time based phenomenon. When it starts it 'takes the floor' and holds it.

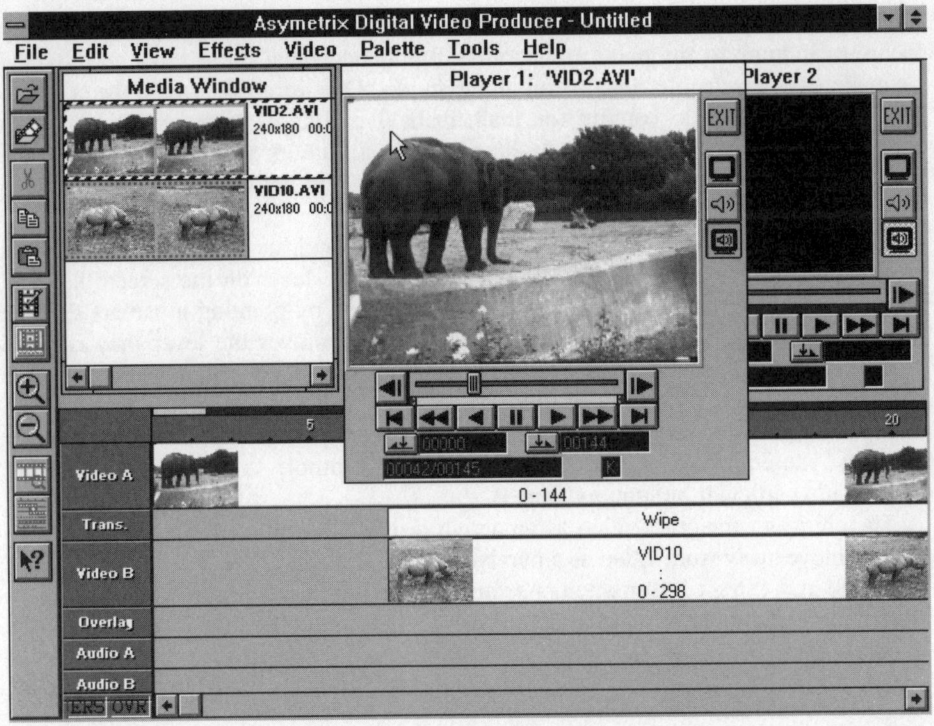

Figure 12.5 Video editing in Digital Video Producer

until it is finished. This aspect of video has to be handled carefully. Multimedia involves a balanced integration of many kinds of media objects. Video, however, is a multimedia experience in its own right. It has to be 'tamed' and reshaped to become a balanced component in interactive multimedia learning.

The first important step in this process is to give the user control over the video. The learner should be given the maximum amount of control consistent with the learning goals of the context. Video sequences should normally be interruptable. Learners should not be held in a time-trap by a video sequence over which they have no control. If a video is running and the user chooses to leave this screen the video should automatically stop. The user may be given direct control of the video. In DOVE the users are supplied with a full set of video controls (Plate 5).

Video should be treated as far as possible as a declarative resource. A 'declarative' resource is one that can be entered at a number of points and traversed in a number of ways. A map is a classical example of a graphic declarative resource. A procedural resource, by contrast, runs along a set path. Video is naturally a time based procedural phenomenon. In interactive multimedia this resource can be moved in a declarative direction. This involves breaking up the monolith of the video sequence. Technically the user can jump to any point in the video. But a conceptual frame must be provided to make this a sensible and useful thing to do. One example would be a video providing an authentic context for mathematical problems. It becomes natural to access this video in a highly flexible, active way. Faced with a particular problem the learner may jump to the relevant video segment. This active access may involve supplying tools to annotate the video.

The Cytofocus system developed by Roy Stringer and his colleagues illustrates a move in this direction (Plate 4). As the user moves the lever on the screen they can adjust the focus on the slide. This effect was achieved by pointing a camera down a microscope as the focus was adjusted. When the user moves the lever they run this video sequence. The video has become a manipulable object under user control as opposed to a passive procedural display. Many users may not even realise that they are manipulating a video sequence. The 'focus pull' technique has been extended to other domains. The circles on the view of Liverpool, for example, are hotspots that trigger zooms onto particular buildings (Plate 3).

The ability to integrate video as an active resource has immense possibilities. We need to move away from video as a purely procedural display. We need tools to access the video and extract information. As this process progresses video will come to be treated more and more as a declarative resource that can be flexibly accessed and used in many ways.

12.5 Summary

This part of the book has discussed the issues involved in presentation design. The basic characteristics of perception were reviewed and composition principles for holistic design outlined. These principles ensure unity and harmony across the presentation of the system. Visual balance and visual flow help to guide the design of individual screens. The design of the individual media components should fit into this harmonious framework.

Tools are used to shape and integrate the media materials. The multimedia toolset can be represented on a series of layers. These layers move from hardware platform up to high level authoring tools. A number of themes were discussed to help guide the choice of tools in this rapidly developing area.

Much of the time in a multimedia project involves the design of the individual media elements and their integration into the system. Principles from the traditional disciplines dealing with text, graphics and video can help inform design decisions. These guidelines need to be re-examined, however, in the new multimedia context. New issues of media integration and complementarity emerge. The ability to act on objects in a highly flexible way opens up opportunities and challenges. The interplay of received wisdom and the new challenges pushes the development of new aesthetics for multimedia composition.

Part Four

Project development, evaluation and delivery

In dreams begins responsibility

quoted by W. B Yeats at the start of his book of poems *Responsibilities*

Chapter 13

Project development

13.1 Introduction

In problem solving we abstract out certain patterns. We then use these abstract frameworks to make sense of, and impose order on, the flux of our experience. We carve experience into categories and say this is how it is, or this is how it should be. When applied to project development the results of such an analysis are often labelled a 'method' that gives prescriptive guidance on how things should be done. There is, however, an inherent tension between prescription and creativity. Kommers has argued that good multimedia designers are 'green-fingered' (Kommers 1993). Prescriptive methods may hinder this creativity. Methods and techniques may be regarded, however, not as prescriptions but as resources for action. The ultimate choice of which resources to use is made by the local design group. To make an informed choice we need a review of the resources available, and heuristics for guiding choice. This chapter (and the remaining chapters in this part of the book) provide a review of this area.

The designer needs to think about the nature of the project in making the choice of methods. Projects differ significantly in scope, setting and what counts as success. At one end of the range there are commercial projects where there is a contractual relationship between supplier and customer. The customer may be the end user of the product, or may be a multimedia publisher. In this commercial setting the emphasis is likely to be upon a fairly tight specification of project objectives. There is usually (though by no means always) a structured methodology to guide and control the process of project development. In many educational settings there is an emphasis on using multimedia in innovative ways in teaching and learning. The form of the project will depend on how the nature of this innovation is envisaged. Such projects require a balance that will support innovation while still producing a workable product in the end. Research projects emphasise innovation as a primary objective. Prototypes simply represent implementations of interesting techniques.

All projects have to deal with the functions of analysis, design, evaluation and implementation. For each design team there is a need to review the options for project management and to select the configuration that best suits local needs and preferences. In making this choice there are a number of issues which need to be addressed. Some of these issues are as follows:

1. What is the overall management framework of the project?
2. How is the specification of the system to be represented?
3. How are design ideas captured and communicated?
4. What is the role of evaluation in project development and delivery?
5. Which parallel activities in design and development can be identified so that the group can work more effectively?
6. How is the project to be signed off and delivered?

The issues of evaluation and delivery are dealt with in the following chapters. The present chapter deals with the other significant issues. The first question is how to structure the overall management of the project.

13.2 The structure of project development

In this section two contrasting approaches to project management will be outlined. These approaches highlight the major functions that have to be addressed, and the dynamic relationship between them. The first approach is the classic Waterfall representation of project functions. The second approach is one of iterative prototyping.

13.2.1 The Waterfall method

The Waterfall method represents a highly structured approach to project development. Its purity of representation marks out clearly and sharply the main phases in the project. It represents in a very strong form the 'plan before you do' approach. This method is illustrated in Figure 13.1. This visual representation shows how it got its name. This approach divides project development into a number of distinct phases. Each phase has a clearly defined output. This output provides the input to the next development phase. The function of the first phase, analysis, is to produce a specification of the new system. This states what the new system should do, but it is

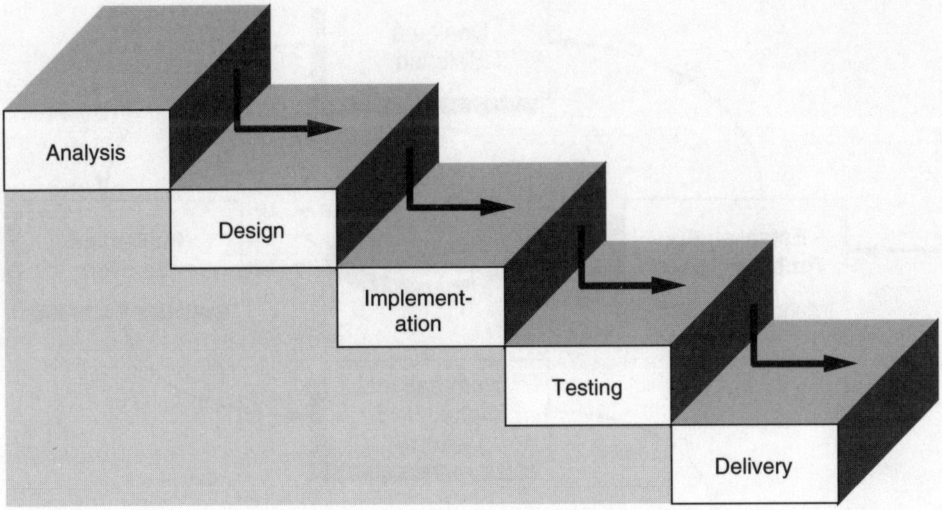

Figure 13.1 The Waterfall approach

not concerned with how this is accomplished. The design stage has to translate the requirements into a (paper based) design of the system. A team of programmers then takes this design and implements it as code. This code is thoroughly tested to verify that it works correctly, conforms to the design, and meets the requirements. Finally the system is handed over to go 'live'.

In this approach the major functions of software development are represented as distinct phases. Each phase produces an output. This output needs to be validated to check that it is correct. Each of the phases has an associated set of specialist tools and techniques. In the analysis phase, for example, data-flow diagrams are used to provide pictorial representations of the analysis of the old system and specification of the new.

There have been many criticisms of this approach. The major criticism is that it is much too rigid. For many software projects it is not possible to specify the objectives in detail until the problem has been explored more fully. Exploring the problem involves building a prototype, showing it to users, and using this prototype to refine the specifications. In building multimedia systems we normally need this more dynamic approach. There are, however, certain salient points that may be carried over from the traditional Waterfall method. The emphasis upon distinct forms of representation for the output of each major function and, in particular, the distinction between design and implementation are significant points. There is also a strong

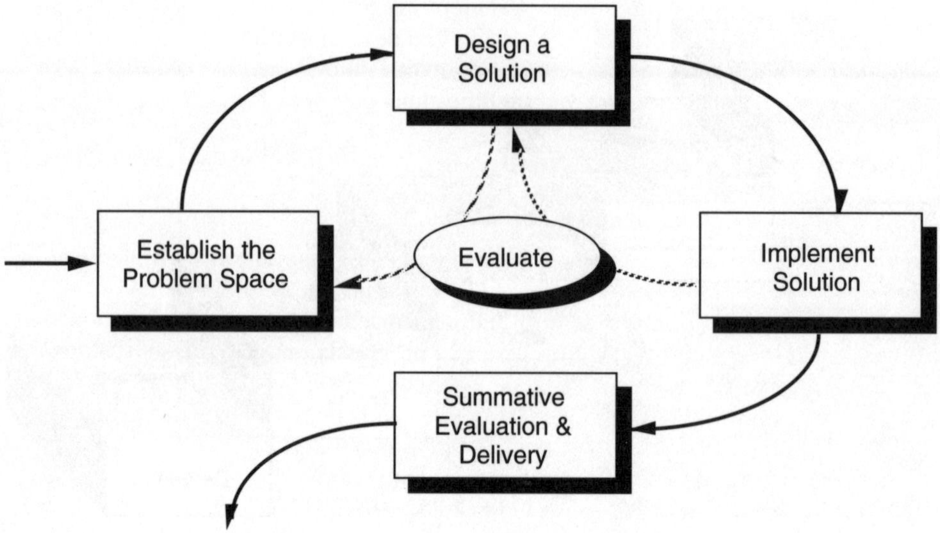

Figure 13.2 Iterative prototyping

emphasis upon validation – the design of the system should be validated against the requirements. Finally there is a strong emphasis upon delivery, e.g. training staff, ensuring a correct delivery infrastructure, and managing the hand-over period. These are useful lessons for multimedia projects.

13.2.2 Iterative prototyping

The most natural form of project development of multimedia systems is iterative prototyping. Iterative prototyping supports an interleaved rather than a linear form of project development. Prototyping allows the team to visualise and evaluate system possibilities. This allows a more 'situated' approach to analysis and design.

Prototyping supports two major forms of interleaving in project development. The function of early prototypes may be to refine the objectives of the system. The prototypes become an object of communication between the designer and the users. It helps the users to decide what they would really like. Requirements become clarified in the light of the design possibilities. Misconceptions between the designer and the clients should also come to light at this stage. Prototypes support *multimedia communication* as part of the negotiations in project development. Commercial customers may demand that this process is incorporated in the project as the production of a 'demonstrator'. The evaluation of this demonstrator provides the basis for clarifying the specification of the system or even whether the project proceeds or not. In the later stages of the project, prototype development supports the mapping from design to implementation. The prototypes allow one to visualise design possibilities, e.g. colour schemes and modifications of screen layouts. The evaluation feeds back to guide design decisions.

The Waterfall approach is basically a linear approach to project development. One block of work is completed before proceeding to the next. Exhortations in the literature to the effect that it is never quite like this abound, but the model does not formally deal with these non-linear decisions (i.e. clarifying objectives in the light of design exploration). The iterative prototyping approach, by contrast, is more of a spiral model (Figure 13.2). Our knowledge of requirements, design and implementation may be incomplete in any one cycle. But there is a progressive building up of a structure which will lead to the completed system. The requirements of the system will be the first to be filled out. Prototype design structures that help clarify the requirements can then be filled out into a more complete system architecture. Finally, the details required for robust use, e.g. error trapping and removal, are implemented. The iterative prototyping approach retains the major system development functions and the broad order in which they are satisfied. But it presents a much more flexible, interleaved model for attaining these ends.

13.3 The Dynamic Systems Development Method (DSDM)

13.3.1 Background

Flexible methods of project development based upon iterative prototyping have become increasingly popular in commercial software development. Collectively these are known as RAD (Rapid Application Development) methods. These methods were developed in reaction to the perceived limitations and rigidities of established variants on the Waterfall approach. These traditional methods force users to fix their requirements early in the project and then wait for the system to be delivered several months (or even years) later. RAD methods are characterised by user-driven iterative prototyping. There is an emphasis on coverging on a system to meet business requirements rather than following a pre-set procedures. In 1995 a standard non-proprietary RAD method was introduced called the Dynamic Systems Development Method (DSDM). This is supported by a consortium of nearly 100 companies. The manual produced by this consortium defines DSDM as a method that 'provides a framework for building and maintaining systems which meet tight time constraints through the use of incremental prototyping in a controlled project environment' (DSDM 1995, p. 15). The emphasis on attaining the right balance between creative freedom and project control matches well the needs of multimedia projects.

Mortimer (1995) describes DSDM as a toolkit rather than a cookbook. A cookbook provides a set of recipes that, if followed correctly, in principle guarantees a correct product. A toolkit, by contrast, provides a set of tools and techniques that are applied to meet the needs of individual situations. The essence of this approach is that there must be sufficient guidance without undue constraint. DSDM seeks to achieve this by providing a set of principles, a framework for project development, and a set of supporting techniques.

13.3.2 DSDM principles

The DSDM manual gives a set of nine principles (DSDM 1995). There are three central principles which define the essence of the method:

1. The use of iterative prototyping
2. A high degree of active user involvement, i.e. the user should be part of the design team
3. A product-oriented rather than a process-oriented ethos.

The principles are interrelated. Iterative and incremental development lead to convergence on a correct 'business' solution. The business or educational solution is not the same as the 'flashy' multimedia solution. The achievement of this target is heavily dependent upon the second critical factor – a high degree of active user involvement. When prototypes are assessed it is the users who provide the critical assessment information. The form of the evolving prototype is shaped to meet the needs conveyed by the users. The system develops through a set of incremental prototypes which *converge* on the system that really meets the users' requirements. This pattern of development differs decisively from traditional approaches that demand a detailed specification of requirements before design commences.

The other DSDM principles support this dynamic approach. Initial requirements are settled at a high level. This statement of requirements defines the purpose and general scope of the system. More detailed requirements can be investigated and specified at later stages in the project. The design team must be empowered to make decisions on these detailed functional targets. Incremental development depends on frequent prototype evaluation, and thus testing is integrated throughout the life cycle. All changes during development should be reversible. If one line of development is not working the team ought to be able to backtrack and try another. This requires good configuration management. Earlier prototypes need to be stored with a clear version control system in place. To make this dynamic approach work a collaborative and co-operative approach between all stakeholders is essential.

13.3.3 The DSDM project life cycle

There are four main phases in the DSDM life cycle. These stages provide the broad structure of project development, though there is fair degree of flexibility in moving between them. The four phases are:

1. Feasibility and 'business' study
2. Functional prototype iterations
3. Design prototype iterations
4. Implementation.

The main aim of the feasibility/business study is to define the high level functional requirements of the system. Functional requirements refer to the business (educational) requirements the system should satisfy. This phase should also produce an outline prototyping plan and establish the main non-functional requirements, e.g. the hardware required to deliver the system. The DSDM manual states that this phase should only take a few weeks. This is because the detailed functional requirements are clarified during the development of the project.

The main part of the project consists of two prototyping phases. The main aim of the 'functional prototype iteration' phase is to clarify the detailed requirements for the system. The output of this phase is a prototype that demonstrates the main functionality of the system. This is a radical departure from traditional approaches where requirements are specified on paper before software development takes place. It is an approach well suited to multimedia projects using powerful authoring tools. The advantage of this approach is that the visual prototypes support the creation of a deep understanding between designer and user. The user gradually understands what can be achieved with the technology. This permits the creation of a *new* solution that effectively exploits the technology, rather than a computerised version of the old way of doing things.

The aim of the next phase is to refine the functional prototype into a robust product. This involves satisfying all the non-functional requirements, i.e. producing a system that will work effectively on the target hardware in the organisational setting. There is not a sharp division between the first two phases. They have distinct functions, but the exact configuration of the project to satisfy these functions is decided by the design team. The default project plan provides a standard way to structure the life cycle. The DSDM manual makes it clear that this phase order is not mandated, 'and it is expected to be tailored to meet the requirements of a particular product' (DSDM 1995, p. 31).

All the components of the system do not have to be developed in unison. Some parts may move on to the design and build phase while others are still at the functional clarification stage. The imperative of producing a product within the schedule provides the overriding criterion for how the work is pursued.

The implementation phase involves placing the system in the user environment, carrying out any required training, reviewing the system and assessing further developments. The output of this phase is a delivered system, user manuals and a project review document. Where required there will also be a trained user population.

13.3.4 Time boxing

DSDM offers a number of techniques to facilitate project development and control. 'Time boxing' emphasises setting sharp time boundaries for deliverables. This requires a clear prioritisation of the deliverables for a given period. Items must be classified as essential or desirable. The critical requirement is to deliver the prototype in time. The deadline should not be missed but rather the deliverables simplified, i.e. desirable but non-essential features are left out. This imposes a discipline on the development team. A range of supporting techniques is discussed in the manual (DSDM 1995). DSDM, however, is fairly eclectic. It is prepared to assimilate a variety of techniques providing they fit within the framework of fast, disciplined delivery of prototypes leading to a final product.

RAD and DSDM have emerged from mainstream commercial software development (e.g. Mortimer 1995). DSDM may need to be tailored to meet the needs of multimedia educational projects. The ethos of DSDM, however, encourages such flexible adaptation to suit particular circumstances. The remaining sections in this chapter explore some of the more specific issues to be resolved in IMLE development.

13.4 Analysis and the specification of objectives

13.4.1 Specifying the nature of the problem

The first major task in project development is to analyse the nature of the problem and plan the project. This task is given different names by different authors. This reflects not just a difference in terminology, but different perspectives. These different perspectives are derived from distinct lines of approach. In traditional software engineering this is referred to as the analysis phase. Vaughan (1994), a commercial multimedia designer, refers to this as the 'planning' phase. Laurillard (1993), an educationalist, calls it 'the definition of objectives and analysis of student needs'. All of these approaches intersect on the need to clarify objectives. The degree to which the objectives are more or less fully specified, and the supporting activities emphasised, varies depending on the perspective adopted. Two contrasting approaches are reviewed in this section – those represented by Laurillard (1993) and Vaughan (1994). They represent the extremes that may be accommodated within an iterative prototyping approach.

A particularly strong and clear expression of the activities at this stage is given by Laurillard (1993). She argues that the production of a clear set of educational objectives at the start of a project is crucial. On this point she echoes the emphasis of traditional Computer Aided Instruction. This assertion provides a good starting point for the discussion of the activities required at this stage.

Laurillard proposes two major activities that feed into the specification of objectives. The first is a statement of the perceived requirements for a course in a particular area. This will be specified by an expert in that subject area. This analysis is primarily curriculum based. The initial broad aim has to be broken down into objectives that are:

- precise
- necessary
- complete.

Each objective should be stated precisely so that it can be clearly agreed when the student has achieved this objective. The objective should be necessary to achieve the aim, and the achievement of all the objectives should be enough to satisfy the aim. These objectives specify the appropriate outcomes, i.e. knowledge and skills in certain content areas, for students taking the course. The objectives should specify outcomes that are measurable. The success of the project can then be decided by measuring how well the outcomes have been achieved.

The curriculum derived objectives specify where the students should be at the end of the course. The second main activity is to assess where the students are now, i.e. the students' conceptions and skills at the beginning of the course. Laurillard focuses on the problems and misconceptions the students may have. She suggests a range of techniques, including tests, assignments and interviews to reveal the problems students have in tackling the subject. The research literature for particular subject areas may also be illuminating. Having clarified the target attainment and the students' problems the educationalist is now in a position to design the learning materials.

Vaughan (1994), a commercial multimedia designer, paints a rather different picture of this phase. For Vaughan, in the beginning is the inspiration. The initial idea may spring from a variety of sources. The designer may think of a new way to do something. A customer may identify an interesting problem. Once the idea is conceived it acts as the seed for subsequent developments. Vaughan quotes the example of a few notes scribbled on a table napkin that provided the starting point for a major instructional project. The process of developing the idea involved meetings to discuss and refine the idea. The interest from the customer meant that the resources for developing the idea further were made available. A prototype was constructed to clarify what was involved. Examination of this prototype provided a much sharper idea of the direction, scale and feasibility of the project. The objectives of the project, for Vaughan, are thus something that evolve from an initial inspiration. There may be a considerable amount of work in developing the initial idea into a specification of the objectives for a project.

Vaughan recommends the use of a feasibility phase before the objectives are finalised. This may involve building a skeletal version of the system. The demonstration of this prototype helps clients to clarify what is really required. A number of factors crucial to the success of the project can be pre-tested. The designer can test, for example, whether a particular authoring system and hardware platform will deliver the required performance. Estimates of the storage space required for media such as sound and video can be made. The formative assessment derived from the examination of this skeleton system leads to a clarification of a number of analytic issues. The statement of objectives and supporting information for project management can be finalised as a result of the information obtained.

Laurillard and Vaughan give rather different views of the analysis phase. Laurillard emphasises the statement of educational objectives. Vaughan indicates that this is not enough. A multimedia artefact has to be created in an area of fast moving technology. The educational objectives have to be mapped onto the possibilities and constraints of this technology. It is very difficult to do this in a purely abstract fashion. We cannot easily finalise the objectives without having some visualisation or idea of the design. We need to explore implementation issues to ensure that the project is feasible. The construction of the problem to be solved is itself a creative act. This creative act arises out of the interplay between inspiration and the formalisms which discipline and give shape to the project.

13.4.2 Activities for analysis and project planning

There are a number of important activities at this stage in addition to the elucidation of objectives. A *plan* for the project activities must be produced. The objectives need to be mapped onto a schedule. This provides the planing framework for the project. Progress in project development can be measured against the milestones set out in this schedule. Warning signs of project drift can be detected at an early stage. Failure to do this causes significant problems later on. Gantt charts provide a useful tool for representing this time based information. Parallel activities can be represented and key milestones identified. These can be produced in software management tools such as Microsoft Project.

The *resources* required for developing the project must be identified. This involves identifying both the personnel and the hardware and software tools required. We need to ensure that these are available or can be obtained. This may involve exploratory work. For example, if there is a promising new software tool we may need to gather information and assess its usefulness at this stage.

We need to consider carefully the *delivery* platform and environment. The delivery issues will vary depending on whether we are delivering a product for an open market or a system tailored to a particular environment. For a standard packaged system we need to specify the delivery platform. The higher the specification the narrower the delivery base. For a system aimed at a particular environment the delivery conditions need to be thought through more clearly. For example, when we developed the CLEM system (described in Chapter 5) a key issue was to ensure an adequate delivery environment. Our aim was to use the system with over 200 students on a sustained basis. There was a lab of PCs for teaching first year programming, but the machines were not powerful enough to deliver the system envisaged. A proposal was put to the department and the lab was upgraded at a significant cost. The expense was justified because the project was aiming to introduce new educational technology. In many other cases the project has to be tailored to fit the delivery constraints.

The final requirement is to produce a *costing* for the project. Spreadsheets provide a useful tool for detailed calculations. The planning activities of this phase are not always the most exciting but they are crucial. They represent the project specification. It is against this framework that we can be held accountable by commercial clients or public funding bodies.

13.5 The capture and communication of design concepts

I have forgotten the word I intended to say, and my thought, unembodied returns to the realm of shadows.

Mandelstam, quoted in Vygotsky (1962)

A considerable portion of this book has been devoted to discussing design. The aim of this section is to focus on the specific issue of how to capture, represent and communicate design ideas. We examine first the requirements for a good design notation. This provides the basis for a discussion of methods for representing design concepts.

There are a number of features which are desirable in a good design notation:

1. Ease of capture of design insights
2. Ease and accuracy of communication
3. Representational power
4. Scalable precision of representation
5. Preferably supporting both formal and informal representations.

When we have a sudden idea we need to capture the inspiration in a quick and easy fashion. The capture tool should not impede the expression of the idea. We don't want to be running to find a computer. The tool should allow quick, 'messy' presentation. We should be able to clean up the presentation later in order to communicate the idea to other team members or even clients. It has to have sufficient representational power to capture the idea at the level of precision we want. We want it to be economical, i.e. fairly transparent to use. We don't want a ten ton spanner that would do the job if only

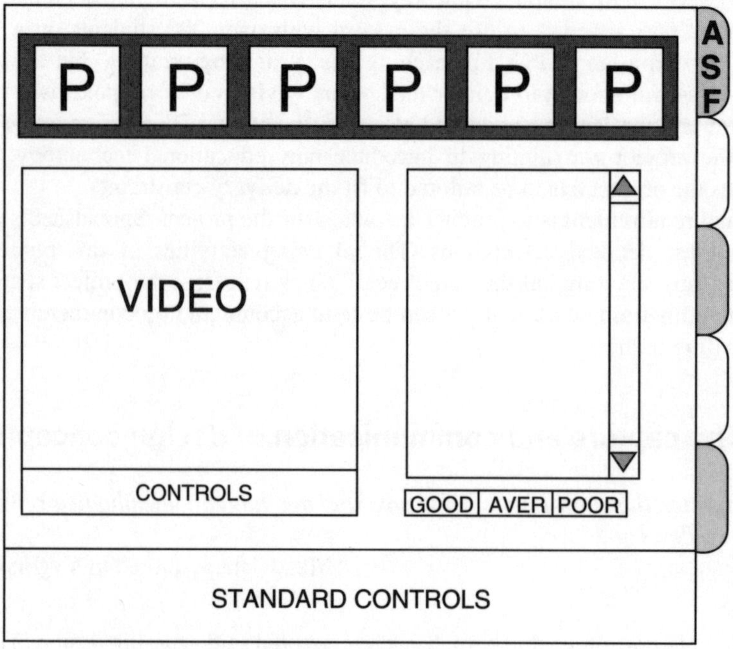

Figure 13.3 A storyboard for a multimedia screen

we could lift it. Finally, if it can support the transition from informal ideas to more formal representations this would be a big bonus.

There are two major aspects of the design that need to be represented. Design ideas about the form and appearance of the system need to be captured. We also need to represent the navigational and control structures for the learner. These are normally represented by two different forms of notation.

Storyboarding is a simple and powerful method for capturing ideas about the form and appearance of the system. This technique is derived from film and video production. In planning a scene a storyboard is created representing the different shots that will be linked together to form the scene. This provides a cartoon-like representation of the structure of the scene. This technique carries over well to multimedia design. A line drawing can identify the main features of one screen. This screen can be drawn at the chosen level of precision. A series of drawings can illustrate the links and transitions between screens. Storyboard pictures are drawn in outline form, as illustrated in Figure 13.3. Figures 9.4 and 9.5 are also in the outline format used for storyboards. The drawings usually have annotations to indicate the functions of the various elements. At early stages of development they may be considerably rougher than the neat outlines of these figures.

Storyboarding supports scalable levels of precision. This makes it a very flexible tool. You can provide a basic outline sketch or fill out the details to develop a fairly formal representation of the system. Storyboards can be drawn on paper or produced on the computer. These storyboard screens may be produced using the same multimedia authoring tool used to develop the prototype. The computer based storyboards may be filled out to become components of the system prototype. There is thus a blurring of the distinction between storyboard and prototype proper. This may offend people with a preference for formal divisions, but it can work nicely in dynamic design and production.

The representation of the navigation structure of the system can be more tricky. Hierarchical and linear structures are easily represented as 'structure charts'. Hypermedia technology, however, supports very flexible navigation through a system. To try to represent the hypermedia control flow on paper may be more of a hindrance than a help. A multimedia system, however, should have a clear conceptual structure. The navigation structure depends on this 'driving vision' for the system – the context or metaphor used to impose coherence. The stronger this is, the simpler and clearer will be the representation of the navigation options.

A second approach to representing navigation options is to annotate the cards in a storyboard. A drawing of the proposed controls can be annotated to indicate the nature of the links. In electronic book systems, for example, standard buttons are often provided for the functions – 'page forward', 'page back', 'jump to contents page' and 'backtrack'. Specific hotspots on the storyboard frame can be annotated with the link destination. The combined use of storyboard annotations and structure charts can provide a powerful and flexible way of representing navigation options.

13.6 Obtaining multimedia content

Producing and editing content in parallel to developing the interface is often the most efficient way to proceed. This parallel production needs to be planned at an early stage. This should produce a schedule showing the interrelationships between these activities, and the milestones for integrating the system. In some systems the content is available at the beginning of the project. Even in these systems a considerable amount of work is required in capturing, retouching and editing the source material.

Content may be gathered in four main ways:

1. Produced by members of the project team
2. Acquired from sources internally available to the team
3. Acquired from the public domain
4. Acquired through clearance of copyright material.

If one of these options for action is blocked then another option may have to be followed. An example is the Carnival des Animaux CD ROM. At a conference in Moscow Richard Millwood gave a few of us an informal demonstration of the system. I asked him why they had used MIDI (Musical Instrument Digital Interface) files for the music. I thought it might have something to do with saving space. Richard replied that the main reason was the difficulty of getting copyright clearance. They had a member of the group who was skilled in MIDI. So he created a MIDI version of Saint Saens's 'Carnival des Animaux'. We are not all fortunate enough to have MIDI wizards in our group, but there are usually people with particular talents whose skills can be productively used.

The DOVE system provides an example of a contribution to a project from an internal source. We developed this project in collaboration with the biology department at our university. The project involved creating a virtual environment for the observation of animal behaviour. They had a number of videos illustrating aspects of animal behaviour. These provided the bedrock content for the first phase of the project. As the project developed the need for video clips grew. Some videos were then recorded specifically for the project. As the system grew we then approached copyright holders for permission to use their material.

There is a range of public domain resources. Authoring tools often have small attached libraries of content and programming resources. Clip art and clip music CD ROMs provide media that may be reused in multimedia productions. You need to check carefully the conditions stated for reuse to ensure they match your requirements. You may 'surf' the Internet for available resources. However, you need to check that the material is public domain, and also that you have the right to reuse it in your work.

13.6.1 Dealing with copyright

The next option is to obtain clearance for the use of copyright material. Gaining copyright clearance can become very complex and time consuming. Dickens and Sherwood-Edwards (1993) point out that copyright clearance for just one piece of music could involve multiple rights holders with international variations in how those rights applied. Certain institutions, such as the Open University in England, have Rights Departments to deal with these issues. Many multimedia developers do not have this type of administrative support. There is a further complication with multimedia production. The developer may not simply want to reproduce a media element. He may want to 're-purpose' it, i.e. modify it to achieve a new effect or to fit better into the new multimedia gestalt. In a sense this is what we have always done with written materials. The legal framework for applying re-purposing to other media materials, however, is by no means clear.

Given these problems in cost, complexity and re-purposing how can one proceed? There are two basic levels in answering this problem: immediate practical steps, and the development of schemes that will remove much of the burden from the individual.

The various options for acquiring content were outlined earlier in this section. One option is to avoid having to acquire copyright material. Richard Millwood recounts a rather dramatic example. In some cases a proposed line of development may have to be abandoned if the cost becomes too great. Joel Greenberg, speaking at Ed Media '94, described the attempt by the Open University to convert one course from print based to an electronic format. This required renegotiation of clearance rights with all the copyright holders since they had clearance for only hard copy reproduction. When the cost became too great this particular project was shelved.

Practical advice on how to proceed to gain copyright clearance is contained in a pamphlet produced for the Teaching and Learning Technology Programme in Britain (TLTP 1994). This has practical advice and sample letters that may be sent out. Vaughan (1994) provides an overview from an American perspective. There are also several advice points on the Internet.

The present copyright situation clearly need to be improved for the benefit of both media providers and consumers. Two ways forward will be discussed. The first approach, collective licensing schemes, is an approach that has already been successfully applied in other areas. The second prospect is a proposal by Ted Nelson for what comes close to copyright heaven.

Collective licensing schemes are seen by many as the way forward (e.g. Dickens and Sherwood-Edwards 1993). There are problems in setting up these schemes. The comments of representatives of rights holders at conferences exploring his theme are indicative of one problem. These representatives see great opportunities in the new media. However, they are worried about the ramifications of distribution over new media that they do not fully understand. Licences for networked use have proved a particularly difficult point. However, there are clear advantages for all concerned in a 'one stop' shopping system. Rights organisations would hold the clearance rights for whole areas of media resources. They would act as a shop for anyone wanting to gain clearance rights for the material they covered. This greatly facilitates the setting of national licensing schemes. In this approach a payment is made to cover a whole community of users (e.g. all schools or universities in a country). Problems remain, e.g. the distinction between educational use and commercial reuse. But this approach seems a promising way forward.

New problems in new opportunity spaces might best be resolved through new thinking. Ted Nelson has produced an attractive idea for solving the problem. He is concerned with networked publishing and the problem of copyright. He has put forward the vision of open publishing based on the idea of 'transclusive copyright'. The idea is that anyone could use material or resources on the Internet. There will be no copyright barrier to publication (Nelson 1994). When the new artefact is used commercially a small payment is made automatically to the original producer of the material. This is possible because the 'new' material contains an embedded pointer to the original source material. Nelson has argued that this is technically feasible. The beauty of this system is that it frees developers to be as creative as they want with a vast range of media resources. A payment is only made if the new system is successful. Then everyone benefits. It is rather like an automatic, technologically managed royalty system.

13.7 Summary

There is a tension in multimedia projects between creativity and control. Getting the right balance is essential for effective project development. Iterative prototyping provides a flexible framework for multimedia projects. DSDM provides an approach to project development based on iterative prototyping and a high degree of user involvement. This approach provides a useful method that can be tailored to meet the needs of individual projects.

At the early stage of project planning certain issues must be considered. These involve the specification of objectives, drawing up a schedule, ensuring that the resources required will be available, and costing the project. These issues may not be the most exciting in multimedia development. They are, however, essential for effective project control.

Storyboarding and structure charts provide methods for capturing and representing design ideas. They can be used to visualise both screen layouts and the overall navigation of the system. The multimedia elements to be included as components of the system may be obtained or developed in parallel. Copyright clearance is an area that requires special attention.

Evaluation and delivery are crucial aspects of project development These two areas are dealt with in the following two chapters.

Chapter 14

Evaluation

14.1 Introduction

Evaluation is interleaved throughout the development process, and the nature of the evaluation will vary depending on the phase of the project life cycle. It is conventional to divide evaluation into two types:

- formative
- summative.

Formative evaluation is carried out during the development of the system. The information obtained is fed back to influence on-going development. Summative evaluation is conducted at the completion of the system. It tells us whether the system has succeeded in its overall aim. Both formative and summative phases evaluate the effectiveness and usability of the system. The effectiveness of the system depends on whether it achieves its learning objectives. Usability refers to the ease of learning and ease of use. These factors are crucial if the system is to operate as an effective learning environment.

Evaluation methods yield two broad types of information – qualitative and quantitative. Qualitative evaluation provides rich information that is especially useful for shaping design. Quantitative information gives hard figures based on systematic sampling. This provides a more objective measure, but the information may lack the richness of insight provided by qualitative information. In many cases a judicious mixture of the two types of information will provide the best overall insight.

The chapter begins with a discussion of strategic perspectives on evaluation. There is no absolute criterion for what counts as good evaluation. The evaluation framework is selected to suit the purpose of the project, and to satisfy the legitimate demands of different interest groups. Several methods for collecting evaluation data are then reviewed. A description of each technique is followed by comments on its relative advantages and disadvantages. The principal techniques discussed are: observation, interviews and questionnaires. The choice of an appropriate range of methods should provide information that supports both formative and summative evaluation.

14.2 Strategic views of evaluation

There are different strategic views of evaluation. In educational institutions the successful completion of courses is assessed through formal procedures such as assignments and examinations. These procedures are used to validate the 'products' of the institutions for the wider society. The first approach to evaluating IMLEs adopts this framework. The success of IMLEs should be measured by objective measures of attainment in the domain. This approach may involve a proper comparative evaluation with a control group. It should be shown on tests of competence independent of the learning situation that the IMLE students do better than the control group.

The radical contructivist theorists have attacked this approach. They argue instead for what they term 'authentic assessment' strategies (e.g. Grabinger and Dunlap 1995). The contructivists believe that learning should be based on tackling authentic tasks in context. This tends to change the focus on what is learned, and the view of how this learning should be assessed. The contructivists emphasise *processes* such as analysis, reflection, co-operation and communication. They argue that these active skills can only be assessed in context (Cunningham 1991, Grabinger and Dunlap 1995). These assessments will most likely be conducted by the teacher in the learning context and they may involve subjective judgement.

Given this sharp divergence between 'authentic' and formal evaluation, which approach to evaluation should be adopted? To answer that question we must first look at the perspectives of the different interested parties. There are three main groups with an interest in evaluation:

- designers
- managers and funding agencies
- users.

There are many forms of evaluation. The form of evaluation adopted depends upon the purpose of the system and the relative input of the interested parties.

Designers are primarily interested in evaluative feedback that helps improve design. To a certain extent the distinction between formative and summative evaluation becomes artificial. All evaluation feeds back to influence design practice. Projects, however, have to be funded, and implementations affect users. Designers are therefore sensitive to the forms of evaluation that are central for these other two groups.

Managers are nervous about innovations that may fail. They want more 'objective' measures of success. These measures may include recordings of improvements in learning (e.g. test scores) or in efficiency (delivering the same material while using less staff resources). Managers and funding agencies are more likely to think in cost–benefit terms (e.g. MacFarlane 1992, Appendix D). They want to know whether the output achieved justifies the cost. In order to make these judgements they want clear quantified measures of success.

The end users are most likely to be concerned with whether the system helps them achieve their goals. This will be strongly influenced by the assessment regime in place. As long as traditional assessment measures are in place end users will judge IMLEs in relation to this framework. Broader issues of usability and acceptability are also important. These areas have been extensively explored in the HCI (human computer interaction) literature.

The evaluation regime adopted should meet the needs of the interested parties in a cost effective way. The following sections examine a range of evaluation methods. Each method is discussed in terms of the costs and benefits involved. An effective evaluation regime is likely to involve the use of more than one of these methods. The appropriate mix often produces the best results.

14.3 Observation

The most direct way to gather data for evaluation is observation. In formative evaluation the user is observed working with prototypes or mock-ups of the system. The designer can check whether the user performs on the system as expected. Problems can thus be detected early and rectified.

Observation can be conducted in an informal or a highly structured way. In structured observation a set of tasks is set and the performance of the users is observed. A check list of points for observation may be drawn up beforehand. The performance of the user on the system is recorded against this check list. Informal observation in the field is often conducted to assess system acceptability. This is a useful general check. The reporting of results from this form of observation, however, is often rather vague. Norman and Spohrer (1996) comment that the assessment of too many studies relies on reports that teachers and students 'liked the system'.

The recording of observations can vary along a cline of sophistication. The simplest form of recording is noting events using pencil and paper. More sophisticated analysis can be conducted if a video record is made. Two cameras may be used. One camera is pointed at the user; the second records what is happening on the screen. The second camera may not be necessary if computer logging of the user's actions is made. Thorough analysis of this data, however, can be very time consuming. Preece (1993) quotes a ratio of 5:1 relating analysis time to recording time. For many systems this cost is too high. The form of recording should be selected that best suits the type and cost of the system being developed.

The main advantages of using observation for evaluation are that it:

- provides direct evidence of system effectiveness and usability
- is easy to use informally
- can be applied as a structured technique with sophisticated recording of behaviour.

The disadvantages include:

- the information provided relates to surface behaviour
- more sophisticated recording leads to high transcription and analysis overheads.

The most effective information is often obtained when observation is used in tandem with interviews.

14.4 Interviews

Interviews are a useful way to gain a rich understanding of users' reactions to a system. This information is particularly important during formative evaluation. In order to get the maximum benefit from interviews they should be clearly planned, and they may need to be linked to other forms of data collection.

It is difficult to ensure that the small sample used for interviews is typical of the user population. Subjects in the extreme of the population should be included, e.g. strong and weak students, as well as representatives of the mainstream. Given that there is a fixed time available for interviews some degree of trade-off is possible between sample size and interview time. By shortening the interview more subjects may be covered. Newman and Lamming (1995) suggest a length of thirty minutes to one hour for interviews to gain information for software development. From my experience I would aim for interviews at the shorter end of this range. Interviewees are usually there on a voluntary basis. It is best not to prolong the interview too much. The optimal length of a particular interview depends on its purpose, and how it is linked with other forms of data collection.

A structured interview consists of a set of preplanned questions. An informal, unstructured interview, by contrast, allows the conversation to follow its own course. Some degree of structuring is recommended to ensure the interview covers certain key topics, and to provide a basis for comparison between respondents. However, the flexibility to follow comments made by the respondents is one of the great advantages of this method. A clear structure, with the freedom to follow interesting points, often provides the best balance. Points may be pursued in depth using probes, e.g. –

'Why do you prefer ... ? What if we changed ... ?'

Follow-up questions can also be used to check the strength of the subject's response. This helps avoid social facilitation effects where the respondents give answers that they believe the interviewer is expecting.

Interviews may be combined with other forms of data collection to provide more penetrating information. In the early development of the Braque system, for example, users were shown candidates for new design notations mocked up in a graphics package. They were asked to work through certain problems. Their performance was observed, and the subsequent interviews probed their views on the usability and effectiveness of the notations. This feedback was used to inform the final decisions on the notations used in Braque (Plate 7). Observation and interview provide a useful combination to evaluate prototypes in the development of a system.

Laurillard (1993) recommends a combination of observation, interview and a trace of the student's performance as a particularly effective combination. This approach is proposed as a general method for finding out about processes in learning, not just the technique for prototype evaluation. She argues that students should be allowed to complete a task undisturbed. They then give a retrospective account of their experience in working through the exercise. A trace of the student's performance, e.g. a worked example or a video tape, is used by the interviewer to focus the students' explanation on what they did and why. Jones et al. (1996) provide a good example of a variant on this approach. They studied the use of a hypermedia learning environment for chemistry with a sample of 200 university students. Information on the students' choices in the hypermedia system was recorded automatically in log files. Preliminary analysis of the log files was used to generate questions for interviews with twelve students. The information from these interviews was then used to elucidate and interpret deeper patterns in the log files.

The strengths of interviews may be summarised as being:

- able to produce rich information on student reactions
- easy to administer
- very useful for formative evaluation
- effective in conjunction with other methods.

The potential weaknesses of interviews are:

- the sample may be unrepresentative
- the recording of interview data may be contaminated by subjective factors
- the collation of results from several individuals to give a clear overall picture may be difficult.

14.5 Questionnaires

Questionnaires are useful in providing overview information in a quantitative form. This technique is valuable for summative information. The quantitative summary data provide an overview of the impact of the system. This information may be supplemented by richer data based on more intensive techniques such as individual interviews.

The value of the information derived from the questionnaire will depend upon how well it is designed. Questions should be precise and unambiguous. Leading questions which point towards a certain answer must be avoided. An appropriate mix of question types should be included to suit the purpose of the questionnaire. There are two broad types of questions – open and closed. Open questions ask respondents to express replies in their own words. This permits richer answers to more open questions, e.g. 'how do you think the system could be improved?' The responses, however, can be difficult and time consuming to quantify. This involves setting up a coding frame that divides the possible responses into distinct categories. The coding may be undertaken by one individual providing that a sample of the responses is checked by another independent judge. The correlation of the coding between these judges must be high in order for the results to be meaningful. An alternative approach is to subjectively scan the responses. This may be used to supplement the information from the closed questions.

There are a variety of forms of questions which produce responses that can be directly quantified. The selection of the question types depends on the information to be elicited. Where the responses fall into a number of categories multiple choice questions may be used. Continuous scales can sometimes be divided into discrete categories as in Figure 14.1. This shows a multiple choice question used to code the use of the help system in a package. Binary choice questions ('male/female'; 'yes/no') are sub-sets of this question type.

Questions with *rating* scales are useful in eliciting subjective reactions to a system. Questions may be asked about general or specific features. General features could be the 'enjoyability' of the system, or its overall effectiveness. Rating of general features often leads to more conservative responses. It is useful to supplement them with more precise questions, e.g. 'how well did you enjoy the last learning exercise you completed?' Common rating scales employ four or five points. Figure 14.2 gives an example of a five point scale. Four point scales force the user to go for either a positive or negative reply. The five point scale can have a neutral midpoint. If in doubt employ the scale which poses the least constraint on the respondent.

There are variants in the use of scaled questions. A semantic differential approach uses a series of bi-polar adjectives ('exciting/dull'; 'easy/difficult'). If the questions are listed directly one under another, a profile can be created by joining the response points. This profile represents the rating of the item across the semantic space sampled. Multiple choice and scaled questions can produce a good sampling of factual and attitudinal questions. Other question types may be included if required. In

How often did you use the Help System in the package?

a) never ☐

b) 1-3 times per week ☐

c) 4-6 times per week ☐

d) 7-9 times per week ☐

e) 10 or more times per week ☐

Figure 14.1 Question used to elicit information on students' use of a help system

'ranking' questions the user is asked to rank a number of alternatives in order of preference. The number of alternatives should not be too great or the respondents may become confused.

The team may construct their own questionnaire or purchase a commercial system, e.g. the Software Usability Measurement Inventory (SUMI) (Kirakowski and Corbett 1993). When constructing your own questionnaire it is useful to test it on a small sample before using it on the full group. Problems with the questionnaire, for example unclear or ambiguous questions, can be detected and rectified at this stage. Various statistical packages, e.g. SPSS (Statistical Package for the Social Sciences), can be used to analyse the data. Using these computer packages it is easy to produce summary descriptive results and carry out inferential statistical analysis. These results can be very useful in producing a summative report on a product.

As with all evaluation techniques questionnaires have advantages and disadvantages. The main advantages are that they:

- are easy and economical to administer

How interesting is the system to use?

Very interesting ☐ ☐ ☐ ☐ ☐ Very boring

How well do you think you have understood the topics covered in the system?

Very well ☐ ☐ ☐ ☐ ☐ Very poorly

Figure 14.2 Question with a five point rating scale

- support both open ended and closed questions
- provide quantitative data
- are comparatively easy to analyse
- are valuable for summative evaluation.

Questionnaires also have certain limitations.

- They may provide surface level information only.
- They do not normally reveal the reasons for the responses.
- The reporting of summary results may obscure variations within the data.

Questionnaires may be used in judicious combination with other techniques to get an effective evaluation of a system. In the summative evaluation of the CLEM system (described in Chapter 5), for example, we supplemented the questionnaire with focus group discussions. Each focus group discussion lasted about one hour with groups of approximately fifteen students. This permitted in-depth probing about the results found in the questionnaire. Focus group discussions give the type of rich, supplementary information provided by interviews. They are, however, more economical to conduct.

14.6 Choice of method

A number of factors influence the selection of evaluation methods:

1. The purpose of the project
2. The stage in the project when the evaluation occurs
3. Cost–benefit considerations
4. Appropriate mix of methods.

Projects vary in both type and setting. The needs of the project should be matched to the type of information generated by particular methods. Carroll (1990), for example, reports that in the research studies underpinning the development of Minimalism the team used rich, qualitative methods. They believed that these would lead to greater understanding of underlying learning processes. For a multimedia product that is to be delivered on a large scale more formal methods of evaluation need to be applied.

The preferred methods of evaluation vary with the stage of project development. At the earliest stage evaluation may depend on the judgements of experts in design or experts in the subject domain. Once a prototype has been constructed formative evaluation can be based on the observation of users supplemented by post observation interviews. Summative evaluation usually requires more quantitative data. This may involve measures of success in using the system, supported by questionnaires. In certain cases, usually involving research into new techniques, this may entail a full experimental comparison.

Cost–benefit considerations are important in devising an evaluation regime. The cost in time and resources of carrying out an evaluation needs to be matched against the value of the information obtained. It is important at the project planning stage to decide on the appropriate evaluation regime. Projects differ in purpose and scale. The choice of regime must satisfy the purpose within the resources available for project development.

The appropriate *mix* of evaluation methods should be selected. Different methods yield different types of information. Combining methods can give the multi-faceted information required. Observation, for example, may indicate certain areas of difficulty. Supporting interviews can then probe for the reasons underlying these difficulties. Questionnaires and general performance measures may yield overall quantitative information for summative evaluation. Focus group discussions or interviews can then provide richer information for interpreting the numerical results.

All information needs to be interpreted. In formative evaluation the feedback is used to guide design decisions. There are usually several design possibilities. The evaluative feedback informs but it does not dictate the design decision. This creative leap is the responsibility of the designer. Summative evaluation should involve a separation of data and interpretation. This is especially important when claiming general significance for the findings, e.g. evaluation of a design technique as opposed to a particular system. A problem for 'authentic evaluation', as proposed by many constructivists, is that it is not clear that this separation can be achieved. Independent interested parties ought to be able to examine the evidence and judge whether they agree with the interpretation proposed by the project team.

14.7 Summary

Evaluation is a crucial part of project development. The framework selected will depend upon the purpose and setting of the project. There are two main phases in evaluation: formative and summative. Formative evaluation helps to shape the evolving design of the system. This involves testing both the effectiveness of the prototype at that stage and the usability of the system. Techniques that yield rich qualitative information are normally employed. A combination of observation and interview is a common format. If access to end users is not possible then simulations using available personnel may be conducted. This is not as satisfactory as a sample of end users, but it can yield valuable information. Iterative prototyping and formative evaluation play complementary roles in project development.

The form of the summative evaluation also depends on the nature of the project. Quantitative data on the success of the system may be required. Questionnaires provide a comparatively cheap way to gather information on the users' assessment of the system. This data may be easily analysed using software packages such as SPSS. In a research setting a full experiment may be conducted to formally evaluate a new design technique.

Books on human–computer interaction usually discuss evaluation in reasonable detail (e.g. Dix et al. 1993, Preece 1993, Newman and Lamming 1995). These books are a useful source for further reading on the subject. They often discuss experimental methods. These methods have not been covered in this chapter as formal experiments have not been widely used in the evaluation of multimedia systems. They also require considerable skill to set up correctly. Newman and Lamming (1995) provide a good initial source for those interested in this technique.

Chapter 15

Delivery

Two sentences by the course tutor had more effect than hundreds of hours of design and development.

(Steve Draper speaking at CAL '95)

15.1 Introduction

At CAL '95 Steve Draper described the evaluation of a multimedia CAL system at Glasgow University. The system was introduced as an optional part of the course and almost no use was made of the system. The course tutor then announced that the system was a compulsory part of the course. The use of the system shot up dramatically, and the system proved to be quite effective. Steve Draper's comment highlights the fact that the delivery conditions may be the most important factor in the success of a CAL system. This point is elaborated in the paper based on this talk (Draper et al. 1996). Good design is essential, but it may not be enough. The delivery conditions can make or break any CAL system. The aim of this chapter is to discuss the issues that can arise in system delivery, and to discuss ways of dealing with these problems.

There is a range of scenarios for the delivery of IMLEs. The specific set of problems varies according to the situation. The first section in this chapter outlines some of the major types of delivery scenario. The integration of the system into the delivery environment offers a significant challenge. At one level there are technical issues – packaging the system and making sure that the appropriate delivery infrastructure is in place. At a deeper level it may require significant organisational changes for the full benefits of multimedia education and training to be realised.

In the chapter each of these themes is discussed in turn. The first section outlines the major delivery scenarios. This is followed by a review of the issues involved in effective packaging. The discussion of the delivery environment falls into two main sections. The first considers the physical delivery environment – ensuring the correct hardware and software set up required to deliver the system. The second deals with the organisational environment. This discussion delineates some of the major issues involved in the effective delivery and integration of the multimedia system.

15.2 Delivery scenarios

There is a range of delivery scenarios:

- a commercial published system
- a bespoke system for a specific organisation
- other scenarios, e.g. educational systems developed through grant aid.

A published system is likely to be delivered on CD ROM, though increasingly network delivery will be a feasible option. The system can be packaged as a self-contained unit. The most popular delivery environments are Windows based PCs and Macintosh computers. Multimedia standards help to ensure delivery to a wide market. The MPC standards provide this for Windows based systems. There is often a trade-off between multimedia power and the size of the potential market. Older standards such as single speed CD ROMs continue to be supported because they provide a larger target audience.

This approach can be used by both commercial and educational producers. Commercial products such as multimedia encyclopaedias are well established. This approach also provides an avenue for educational developers. Certain products from the TLTP initiative have been published as CD ROMs, e.g. the Crucible system. The advantage of this approach is that marketing and delivery may be handled by a third party – the publishers. This can be quite an attractive option for designers. However, many publishers are still finding their way in this area. The full infrastructure and division of responsibilities required to support multimedia publishing is still evolving.

Traditional software systems are often developed as bespoke systems for specific organisations. A multimedia system may be developed in the same way. For economic reasons, however, there is often pressure to deliver the system beyond the original situation. This demand can complicate the delivery factors considerably. CLEM (see Chapter 5) is an example of a system developed for a specific delivery environment. The aim was to develop a system to be delivered in a specific university department (though it was later sold to other universities). This delivery scenario meant that the system could be designed in a certain way. The learning environment, for example, was coupled to a commercial compiler available within the department. The system also exceeded the limitations of the 'reader' provided with the authoring tool. The full authoring environment was used for delivery as the 'reader' was considered too restrictive. These decisions optimised the system for delivery in a certain environment. This permitted certain design features to be built-in that otherwise could not have been included. The price paid for this optimised tailoring is that it becomes difficult to deliver the system more broadly.

There are a large number of educational systems developed through grant aid. The conditions of the grant often require the dissemination of the system. Experience has shown that there are often significant problems in delivering these systems. These projects are often developed in university departments that are geared to teaching and research. They do not have the support mechanisms in place for delivering and maintaining multimedia software. One of the clear lessons from initiatives such as the TLTP is that considerably more attention needs to be made to delivering and maintenance. This may be provided through special support units, as in the Open University, or through collaboration with commercial software houses. There is a clear need to develop organisational support structures to help academics to deliver more effectively the systems they develop.

The Internet is viewed by many as the most attractive option for publishing a system. If this system is developed using HTML it can be delivered on the World Wide Web. The attractions are an 'easy to use' authoring system and a guaranteed delivery platform. These attractions, however, may be paid for by limitations in educational design. Woolston (1995) argues that educational systems based on HTML can be quite limited. Much more powerful authoring tools are available but then serious concern has to be given to local hardware and network constraints. The Internet offers the prospect of becoming the primary delivery medium of the future. For the present, however, there are significant problems in ensuring adequate delivery of multimedia systems.

There is a tension between power and imagination in design and the constraints of delivery. The resolution of this problem depends upon decisions made very early in system development. The key question is – what is the purpose of the system? What aim is it meant to meet? The key choices made in the trade-off between design power and delivery constraints depends upon the answer. One of the key project tasks is to plan for delivery. Problems in effective system delivery are most likely to occur when this question has not been clearly tackled.

15.3 Packaging for delivery

The system needs to be presented in a way that it easy for the user to load and run. If the system is not directly accessed over the Internet this involves the physical installation of the system. It also involves the provision of guides on how the system is to be used.

15.3.1 Installation information and utilities

The user should be supplied with a clear guide to installing the system. This should specify the requirements for the delivery machine, e.g. processor, RAM and hard disk requirements. A given delivery standard may be specified, e.g. MPC level 2. The installation procedure should be clearly described, including preferably an automated installation routine. Many authoring systems now provide the facility to package

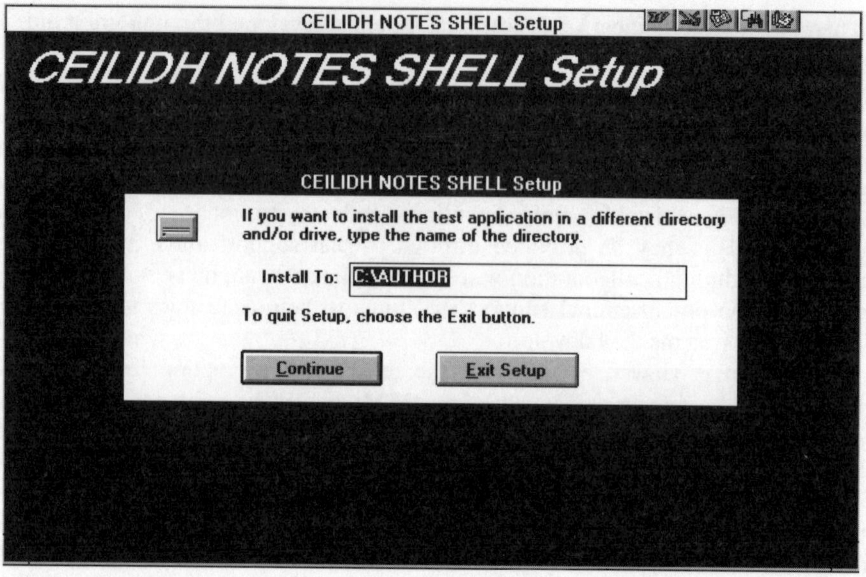

Figure 15.1 Opening screen of an automated installation

systems for automatic installation. Figure 15.1 shows the opening screen for installing an authoring system called the Ceilidh Notes Shell. This system was developed in Visual Basic and packaged using the VB installation tool kit. The developer writes a script which specifies the installation steps, e.g. copying files to specified directories. The installation utility executes this script and installs the system. The installation system needs to be thoroughly tested on a variety of machines. This should preferably involve a Beta test phase when the system is tested by a sample of the typical user population. Though this is not always possible it is very helpful in ironing out bugs in the system.

15.3.2 End user guides

There is a variety of types of multimedia learning environment. For many systems the overheads in learning about the system should be minimised. An electronic book, for example, should be usable almost immediately. The system should be as transparent as possible since the focus is not on the system but the content delivered. Such simplicity and transparency is a product of good design. In other projects the system itself may be an important focus of attention, e.g. a software tool. In these circumstances more extensive help and assistance may be required.

Guides to software are traditionally divided into two areas – tutorial and reference

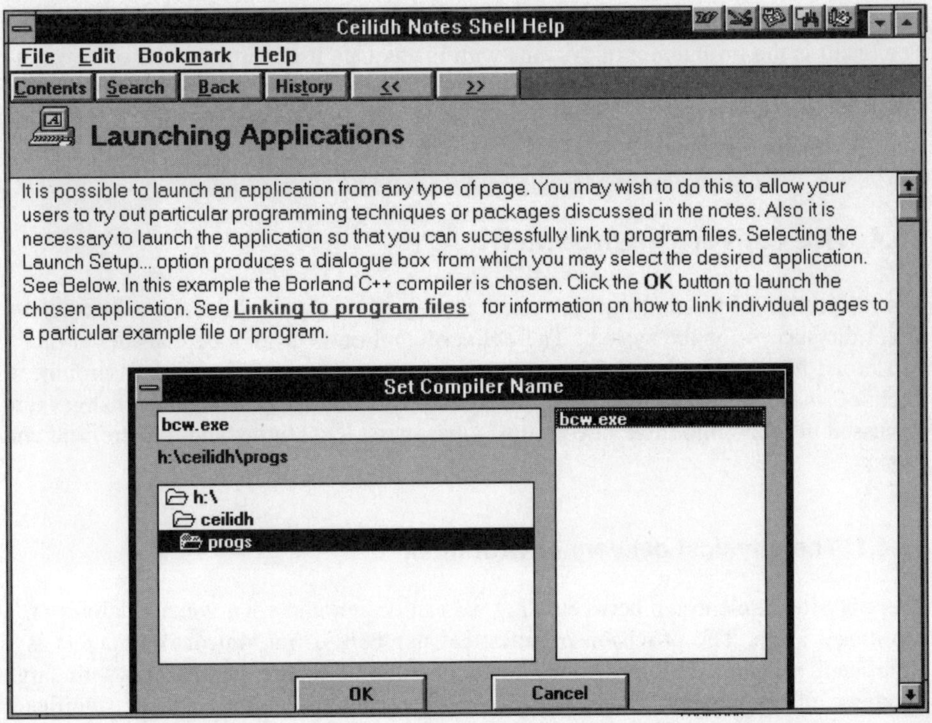

Figure 15.2 A help page from the Ceilidh Notes Shell

information. Complex multimedia systems may have a tutorial guide. Authorware, for example, has an effective tutorial based on building a multimedia system. ToolBook provides on-line tutorials to the main features of the system. Developing full tutorials is very demanding. Detailed tutorials are normally only provided for systems with complex functionality.

More general help information may be provided in hard copy or on-line form. Software tool assistance is available for producing on-line help. Help files for Windows based products, for example, may be developed in a word processor. Mark-up symbols in the text are interpreted by the Windows help compiler to produce a standard hypertext help system. Figure 15.2 illustrates a help page produced from a marked up text file produced in a standard word processor.

Producing guides and help for a system is a demanding task. This task may be minimised by the design of the system. A system that is easy to learn and use may be developed by employing familiar metaphors and standard screen layouts. For more complex systems greater help may need to be provided. The key point is not to deliver a system with inadequate guidance to the user. Given that the help systems are written last, unfortunately this is the area most often squeezed by time and budget constraints. The result is the production of systems with inadequate user support. The only way to avoid this problem is to develop greater awareness of the requirements for good software delivery. These requirements need to be clearly budgeted for at the early stage of project planning.

15.4 The delivery environment

The integration of the multimedia system into the delivery environment will crucially affect the success of the system. The delivery environment may be considered under two broad headings – the physical environment and the organisational environment. Each of these areas will be considered in turn. The organisational changes are discussed in relation to three key groups – managers, local tutors and trainers, and end users.

15.4.1 The physical delivery environment

There is often a clear gap between what we can design and what we can deliver on a significant scale. The provision of sufficient numbers of multimedia computers is a significant problem in many educational institutions. Those institutions with large numbers of computers have them networked together. This offers significant advantages. It also makes the delivery of multimedia material more problematic. Standard local area networks are often not adequate for delivering multimedia material to large groups. Educational multimedia products must be designed with these delivery constraints in mind. This can be frustrating for the designer. However, it is even more frustrating for the user to attempt to use a system with poor performance and long response times.

I can recall both good and bad examples in our own work of this match of system and delivery environment. When the CLEM system was developed it was clear that the machines in the departmental programming laboratory were not powerful enough. At a very early stage this problem was acknowledged and a decision taken to upgrade the target laboratory. This planning meant that an adequate delivery infrastructure could be guaranteed.

In other situations the match of system and delivery environment was less harmonious. The group was asked to develop a set of CAL packages for IT skills to be installed on a new network. The network was not in operation during the development of the system. Network and CAL systems went live together. There were significant problems in performance. It is very problematic when you do not have a clear idea in advance of the performance levels of the delivery system. In developing a system it is preferable to regularly check the performance of the prototypes on a *delivery* specification machine. It is this performance, not that of the development platform, that is crucial. I remember the plaintive comment of one person (in a different context) that the delivery network had 'poisoned' his system.

The designer must be clear about the intended delivery platform for the system and the likely performance on that platform. For an in-house project one task for the development team is to ensure that an adequate delivery platform will be available. For delivery to a general market the designer must clearly specify the required platform. There are rapid advances in technology. For a system that is to be delivered within a time span of two or three years (as in systems developed under educational grants) the designer has to estimate the likely platform that will be available.

15.4.2 The organisational environment

There is a dynamic relationship between the new learning technology and educational organisations. Organisations face not just the task of assimilating the new technology but also the challenge of accommodating their structures in order to effect this change. This process is one that will be carried out well into the twenty first century. There is a variety of approaches to this issue. These range from the relatively conservative (emphasis on assimilation) to the highly radical (emphasis on change). Hall et al. (1995, p. 625) argued that '...a natural progression from current practices...can help break down some of the perceived barriers'.

Hall et al. (1995) proposed a resource based approach. They argue that preparation of traditional lectures and teaching material is a resource based activity. They propose that presenting multimedia as an extended set of educational resources is likely to lead to a much wider uptake of the new technology. This approach places minimal constraints on how the resources are used by the local tutors. This makes the resource based approach less threatening and hence more likely to be adopted. The architecture proposed for this resource based approach is reviewed in Chapter 3.

Other researchers argue for radical changes in how education should be provided. Papert (1980, 1993) has consistently argued for the role of learning technology in facilitating radical change in educational process and provision. Many of the constructivist theorists reviewed in Chapter 6 propose similar arguments for radical change. The projects reviewed in that chapter point to possible prototypes for the new forms of education.

If a multimedia system demands radical changes it may well be rejected. If the system is too conservative it will fail to exploit the potential of the new technology. To make a product successful it must be acceptable to its users. This task is greatest when there is a degree of challenge to the traditional way of doing things. The remainder of this section discusses the barriers and opportunities in winning over the key groups of people involved in delivery.

Management support

Management support is crucial for the effective delivery of computer based learning. This is vital to ensure that the correct delivery infrastructure can be set up and tutors supported in delivering the product. If a system is to be developed for in-house delivery an important early step is to achieve the support of the relevant managers. The success of the system will depend crucially on the strength and robustness of the support.

In organisational settings there are multiple agendas. There is a danger of partial support, especially if the innovation is being driven from below. This can make effective implementation difficult, which produces an adverse reaction from the users. If the system is judged a failure it is the *system* rather than the implementation conditions that will be blamed. Strong management support is thus a vital factor in successful system implementation.

Local tutors and trainers

There is substantial evidence of resistance to educational technology from teachers and trainers (Cummings 1995, Hammond et al. 1992). Hostile or indifferent local tutors can substantially undermine the effectiveness of multimedia education system. A strategy for dealing with these problems is necessary for the effective delivery of systems.

There are a number of barriers, or what Cummings (1995) calls resistance factors, to the use of educational technology:

1. Lack of organisational incentives for engaging in the work
2. Lack of confidence in using computers as a teaching medium
3. Demands for changes in teaching style and technique
4. Lack of a good delivery infrastructure
5. Fear that computers will replace the teacher/trainer.

Many of these factors relate to the organisation of education and training. The long term solution of these problems involves fundamental changes in educational organisations such as those envisaged in the MacFarlane report (MacFarlane 1992). The developer of an individual system has a limited amount of leverage. There are two types of action open to the developer delivering a system to a specific organisation:

- ensure at the feasibility stage that the main conditions for successful delivery are in place
- provide the training and support required for local tutors to make the adjustment.

The simplest way to deal with many of these problems in an in-house development is for the development team to deliver the system. Although this seems a strange notion in broader software development terms it has frequently been employed in CAL development. Collis (1995), in reviewing early work in CAL, comments on the number of implementations where the implementors were directly involved in the development of the system. Radical learning technology has a forcing function in changing educational practice. The commitment required to carry this through is often more easily found in the educational team that developed the system. When a successful implementation has been demonstrated, system delivery may be transferred to other personnel.

This approach ties down the development team and constrains the scope of delivery of the system. The use of the DSDM approach suggests a transition to how this approach might be more broadly applied. DSDM emphasises the incorporation of end-users of software systems in the development team. This technique helps to break down many of the barriers to system acceptability. It also means that knowledgeable people are available to guide and sustain the implementation process.

The DSDM approach offers many advantages in developing a system for delivery within a specific organisation. Whether or not users are incorporated in the team they need to be consulted. A number of questions need to be addressed, for example:

- Have the local tutors elected to use the system, or are they responding to management pressure?
- To what extent are they prepared to change their role?
- To what extent will the system be incorporated into the course or simply provided as an extra?

Consultation with tutors and a demonstrated willingness to make changes can help gain the support of local staff. There is often some tension between what local tutors will request and the orientation of the design team. Design teams inspired by constructivist principles may want to give greater autonomy to students; the tutors may want to retain or even extend teacher control, e.g. through computer based monitoring. In one system, for example, we wanted to make the system available for home use by students. One tutor urged us not to do this. He had his class organised on a fairly tight basis. He believed many students would simply use the excuse of the home system not to attend classes, while not doing the work. Designers cannot simply override these requests if they want the co-operation of the tutors. Genuine negotiation has to take place and compromises made if the system is to be acceptable to local tutors. This acceptability is usually crucial for effective system implementation.

The end users

Certain assumptions about the knowledge, skills and orientations of end users are built into the design of IMLEs. If these assumptions are invalid the effectiveness of the system will be markedly reduced. A number of issues need to be clarified:

- Are students prepared for working in a 'learner centred' way where they are responsible for their own progress?
- How does the system accommodate individual differences in skill and prior experience?
- How does the multimedia system relate to the rest of the course from the students' point of view?
- Will there be adequate access to the system?

The design of the system must take into account the prior experience and abilities of students. The designer needs to be sure about what skills are assumed as a pre-requisite for using the system. The designer should check that these skills are present in the target learner cohorts. It is also important to check how the system fits into the wider course from the students' points of view. The significance of the system for the students often depends crucially on how it fits in to this wider context. Finally, adequate access to the systems must be ensured for the students. Consideration should also be given to the needs of weaker students who may need extra time to deal with the learning demands placed upon them.

15.5 Summary

Effective packaging and delivery is a crucial phase in producing multimedia systems. The failure to deal adequately with these tasks is probably the single greatest cause of system failure. Planning for delivery involves turning the system from the designer's product into the user's product. This involves a number of tasks. The salience of individual tasks will vary with the delivery scenario.

The system must be packaged for the users. This involves providing installation information. An automated installation routine may be provided to ease this task for the user. End user guides and reference information should be matched to the complexity of the system. 'Edutainment' products that are designed to be easy to use should require minimal guidance. These systems are often specifically designed to minimise the need for extra support. Brief animated guidance to the use of the system may be given. More complex systems, such as software tools, may require greater assistance for their full potential to be realised. Tutorials may be provided in hard copy or on-line form. Software tools are available to facilitate the production of standard hypertext help.

The nature of the delivery environment needs to be considered in detail for systems developed for specific organisations. Strong management support for the project is crucial. This support can ensure an adequate delivery structure and support for tutors delivering the system. The co-operation of local tutors and trainers is important for effective delivery. Achieving this support involves consultation and the willingness to make adjustments. Some of these adjustments may require compromises by the designer in order to get the system accepted. The students or trainees are the end users of the system. The system must be planned to take account of their prior experience and skills. The system should be delivered in a way that provides adequate access and support to these users. End users will judge the system on the way it is delivered to them. The culmination of good design is effective delivery.

References

Alpert S. R., Singley M. K. and Carroll J. M. (1995) Multiple multimodal mentors: delivering computer-based instruction via specialized anthropomorphic advisors, *Behaviour and Information Technology*, 14, No. 2, 69–79.

Ambron S. and Hooper K. (eds) (1990) *Learning with interactive multimedia: developing and using multimedia tools in education*. Microsoft press.

Anderson J. R. (1990) *The adaptive character of thought*. Lawrence Erlbaum.

Apple (1992) *Macintosh human interface guidelines*. Addison-Wesley.

Ausubel D. P. (1968*) Educational Psychology: a cognitive view.* Holt, Rinehart and Winston.

Barker P. (1990) Authoring electronic books, *Computer Education*, Nov. 1990.

Barker P. (1993) *Exploring Hypermedia.* Kogan Page.

Barker P. (1995) Electronic books: a review and assessment of current trends. Paper presented at WCCE '95, Sixth World Conference on Computer in Education, Birmingham, England, July 1995 (to be published in Educational Technology Review).

Bates A. W. (1994) Educational multi-media in a networked society. In T. Ottmann and I. Tomek (eds) op. cit.

Belkin N. J., Borgman C. L., Brooks H. M., Bylander T., Croft W. P., Daniels P., Deerwester S., Fox E. A., Ingwersen P., Rada R., Sparck Jones K., Thompson R. and Walker D. (1987) Distributed expert based information systems: an interdisciplinary approach, *Information Processing and Management*, 23, No. 5, 395-409.

Booth J., Foster J. and Wilkie D. (1994) Developing CAL courseware: practice versus theory, *ALT C Conference Abstracts*, Hull, Sept. 1994.

Boyle T. and Drazkowski W. (1989) Exploiting natural intelligence: towards the development of effective environments for learning to program. In A. Sutcliffe and L. Macauley (eds) *People and Computers V.*, Cambridge University Press.

Boyle T. and Margetts S. (1991) *Pascal by active learning using the CORE approach.* D. P. Publishing.

Boyle T. and Margetts S. (1992) The CORE guided discovery approach to acquiring programming skills, *Computers and Education,* 18, 127-133.

Boyle T., Gray J., Wendl B. and Davies M. (1994) Taking the plunge with CLEM: the design and evaluation of a large scale CAL system, *Computers and Education,* 22,19-26.

Boyle T. and Thomas G. (1994) Build your own virtual computer: a computer simulation using an active learning approach. In Brusilovsky P. (ed.) *Proceedings of the East-West Conference on Multimedia, Hypermedia and Virtual Reality, MHVR '94*, Moscow, Sep. 1994.

Boyle T., Stevens-Wood B., Zhu F. and Tikka A. (1996) Structured learning in virtual environments, *Computers and Education*, 26, 1/3, 41-49.

Boyle T. and Davies M. (1996) Hypermedia environments for learning to program. In P. Brusilovsky, P. Kommers and N. Streitz (eds) *Multimedia, hypermedia and virtual reality*. LNCS 1077. Springer.

Brown J. S. and Burton R. E. (1978) Diagnostic models for procedural bugs in basic mathematical skills, *Cognitive Science*, 2, 155-192.

Bruner J. S. (1964) The course of cognitive growth, *American Psychologist, 19, 1-15.*

Bruner J. S. (1975) The ontogenesis of speech acts, *Journal of Child Language*, 2, 1-19.

Bruner J. S. (1990) *Acts of meaning*. Harvard University Press.

Brusilovsky P. (1994) Adaptive hypermedia: the state of the art. In P. Brusilovsky (ed.) *MHVR '94, Proceedings of the East-West Conference on Multimedia, Hypermedia and Virtual Reality*, Sept. 1994, Moscow.

Carroll, J. M. (1990) *The Nurnberg funnel: designing Minimalist Instruction for practical computer skill.* MIT Press.

CTGV (Cognition and Technology Group Learning Technology Centre Peabody College of Vanderbilt University) (1991) Technology and the design of generative learning environments, *Educational Technology*, 31, No. 5, 34-40.

CTGV (Cognition and Technology Group at Vanderbilt) (1993) Designing learning environments that support thinking: the Jasper series as a case study. In T. M.

Duffy, J. Lowyck, D. H. Jonassen and T. M. Welsh (eds) *Designing Environments for Constructive Learning*. Springer-Verlag.

Collins A., Brown J. S. and Newman S. E. (1989) Cognitive apprenticeship: teaching the crafts of reading, writing and mathematics. In L. B. Resnick (ed.) *Cognition and instruction: issues and agendas*. Lawrence Erlbaum Associates.

Cummings L. E. (1995) Educational technology - a faculty resistance view. Part 1: Incentives and understanding, *Educational Technology Review*, No. 4, Autumn 1995.

Cunningham D. J. (1991) Assessing constructions and constructing assessments: a dialogue, *Educational Technology*, 31, No. 5, 13-17.

Cunningham D. J., Duffy T. M. and Knuth R. (1993) The textbook of the future. In C. McKnight, A. Dillon and J. Richardson (eds) *Hypertext: a psychological perspective*. Ellis Horwood.

Chee Y. S. (1994) SMALLTALKER: a cognitive apprenticeship multimedia environment for learning Smalltalk programming. In T. Ottmann and I. Tomek (eds) op. cit.

Collis B. (1995) IFIP Working Group 3.3: applications of computer related technology; are we making progress? In J. D Tinsley and T. J. van Weert (eds) *World Conference on Computers in Education VI: WCCE '95 Liberating the Learner*. Chapman and Hall.

Darby J. (1995) Editorial: teaching and the Internet, *Active Learning*, No. 2, p. 2, July 1995.

Davies M. and Boyle T. (1996) Hypermedia environments for learning to program. In Brusilovsky P., Kommers P. and Streitz N. (eds) *Multimedia, hypermedia and virtual reality: models, systems and applications*. Springer-Verlag.

De Villiers J. G. and De Villiers P. A. (1978) *Language acquisition*. Fontana.

Dickens J. and Sherwood-Edwards M. (1993) Multimedia and copyright; some obstacles on the yellow brick road. In *Proceedings of Multimedia Systems and Applications, International State of the Art Conference*, Leeds, December 1993.

Dix A., Finlay J., Abowd G. and Beale R. (1993) *Human–computer interaction*. Prentice Hall.

Donaldson M. (1978) *Children's minds*. Fontana.

Draper S. W., Brown M. I., Henderson F. P. and McAteer E. (1996) Integrative evaluation: an emerging role for classroom studies of CAL, *Computers and Education*, 26, Nos 1-3, 17-32.

DSDM (1995) *Dynamic Systems Development Method, Version 2*, Tesseract Publishing.

Duffy T. M. and Jonassen D. H. (1991) Constructivism: new implications for educational technology?, *Educational Technology*, 31, No. 5, 7-12.

Edelson D. C., Pea R. D and Gomez L. M. (1996) The collaboratory notebook, *Communications of the ACM*, 39, No. 4, 32-33.

Feifer R. G. and Allender L. T. (1994) It's not how multi the media, it's how the media is used. In T. Ottmann and I. Tomek (eds) op. cit.

Fisher K. (1992) Semantic networking: the new kid on the block. In P. A. M. Kommers. D. H. Jonassen and J. T. Mayes (eds) *Mindtools: cognitive technologies for modelling knowledge*. Springer-Verlag.

Ford A. (1995) *Spinning the web: how to provide information on the Internet*. International Thomson Publishing.

Gagné R. M. (1965) *The conditions of learning*. Holt, Rinehart and Winston Inc.

Gagné R. M. and Briggs L. J. (1979) *Principles of instructional design*. Holt Rinehart and Winston.

Gates W. H. (1995) *The road ahead*. Viking.

Gibbons H. (1992) Murder One - developing interactive simulations for teaching law, *CTISS File*, No.14, Oct. 1992.

Goldman-Segall R. (1991) A multimedia research tool for ethnographic investigations. In S. Papert and I. Harel (eds) *Constructionism*. Ablex.

Goldman-Segall R., Elder K., Riecken T., Francis-Pelton L., Tinney J., Roche L., Godrey K. and Hoebel M. (1994) Virtual Clayoquot video database: the Bayside middle school implements a networked multimedia socio-scientific study about a British Colombia rainforest. In T. Ottmann and I. Tomek (eds) op. cit.

Grabinger R. S. and Dunlap J. C. (1995) Rich environments for active learning: a definition, *ALT-J Association for Learning Technology Journal*, 3, No. 2, 5-34.

Guzdial M., Kolodner J., Hmelo C., Narayanan H., Carlson D., Rappin N., Hubscher R., Turns J. and Newsletter W. (1996) Computer support for learning through complex problem solving, *Communications of the ACM*, 39, No. 4, 43-45.

Hall W. (1993) Hypermedia tools for multimedia information management, *Proc. 'Multimedia Systems and Applications'*, Leeds, Dec. 1993.

Hall W., Hutchings G. and White S. (1995) Breaking down the barriers: an architecture for developing and delivering resource based learning materials. In J. D. Tinsley and T. J. van Weert (eds) *World Conference on Computers in Education VI: WCCE '95 Liberating the Learner*. Chapman and Hall.

Halliday M. A. K. (1973a) The functional basis of language. Appendix in B. Bernstein, *Class codes and control*, Vol. 3. Routledge and Kegan Paul.

Halliday M. A. K. (1973b) *Explorations in the functions of language*. Edward Arnold.

Halliday M. A. K. (1975) Talking one's way in: a sociolinguistic perspective on language and learning. In A. Davies (ed.) *Problems of language and learning*. Heinemann.

Hammond N. (1993) Learning with hypertext: problems, principles and prospects. In McKnight C., Dillon A. and Richardson J. (eds) op. cit.

Hammond M. (1995) Learning from experience: approaching the research of CD-ROM in schools. In J. D Tinsley and T. J. van Weert (eds*) World Conference on Computers in Education VI: WCCE '95 Liberating the Learner*. Chapman and Hall.

Hammond N., Gardner N., Heath S., Kibby M., Mayes T., McAleese R., Mullings C. and Trapp A. (1992*)* Blocks to the effective use of information technology in higher education, *Computers and Education*, 18, 155-162.

Hand C. (1996) Other faces of virtual reality. In P. Brusilovsky, P. Kommers and N. Streitz (eds) *Multimedia, hypermedia and virtual reality*. LNCS 1077. Springer.

Hardman L. (1990) Introduction to Hypertext and Hypermedia*, CTISS File*, No. 9, Feb. 1990.

Harel I. and Papert S. (eds) (1991) *Constructionism*. Ablex.

Hartley J. (1994) *Designing instructional text*, 3rd edn. Kogan Page.

HEFCE (1993a) *Teaching and learning technology programme: a report of 43 projects funded under the Teaching and Learning Technology Programme,* Higher Education Funding Council England, May 1993. (The contents of this report are published in the CTISS File, No. 15, April 1993.)

HEFCE (1993b) *Teaching and learning programme: Phase 3, a report of 33 additional projects funded by HEFCE, SHEFC, HEFCW and DENI under the Teaching and Learning Technology Programme,* Higher Education Funding Council for England, Nov. 1993.

Henderson J. V. (1995) Needed: new models for network-based learning. In H. Maurer (ed.) *Educational Multimedia and Hypermedia 1995, Proceedings of Ed-Media '95 – World Conference on Educational Multimedia and Hypermedia*, Graz Austria, June 1995. AACE.

Heppel S. (1993) Eyes on the horizon, feet on the ground. In C. Latchem, J. Williamson and L. Henderson-Lancett (1993) *Interactive multimedia - promises and pitfalls*. Kogan Page.

Hodges M. E and Sasnett R. M. (1993*) Multimedia computing: case studies from MIT Project Athena*. Addison-Wesley.

Ingwersen P. (1986) Cognitive analysis and the role of the intermediary in information retrieval. In R. Davies (ed.) *Intelligent information systems*. Ellis Horwood.

Jackson S. L., Stratford S. J., Krajcik J. and Soloway E. (1996) A learner-centred tool for students building models, *Communications of the ACM*, 39, No. 4, 48-49.

Jacobs G. (1995) Editorial, *ALT-J Association for Learning Technology Journal*, 3, No. 2, 5-34.

Johnston P. (1992) *Human computer interaction*. McGraw-Hill.

Jonassen D. Mayes T. and McAleese R. (1993) A manifesto for a constructivist approach to uses of technology in higher education. In T. M. Duffy, J. Lowyck, D. H. Jonassen and T. M. Welsh (eds) *Designing environments for constructive learning*. Springer-Verlag.

Jonassen D. H and Marra R. M. (1994) Concept mapping and other formalisms as mindtools for representing knowledge, *ALT-J Association for Learning Technology Journal*, 2, No. 1, 50-56.

Jones T., Berger C. and Magnusson S. J. (1996) The pursuit of knowledge: interviews and log files in hypermedia research. In P. Carlson and F. Makedon (eds) *Educational Multimedia and Hypermedia 1996, Proceedings of Ed-Media '96 – World Conference on Educational Multimedia and Hypermedia*, Boston, June 1996. AACE.

Kafai Y. B. (1996) Software for kids by kids, *Communications of the ACM*, 39, No. 4, 38-39.

Karyakin M. I, Eremeyev V. A. and Pustovalova O. G. (1994) On adventure gaming as an interface to an educational microworld. In T. Ottmann and I. Tomek (eds) op. cit.

Kearsley G. P. (ed.) (1987) *Artificial intelligence and instruction*. Addison-Wesley

Kirakowski J. and Corbett M. (1993) SUMI: the software usability measurement inventory, *British Journal of Educational Technology*, 245, No. 3, 2, 210-212.

Klawe M. M, Lawry J., Inkpen K., Sedighian K. and Upitis R. (1994) Can electronic games make a positive contribution to the learning of mathematics and science in intermediate classrooms? In T. Ottmann and I. Tomek (eds) op. cit.

Kommers P. (1993) Ideology, multi-perspectiveness and concept representation for hypermedia design. Paper presented at the International Conference on Computer Technologies in Education, Kiev, Ukraine, Sept. 1993.

Krol E. (1994) *The whole internet user's guide and catalogue*. O'Reilly and Associates Inc.

Kozma R. B. (1992) Constructing knowledge with Learning Tool. In P. A M. Kommers. D. H. Jonassen and J. T. Mayes (eds) *Mindtools: cognitive technologies for modelling knowledge*. Springer-Verlag.

Kuczaj S. A. (1986) Thoughts on the intentional basis of early object word extensions in comprehension and/or production: support for a prototype theory of early object word meanings, *First Language*, 93-105.

Laurillard D. (1993) *Rethinking university teaching: a framework for the effective use of educational technology*. Routledge.

Lemay L. and Perkins C. (1996) *Teach yourself Java in 21 days*. Sams.net Publishing.

Linn M. C. (1996) Key to the information highway, *Communications of the ACM*, 39, No. 4, 34-35.

McEwan S. (1993) Future developments in information publishing. In J. A. Vince and R. A. Earnshaw (eds) *Multimedia systems and applications*. British Computer Society.

MacFarlane A. G. J. (1992) (Report of the Committee of Scottish University Principals) *Teaching and learning in an expanding higher education system.* Scottish Centrally Funded Colleges.

McKnight C., Dillon A. and Richardson J. (Eds) (1993) *Hypertext: a psychological perspective*. Ellis Horwood.

Marcus A. (1992) *Graphic design for electronic documents and user interfaces*. ACM Press.

Microsoft (1995) *The Windows interface guidelines for software design*. Microsoft Press.

Millwood R. and Mladenova G. (1994) Educational multimedia: how to allow for cultural factors. In P. Brusilovsky, P. Kommers and N. Streitz (eds) *Multimedia, hypermedia and virtual reality*. LNCS 1077. Springer.

Mortimer A. J. (1995) Do it right or get it right? A critique of the Dynamic Systems Development Method, BIT '95 Conference, Manchester Metropolitan University.

Nathan, M. J. (1990) Empowering the student: prospects for an unintelligent tutoring system, *Procs. CHI '90*. ACM Press, pp. 407-414.

Nathan M. J. and Young E. (1990) Thinking situationally: results with an unintelligent tutor for word algebra problems. In A. McDougall and C. Dowling (eds) *Computers in Education*. Elsevier Science Publishers.

National Council of Teachers of Mathematics (1989) *Curriculum and evaluation standards for school mathematics*. Reston, V. A.

Negroponte N. (1995a) *Being digital*. Hodder and Stoughton.

Negroponte N. (1995b) 'Being Nicholas', interview with Thomas Bass. *Wired*, Nov. 1995.

Nelson T.(1994) Tomorrow's networked literature and copyright. Invited talk given at

Ed Media '94, International Conference on Educational Multimedia and Hypermedia, Vancouver, June 1994.

Neuwirth E. (1996) The World Wide Web with integrated applications. Invited paper presented at *Ed Media and Ed Telecom '96*, Boston, June 1996.

Newman W. M. and Lamming M. G. (1995) *Interactive system design*. Addison-Wesley.

Nielson J. (1990) *Hypertext and hypermedia*. Academic Press.

Norman D. A. and Spohrer J. C. (1996) Learner-centered education, *Communications of the ACM*, 39, No. 4, 24-27.

Nwana, H. S. (1990) Intelligent tutoring systems : an overview. *Artificial Intelligence Review*, 4, 251-277.

Orwell G. (1945) Politics and the English language. Reprinted in P. Gleeson and N. Wakefield (eds) (1968) *Language and culture*. Charles E. Merrill.

O'Toole I. (1993) *Instructional design for multimedia.* A. V. Consultants.

Ottmann T. and Tomek I. (eds) (1994) *Educational Multimedia and Hypermedia 1994, Proceedings of Ed-Media '94 – World Conference on Educational Multimedia and Hypermedia*, Vancouver, June 1994. AACE.

Papert S. (1980) *Mindstorms: children, computers and powerful ideas*. Basic Books.

Papert S. (1993) *The children's machine*. Basic books.

Perkins D. N. (1991) Technology meets constructivism: do they make a marriage?, *Educational Technology*, 31, No. 5, 18-23.

Piaget J. (1970) Piaget's Theory. In P. H. Mussen (ed.) *Carmichael's manual of child psychology, 3rd Edn.* John Wiley and Sons Inc.

Pirsig R. M. (1976) *Zen and the art of motorcycle maintenance: an enquiry into values.* Corgi Books.

Polson M. C. and Richardson J. J. (1988) *Foundations of intelligent tutoring systems*. L.E.A.

Preece J. (ed.) (1993) *A guide to usability*. Addison-Wesley.

Price R. V. (1991) *Computer-aided instruction: a guide for authors*, Brooks/Cole, Pacific Grove California.

Quiller-Couch A. T. (1916) *On the art of writing*. Cambridge University Press.

Reader W. and Hammond N. (1994) Computer-based tools to support learning from hypertext: concept mapping tools and beyond, *Computers and Education*, 22, No. 1/2, 99-106.

Riddle D. (1990) EcoDisk CD-ROM, *CTISS File*, No. 10, Sept. 1990.

Romiszowski A. J. (1993) Developing interactive multimedia courseware and networks: some current issues. In C. Latchem, J. Williamson and L. Henderson-Lancett (1993) *Interactive multimedia - promises and pitfalls*. Kogan Page.

Rosch E.(1988) Categories and coherences: a historical view. In F. S. Kessel (ed.) *Development of language and language researchers : Essays in honour of Roger Brown.* Erlbaum.

Rosson, M. B., Carroll, J. M. and Bellamy, R. (1990) Smalltalk scaffolding: a case study of Minimalist instruction, *Procs. CHI '90*. ACM Press, pp. 423-429.

Scardamalia M. and Bereiter C. (1996) Student communities for the advancement of knowledge, *Communications of the ACM*, 39, No. 4, 36-37.

Schlusselberg E. (1993) Dans le Quartier St. Gervais: an exploratory learning environment. In M. E. Hodges and R. M. Sasnett op. cit.

Schwier R. A. and Misanchuk E. R. (1993) *Interactive multimedia instruction.* Educational Technology Publications.

Segal J. and Ahmad K. (1991) *The role of examples in the teaching of programming languages,* University of Surrey Computing Sciences Technical Report, CS-91-01.

Sleeman D. and Brown J. S. (Eds.) (1982) *Intelligent tutoring systems*. Academic Press.

Smith D. C., Irby C., Kimball R. and Verplank B. (1982) Designing the Star user interface, *BYTE*, April, pp. 242-282.

Tagg C., Tagg B. and Oram I. (1995) Realising a vision?. In J. D Tinsley and T. J. van Weert (eds*) World Conference on Computers in Education VI: WCCE '95 Liberating the Learner*. Chapman and Hall.

TLTP (Teaching and Learning Technology Programme) (1994*) Copyright guidelines for the Teaching and Learning Technology Programme*. Higher Education Funding Council for England, Bristol.

Trapp A., Reader W. and Hammond N. (1992) Tools for knowledge mapping: a framework for understanding. In P. Brusilovsky and V. Stefanuk (eds*) East–West Conference on Emerging Computer Technologies in Education*, Moscow, April 1992.

Tufte E. R. (1990) *Envisioning information*. Graphics Press.

Tway L. (1992) *Welcome to multimedia*. MIS Press.

Twigg C. A. (1994) The need for a national learning infrastructure, *Educom Review*, 29, Nos 4, 5, 6.

Underwood J. (ed.) (1994) *Computer based learning: potential into practice*. David Fulton Publishers.

Upitis R. (1994) Parent and teacher attitudes towards video and computer games. In T. Ottmann and I. Tomek (eds) op. cit.

Van den Brande L. (1993) *Flexible and distance learning: a special report of the Commission of the European Communities Directorate-General XIII*. John Wiley and Sons.

Van Hoff A., Shaio S. and Starbuck O. (1995) *Hooked on Java*. Addison-Wesley.

Vaughan Tay (1994) *Multimedia: making it work*, 2nd edn. Osborne, McGraw-Hill.

Vygotsky L. S. (1962) *Thought and language*. MIT Press.

Wason P. C. and Johnson-Laird P. N (1972) *Psychology of reasoning: content and structure*. Batsford.

Weingrad P., Hay K. E., Jackson S., Boyle R. A., Guzdial M. and Solloway E. (1993) Student composition of multimedia documents: a preliminary study. In H. Maurer (ed.) *Educational Multimedia and Hypermedia Annual 1993, Procs of Ed Media '93. AACE.*

West C. K., Farmer J. A. and Wolff P. M. (1991) *Instructional design: implications from cognitive science*. Allyn and Bacon.

Williamson M. (1994) Solutions focus: high tech training, *BYTE*, 19, No. 12, 74-88.

Wilson S. (1995) *World Wide Web design guide*. Hayden Books.

Woolston C. (1995) Teaching on the WEB: good, bad or ugly. *ALT-N, Association for Learning Technology Newsletter*, No. 8, January 1995.

Appendix 1

Major access points for WEB based information on multimedia and learning

This appendix outlines some major Web access points for information on learning technology. Two types of information points are listed: organisations concerned with multimedia and education, and tool vendors. The information in this appendix is correct at the time of publication. The Web is a dynamic phenomenon and some addresses may possibly change. The access points, however, soon open into a matrix of cross-related information which provides considerable flexibility of access to sites and information.

Associations and societies involved with learning technology

General annotated index to learning technology resources on the WEB

http://tecfa.unige.ch/info-edu-comp.html

This site is based at the School of Psychology and Education at the University of Geneva. This gateway gives wide access to a large number of Web educational technology sites.

Association for the Advancement of Computers in Education (AACE)

http://aace.virginia.edu/aace

This is a major international organisation which promotes the use of computers in education. There are a number of chapters situated across the world.

ALT (Association for Learning Technology)

http://www.csv.warwick.ac.uk/alt-E/index.html

British based association for promoting the development and dissemination of learning technology.

CTISS (Computers in Teaching Initiative Support Centre)

http://info.ox.ac.uk/cti/

This home page provides links to all 23 subject specific CTI centres in Britain. These centres cover a wide range of academic subjects. They provide detailed information on the use of learning technology in their respective subject areas.

Educom

http://www.educom.edu/

Educom is a major consortium of higher education institutions, based in the USA, concerned with the advancement of the use of computers in education. This site contains information on the National Learning Infrastructure Initiative.

TLTP (Teaching and Learning Technology Programme)

http://www.icbl.hw.ac.uk/tltp/

This site contains information on the 76 projects funded in Great Britain under the Teaching and Learning Technology Initiative. It also provides links to other major UK based learning technology initiatives.

Educational multimedia tool vendors

Asymetrix Corporation

http://www.asymetrix.com

Asymetrix produce a number of multimedia tools including ToolBook and Digital Video Producer.

Macromedia Inc.
http://www.macromedia.com

Macromedia produce a number of multimedia tools including Authorware and Director.

Microsoft Corporation

http://www.microsoft.com/

Sun Microsystems, Inc.

http://java.sun.com/

This is the Java home page. Sun developed the Java language which has had a major impact of Web authoring.

For information on VRML (Virtual Reality Modelling Language)

http://vrml.wired.com/

http://sdsc.edu/vrml/

Index